'Ursula Hoadley is one of the very best of the new generation of writers on curriculum and pedagogy. She is a creative and rigorous researcher with an interest in making a difference – and her research on South African schools and their challenges in the post-Apartheid era is confronting. This book brings together vivid depictions of classrooms, teachers, students and failed education reforms – and it develops fresh thinking about curriculum, pedagogy and place in moving forward. It deserves to be widely read.'

—*Lyn Yates, Foundation Chair of Curriculum, Melbourne Graduate School of Education, University of Melbourne, Australia*

'Ursula Hoadley examines the complex and revealing relationship between societal structuring, the three South African curriculum reforms and pedagogic practices in classrooms, detailing its implications for theory, policy and research. Key among these is the reciprocal relation between reform and teacher development. Without "a significant shift in the cognitive horizons of those teaching in our schools," Hoadley concludes, reform must fail. Hoadley makes a compelling argument for a relational conception of curriculum and pedagogy (or knowledge *in* pedagogy) in thinking about curriculum change. It is argument curriculum studies scholars not only in South Africa but worldwide will want to address.'

—*William F. Pinar, Canada Research Chair in Curriculum Studies, University of British Columbia, Vancouver, Canada*

Pedagogy in Poverty

As South Africa transitioned from apartheid to democracy, changes in the political landscape, as well as educational agendas and discourse on both a national and international level, shaped successive waves of curriculum reform over a relatively short period of time. Using South Africa as a germane example of how curriculum and pedagogy can interact and affect educational outcomes, *Pedagogy in Poverty* explores the potential of curricula to improve education in developing and emerging economies worldwide and, ultimately, to reduce inequality.

Incorporating detailed, empirical accounts of life inside South African classrooms, this book is a much-needed contribution to international debate surrounding optimal curriculum and pedagogic forms for children in poor schools. Classroom-level responses to curriculum policy reforms reveal some implications of the shifts between a radical, progressive approach and traditional curriculum forms. Hoadley focuses on the crucial role of teachers as mediators between curriculum and pedagogy, and explores key issues related to teacher knowledge by examining the teaching of reading and numeracy at the foundational levels of schooling.

Offering a data-rich historical sociology of curriculum and pedagogic change, this book will appeal to academics, researchers and postgraduate students in the fields of education, sociology of education, curriculum studies, educational equality and school reform, and the policy and politics of education.

Ursula Hoadley is Associate Professor in the School of Education at the University of Cape Town in South Africa. She has a particular interest in curriculum, teachers' work and the sociological study of pedagogy.

Routledge Research in Education Policy and Politics

The Routledge Research in Education Policy and Politics series aims to enhance our understanding of key challenges and facilitate ongoing academic debate within the influential and growing field of Education Policy and Politics.

www.routledge.com/Routledge-Research-in-Education-Policy-and-Politics/book-series/RREPP

Books in the series include:

Modernising School Governance
Corporate Planning and Expert Handling in State Education
Andrew Wilkins

UNESCO without Borders
Educational Campaigns for International Understanding
Edited by Aigul Kulnazarova and Christian Ydesen

Education and Political Subjectivities in Neo-liberal Times and Places
Emergences of Norms and Possibilities
Edited by Eva Reimers and Lena Martinsson

Local Citizenship in the Global Arena
Educating for Community Participation and Change
Sally Findlow

Using Shakespeare's Plays to Explore Education Policy Today
Neoliberalism Through the Lens of Renaissance Humanism
Sophie Ward

Middle-class School Choice in Urban Spaces
The Economics of Public Schooling and Globalized Education Reform
Emma E. Rowe

Education and the Production of Space
Political Pedagogy, Geography, and Urban Revolution
Derek R. Ford

Pedagogy in Poverty
Lessons from Twenty Years of Curriculum Reform in South Africa
Ursula Hoadley

Pedagogy in Poverty

Lessons from Twenty Years of Curriculum Reform in South Africa

Ursula Hoadley

Routledge
Taylor & Francis Group
LONDON AND NEW YORK

First published 2018 by Routledge
2 Park Square, Milton Park, Abingdon, Oxon OX14 4RN
52 Vanderbilt Avenue, New York, NY 10017

First issued in paperback 2019

Routledge is an imprint of the Taylor & Francis Group, an informa business

British Library Cataloguing-in-Publication Data
A catalogue record for this book is available from the British Library

Library of Congress Cataloging-in-Publication Data
A catalog record for this book has been requested

Typeset in Galliard
by Apex CoVantage, LLC

ISBN 13: 978-0-367-20406-8 (pbk)
ISBN 13: 978-1-138-92981-4 (hbk)

For Bill and Marie, my first teachers.

Contents

Credits

Figures 6.1, 6.2 and 6.3 were reproduced with the kind permission of MIET Africa (www.mietafrica.com/)

This book is derived in part from an article published in Journal of Curriculum Studies on 20 Nov 2007 available online: www.tandfonline.com/10.1080/00220270701261169

Acknowledgements

The research on which this book is based spans a period of 20 years, pretty much the whole period of my research career thus far. There are therefore many people to acknowledge who have supported, critiqued, encouraged, guided and inspired the work along the way. Heather Jacklin first encouraged me to do research and employed me on the Learner Progress and Achievement Study in 1996, the basis for the first case of policy reform and classroom study in the book. I learnt what I first understood about research alongside Heather and Xolisa Guzula, my co-researcher on the project. The second case in the book is based on my PhD study that followed from 2000 to 2005. Paula Ensor and Joe Muller, my doctoral supervisors, were brilliant mentors. I learnt, and continue to learn a great deal from them and am enormously grateful for their support and friendship over many years and different undertakings. The third case is based on a project that I led from 2011 to 2014, the Schools Performing Against Demographic Expectations (SPADE) project. My long-time collaborator and friend Jaamia Galant was instrumental in the work of the project. Enormous thanks are due to her for her intellectual energy, practical guidance, sharp critique and unfailing support. The research reported in Chapter 11 was initially conceptualized with her. The research in Chapters 6 and 8 was initially a conference paper written with Paula Ensor. I benefited hugely from the conversations and work with her. Chapter 10 also draws on a joint conference paper with Nick Taylor. I thank him for the excellent conversations in preparing that paper, and more generally for the warm collegiality and inspiration he has provided over the years. Chapter 3 emerges from fruitful and challenging work with Servaas van der Berg and Nic Spaull, wonderful colleagues who provide a constant reminder of the importance of directing research for social change.

There were a number of people who were instrumental in encouraging me to write this book, most notably Michael Young, Paula Ensor and Lyn Yates. Their support for the project, as well as comments on the initial proposals, was invaluable. Joe Muller, Wayne Hugo, Jenni Case and Lilli Pretorius read drafts of chapters, and their incisive, critical and encouraging comment made an enormous difference in completing the book. I feel extremely fortunate to have such generous colleagues. There are many others who have along the way commented on and discussed the work in the different chapters, and I am very grateful to all of them, especially Lynne Slonimsky, Yael Shalem, Jeanne Gamble, Penny Vinjevold and Zain Davis. They model excellence in thinking about education and have helped me over the years to sharpen my ideas. Finally, I owe a special debt of gratitude to Joe Muller, for his unwavering support and care, patient goading and at times stinging criticism. His constant and honest engagement with my work has helped me to do better time and again.

At the time of writing this book my children Grace and Malaika, 5 and 7 years of age, were both learning to read. It was one of the most thrilling moments in my time as a parent, watching whole worlds open up to them as they mastered the decoding of text and marveled at the stories this revealed and their ability to reveal them. I thank them for their boundless energy, and for reminding me of how exciting learning can be and why we should be doing everything possible to broaden this experience of schooling. Last and certainly most, I thank my husband David. Without his love and encouragement, and generosity in giving me time to spend on this project, I would never have completed the book.

1 Introduction

Teacher:	Listen, on page 63, how a tree lives and grows. It says that . . . what does it say people? How a tree lives and grows. What does it say?
Learners:	How a tree lives and grows.
Teacher:	What does it say?
Learners:	How a tree lives and grows.
Teacher:	What does it say?
Learners:	How a tree lives and grows.
Teacher:	Umthi uphula njani ukhube nyani. Say it in Xhosa.
Learners:	Umthi uphula njani ukhube nyani.
Teacher:	Say it again in English, how a tree lives and grows.
Learners:	How a tree lives and grows.
Teacher:	There are those who are not talking. I don't hear you. How a tree lives and grows.
Learners:	How a tree lives and grows.
Teacher:	I don't hear some [of you], how a tree lives and grows
Learners:	How a tree lives and grows.
Teacher:	I don't hear you. How a tree lives and grows.

(Grade 3 classroom, Khayelitsha, South Africa, 2003)

For anyone who has done research in schools in a developing country context, this would be a very familiar form of classroom exchange. It entails a heavy reliance on memorization and chorusing, generating a synchrony between teacher and students so that classroom activity is fundamentally communal. No distinctions or judgments are made of individual learners and their activity, and initiative and spontaneity on the part of students is closed down. Pedagogy is a form of marking time, a rite of rote.

The exchange takes place almost 10 years after the transition from apartheid to a democratic regime in South Africa. The apartheid curriculum has been abolished, and the system has already been through two major curriculum reforms. Like many other countries in Africa and the developing world, these reforms have tried to steer curriculum towards outcomes-based forms and pedagogy towards learner-centred practices. The latter has explicitly sought to scotch 'authoritarian' practices in classrooms, which include features described as teacher-centred classrooms, rote and surface learning and collective chanting. It is clear that in many ways the reforms have failed to shift these practices. This book is concerned with dynamics of pedagogic change and stasis in response to curriculum reform. It considers the effects of the wide-ranging efforts of the democratic regime in South Africa to shape teaching and learning through radically different curriculum models. Although being very specific to the particular context, the South African case is representative of shifts and dynamics in curriculum across a wider range of developing country contexts.

The book constructs a historical-sociological account of educational change in South Africa in the first 20 years of the democratic, post-apartheid era. It traces a series of three curriculum reform efforts that represented radically different ideological and pedagogical policies on education. I present an ethnographic study of classrooms conducted just after the implementation of each reform. These studies were conducted in early primary school classrooms in the same poor communities outside of Cape Town.

The account is located in a time of rapid social, political and economic change. The moral order, the mores and conventions that maintained society under apartheid, and then at different stages under a democratic dispensation, were in flux. This changing moral order was reflected in shifting curriculum forms and pedagogic regimes. The book shows how these broad shifts in society were reflected in curriculum and translated in classrooms at different points in time. The dynamics in the classroom represent a microcosm of how power has been distributed and control enacted in the post-apartheid era.

The book considers the developments and the contestations around the reform of the national curriculum in relation to both national and international dynamics. Global discourses around national qualifications frameworks, outcomes-based education (OBE), progressive agendas of learner-centredness and constructivist learning, and more recently standards-based reform and the measurement of learning all had bearing on the nature of reform processes in South Africa across time. The focus in tracking the reforms, however, is on the critical pedagogical relation – between knowledge, the teacher and the learner. Fundamentally, it is the nature and status of knowledge that shifts when the curriculum changes, and relatedly, it is the model (idea) of the teacher and the student, and the social relation between them that shifts in attendant pedagogic reforms.

Knowledge, pedagogy and the 'crisis' in the curriculum field

One of the key arguments emerging from the book concerns pedagogy as a specialized, knowledgeable practice. A number of scholars have recently argued that there is a crisis in the curriculum field in that it has in recent times lost sight of its object: knowledge (for example, Wyse et al., 2014; Muller, 2000; Young, 2013). In pursuit of more socially just schooling for all, and in a political response to prior technicist and elitist emphases on knowledge, many curriculum theorists have concentrated on issues of identity, culture, power and social positioning in questions of curriculum and pedagogy. The emphasis has been on *who* is getting access to knowledge, and *who* is making decisions around knowledge for inclusion in the curriculum. In these important debates, the knowledge itself has been lost. There has recently been a return to the question of *what* knowledge is most valuable for inclusion in the curriculum. The question has been taken up especially in relation to increasingly generic and skills-based curriculum policy formulations as well as the distorting effects of testing. It has also been taken up as a question of social justice: who gains access to formal school knowledge and the possibilities it confers, and who is locked out.

The questions of the book

While Young provides a crisp articulation of the curriculum crisis and clarifies a privileged version of the purposes of schooling and curriculum – "The struggle over schooling has always has been a struggle for knowledge; that is what the debate about the curriculum should be about" (Young, 2013, p. 115), in this book I extend these debates in relation to pedagogy. What does a knowledge-based approach mean for pedagogy, in particular what does it mean for those in classrooms in poor communities? What can we learn from tracing the history of the changing position of knowledge in the curriculum and concomitant pedagogic forms over a period of 20 years in South Africa? Conceptually, how do we think about the relation between curriculum and pedagogy? And how do we understand broader questions of educational change over time in a developing country context as they play out in the micro context of the classroom?

What a long view of curriculum and pedagogical change over time affords is a clearer understanding of change and stasis. The inflexibility of pedagogic regimes in poorer contexts (such as the predominant rite of rote introduced at the start of this chapter) is often attributed to material aspects, such as poor resources, large classes and time constraints. 'Culture' is also often invoked. But each change in curriculum and pedagogic regime entails a disturbance of the life-world of classrooms, of lived, sedimented meanings of what it means to teach and learn. Teachers have an existing set of competences, practices and attitudes, a cognitive horizon (Craig, 1989) that may expand or restrict over time. These cognitive horizons are manifest in the ways in which knowledge is structured and social relations are established in classrooms. In the case of the historical trajectory sketched here, what are these?

The book draws out two features that exemplify the forms of life in classrooms over the 20-year period that have remained resistant to change. The first is a communalizing orientation to instruction, where, similar to the introductory description, the teacher works with the whole class as a homogeneous group, with little or no differentiation of tasks or attention to individual performances. This is contrasted with an individualizing pedagogy that emphasizes more personalized relationships between teachers and learners. This individualizing relation allows for individualized judgments and enactments in relation to what students produce in the classroom in order to produce a shift in learning.

The second enduring feature of classrooms is the emphasis on the outer form of task demands. MacDonald (2002) suggests that in many instances, required forms of learning and knowledge are opaque to teachers, and they therefore can only mimic the surface characteristics of the task. Or, what they can't do is bring to the surface the underlying principles or concepts of the task. Thus, the knowledge substance underpinning or ordering the pedagogy is thin or absent. It is the constancy of these aspects of pedagogy that are put in stark relief when looking at change over time. A learning limbo is engendered in the dislocation between the curriculum requirements of a range of reforms and what is manifestly possible in the classroom.

The process of curriculum reform in South Africa, then, offers a kind of natural experiment in relation to curriculum and pedagogic change, describing the three post-apartheid curriculum reforms and three parallel analyses of pedagogy. The specification and teaching of literacy and early mathematics at the foundation level of school (grades 1 to 3) is taken as a lens through which to refract the central questions of the book. How is knowledge structured in curriculum and pedagogy over time, how is the model of the teacher and the learner and their relation constituted in policy and practice? And what can we learn from these processes of change and stasis about the possibilities of pedagogy in poverty?

The purpose of education and the question of knowledge

Bernard Charlot (2009) gives an example of the difference between the world as a place of experience and the school where the world is treated as an object of thought. He asks us to take a city, in this case Lisbon, but it could be any city. When the geography teacher talks about Lisbon where her students live, the city is considered in terms of its functions, its role as the capital, its physical location, etcetera. This Lisbon is not the same as the Lisbon that the students live in, where students relate to the city in terms of how their families and friends live in and move through the city, what their neighbourhood is like. The students' Lisbon is a place of experience, and school's Lisbon is an object of thought. Charlot asserts that when pupils elide the difference between the two and relate to the latter as if it was the former, they will have problems at school.

The sociologist Basil Bernstein too is concerned with the way in which education specializes consciousness with respect to school ways of organizing experience and making meaning, or a 'school code'. Whereas everyone has access to the commonsense knowledge of everyday life, schooling inducts learners into 'uncommon-sense' knowledge, where an educational identity and specific skills are clearly marked and bounded (Bernstein, 1975, p. 81).

By introducing a strong conceptualizing of boundaries, Bernstein marks out the school as having a particular purpose – the specializing of consciousness through acquisition of knowledge. This is certainly not the only purpose of schooling, but it is the one privileged in this book. As Charlot maintains, "Controlling the relationship between the object of thought and its referents in life's environment, and introducing the pupil to intellectual worlds made up of objects whose meaning does not derive from a relationship with the real world as it is experienced is, under two correlated forms, the overriding problem of the school pedagogy" (2009, p. 91).

Bernstein, whose work offers the central theoretical resources in the book, takes as his central concern how social class, pedagogy as a social practice and forms of human consciousness are related. The issue concerns access to formal (or in Durkheim's terms, 'sacred') knowledge and the potential it holds for individual and collective transformations. Bernstein, like Durkheim, rejects the idea that there is any one particular pedagogic model that is in principle better than any other, a preoccupation that we shall see has dominated debates around pedagogy in developing countries. Rather education systems and processes need to be located within their socio-historical setting, with an understanding of the particularities of the specific social system. Crucial to this understanding is the relation between everyday and formal knowledge, mental and manual, sacred and profane knowledge.

What is it that access to the sacred, or to educational knowledge, affords? Ravich puts it eloquently as helping to "make a chaotic world coherent" (2000, p. 17). But most importantly, educational knowledge entails the ability to think abstractly. And through being able to abstract from immediate, material circumstances, educational knowledge holds the power to enlighten and to liberate. Alternative presents and futures can be conceived when abstraction is mastered. This is the social justice bedrock of access to formal, academic knowledge: it offers possibilities to challenge and change circumstances as they have been determined.

In South Africa this relation, between mental and manual, sacred and profane, or what in the context of schooling is often referred to as school knowledge and everyday knowledge has animated curriculum debates for at least the last 20 years. Over time the issue became fraught with the implications of arguing for strong boundaries in a context where for so long so many were excluded from 'higher' forms of mental knowledge under apartheid.

The distinction, however, between different forms of knowledge and their place in curriculum and pedagogy remains important for two central reasons. The first relates to the emphasis on schooling as a preparation for work. Often taking the form of competency training and outcomes-based education, the stress on relevance to the workplace poses serious threats to more generalized, academic knowledge. This emphasis, some argue, frames schooling as a hollowed out preparation for work (Allais, 2014). The second reason for distinguishing between different forms of knowledge is that persistent reforms oriented towards learner-centred and constructivist pedagogies often privilege the everyday knowledge of the student over the school knowledge they are required to learn. This can result in distorting effects in school learning, especially for students who gain little preparation for school in the home. The concern in all of this is the unequal distribution of different types of knowledge, specialized and everyday or vocational, to different students, often on the basis of social class. This issue is a central thread running through the analyses and discussions in the book.

A note on methodology and validity

Over the course of the book a loose connection between different curriculum reforms and classroom pedagogy is established. The samples of classrooms are very small though representative of South African classrooms in several critical ways. They are all located in schools in very poor communities, in urban townships where the majority of people living there are poor and black,[1] many unemployed or in very low paid low-skilled jobs.

Although it is possible to claim 'face-generalisability' (Schofield, 1993) on the basis of the typicality of the schools and their contexts, the intention is not to generalize from the small number of case studies to all classrooms, nor to make direct links between curriculum reforms and pedagogic practices. This is not a study of policy fidelity or a consideration of the ways in which curriculum is implemented. Rather it is an exercise of setting the intended and the enacted curriculum alongside each other at particular points in time to reflect on the intersection of knowledge, curriculum and pedagogy in times of change. The case studies are set against a wide number of studies both local and international that have experienced similar reforms and recognize the same pedagogic forms. Thus, the small number of case studies speaks to a much wider context of countries wrestling with the provision of mass schooling under significant resource constraints.

The educational context of South Africa

In 1994 South Africa became a democratic state after a brutal history of colonialism, which had reached its nadir in the apartheid years (1948–94). While much has changed in democratic South Africa over the last 22 years, stark inequalities continue to define the society and South Africa persists in being one of the most unequal countries in the world. Youth unemployment remains one of the biggest challenges, and this is in the face of very weak economic growth, weaker global competitiveness ranking and rising government debt. Although life expectancy has increased, access to basic services has improved and an extensive social grant system has been rolled out, education remains a critical challenge.

Primary net enrolment rates in schooling are high relative to other developing countries. However, participation, especially to the end of high school, is a significant problem, with only about 40% of the starting Grade 1 cohort completing the final school-leaving certificate examination in the requisite 12 years (Spaull, 2013). There are significant racial disparities in schooling outcomes still prevalent in the system. In 2008, four out of five Grade 6 children in former white schools were reading at grade level compared to four children in a hundred in former black schools (Taylor et al., 2013). While some improvement over the last few years has been reported, in general the vast majority of the 12.4 million pupils in more than 24 000 schools are failed by a dual system of schooling. Performance on a range of standardized tests shows a bimodal distribution, where around 80% of schools serve poor black communities and produce very weak outcomes, and 20% are mostly former white and currently multiracial, middle-class schools that produce good outcomes. Wide learning gaps are evident between children in what are essentially two schooling systems (Spaull & Kotze, 2015).

Learning deficits are acquired in the first years of schooling. The vast majority of children cannot read for meaning in their home language by the end of Grade 4. Almost a third of children are functionally illiterate in English, the medium of instruction for the upper levels of schooling, by the end of Grade 6 (Van der Berg et al., 2016). The quality of education delivered in South Africa, and the kind of teaching that students are subject to, still bears the hallmarks of apartheid education.

There are a number of 'binding constraints' that inhibit improvement in the system, including weak teacher content knowledge and pedagogical skill, and wasted learning time and insufficient opportunity to learn (Van der Berg et al., 2016). Early post-apartheid research raised a concern around teachers' content knowledge (Taylor & Vinjevold, 1999), identifying it as a significant contributor to poor academic outcomes for learners. Recent work on 2007 SACMEQ data, currently the only nationally representative assessment of primary school teacher content knowledge in South Africa, shows that almost four out of five (79%) Grade 6 mathematics teachers have a content knowledge level below the Grade 6/7 level, i.e. below the level they are currently teaching (Venkat & Spaull, 2015). Why? A large part of the reason can be attributed to apartheid schooling and teacher training legacies that have continued into the post-apartheid era. In order to become a primary school teacher in a black school under apartheid in the 1980s, you needed a Grade 8 pass. In other words, you only needed to have completed primary school in order to teach it. Training programmes that were established in the post-apartheid era were wholly inadequate in upgrading the knowledge levels of teachers in the system.

But there are also broader societal dynamics at play. Under apartheid, the infamous Group Areas Act restricted the movement of black, coloured and Indian people, allocating different race groups to particular geographical areas. For black people these were either townships on the outskirts of urban areas, or 'bantustans', rural reservations established for different black ethnic groups. Although there have been shifts in the racial make-up of formerly white and more middle-class areas, formerly poor black geographic areas remain defined by class and race. This enduring social separation stemming from group areas means a restriction on the sharing not only of material resources, but cultural and symbolic resources as well. The teachers in the case studies presented in this book all lived in or very near the black townships in which they taught, and they were schooled in similar conditions to those in which they were teaching. Their training occurred in institutions that were at the time, or had very recently been, both race and class-defined. Thus, the opportunities that the teachers had to experience, observe or craft alternative practices to those engendered under apartheid and sustained into the democratic era were limited. They were essentially caught in the 'trap' of low quality education (Van der Berg et al., 2011).

The notion of 'cognitive horizon' with its spatial connotations is thus a useful one in considering the shifts from apartheid through the series of reforms in the democratic era. In the absence of significant opportunities for teachers' cognitive horizons to expand, what chances do reforms stand in shifting entrenched classroom practices and low levels of student learning?

Outline of the book

Chapters 2, 3 and 4 set the scene for the discussion of the reforms in the book.

Chapter 2 reviews the research around curriculum and pedagogy in developing country contexts. The intention is to locate South Africa within these contexts as a developing country case. The chapter identifies dominant curriculum and pedagogic forms in developing country contexts. Curricula are often characterized as traditional or content-based. Pedagogy is 'formalist', 'traditional' or 'teacher-centred'. The chapter considers the nature of reforms across a range of countries that have attempted to change these dominant forms of curriculum and pedagogy. In particular, I consider how learner-centred and outcomes-based reforms were taken up widely and what their effects have been. In terms of the focus of this book the chapter concludes with a discussion of the place of curriculum knowledge in developing country reforms, debates and research.

The next two chapters establish a historical point of departure for the reforms that are discussed in the rest of the book by considering curriculum and pedagogy under apartheid. Chapter 3 gives a history of curriculum under apartheid, as well as providing some description of the provision of education especially for black learners at the time. The chapter shows that the purposes inscribed in the various curricula developed under apartheid shifted over time, through religious conversion, ideological conditioning, vocational preparation and, later, some sense of a liberal education for self-realisation. Throughout, however, it was a determinedly traditional, content-based curriculum with clear knowledge boundaries. While the curriculum for different race groups was very similar on paper, it differed vastly in implementation. Through a process of state neglect, extremely poor quality provision and learners' strong resistance to "education for domestication" (Freire, 1970), black learners were deprived of access to knowledge and meaningful learning. While apartheid succeeded in massifying schooling, it did so at the expense of quality, systematically depriving the vast majority of the population of a proper education.

Chapter 4 extends the account given in Chapter 3 into a consideration of pedagogy under apartheid. It begins by sketching out what attempts were made to shape pedagogy at this time, and why they failed to shift practice. The kinds of pedagogic forms found at this time were very similar to those described across a broad range of contexts in Chapter 2 – traditional forms that involved rote memorization of a low level of subject content with collective chorusing and chanting a common feature. I argue that a paucity of resources, in particular cognitive resources, can explain the dominance of these practices despite attempts to introduce different pedagogic forms.

Chapter 5 precedes the analyses of the post-apartheid curriculum policy reforms and ethnographic studies of the classrooms. It sets out the broad theoretical frame for the analyses in the chapters that follow and discusses the central conceptual resources used. An appendix is linked to this chapter, describing how the theory was deployed in different chapters. The following six chapters of the book alternate between an analysis of the curriculum policy reform and a study of pedagogy under that particular reform. The three curriculum reforms were:

Curriculum 2005 (C2005) implemented 1998–2002
National Curriculum Statement (NCS) implemented 2002–11;
Curriculum and Assessment Policy Statement (CAPS) 2012–current period.

The chapters track the changes in curriculum policy from the radical constructivist C2005 to the more traditional CAPS, showing how the position of knowledge and its specification shifted across the reforms. Under each reform I look at what pedagogic forms were found in classrooms. More detail on each of the chapters is provided below.

C2005 is analyzed in Chapter 6. C2005 was a radical learner-centred, constructivist project set in an outcomes-based curriculum form. C2005 precluded the specification of formal subject knowledge. In this version of a learner-centred reform teachers and learners were expected to select their own content and devise programmes of learning. Given the schooling system of which most had experience, the possibilities of teachers and learners co-constructing a curriculum with no guidance was extremely ambitious. The teacher and learner imagined by this curriculum could not have been further from the reality of those emerging from the degradation of apartheid schooling.

Chapter 7 considers C2005 in implementation looking at four Grade 1 classrooms. The analysis shows how the curriculum failed to disrupt many classroom practices that had been prevalent under apartheid. Without support from the curriculum around what to teach, and with an understanding that the new curriculum no longer required teachers to provide students with content, the pedagogy blocked the potential for students to access formal school knowledge. The case suggests how a radical learner-centred reform was subsumed into existing practice, especially in the face of poor teacher knowledge that could not compensate for the lack of knowledge signaling in the curriculum.

In Chapter 8 I analyze the second curriculum reform, the NCS. Although making some gains in the specification of knowledge, the chapter shows how the curriculum produced in this reform effort was a hybrid, filled with contradictions largely stemming from the play of different interests in the review process. It was also a product of its social and political milieu. Eight years into the new democratic regime the glaring inequalities generated under apartheid remained almost untouched. A strong emphasis on social justice and values defined the new curriculum and at the same time it continued to emphasise the importance of skills and fostering economic participation.

Chapter 9 considers pedagogy under the NCS curriculum regime, showing perhaps predictably that teachers' practice had shifted very little. The chapter describes the form of the pedagogy, drawing attention to the low level of localized, everyday knowledge that continued to predominate in classroom interaction, as well as a 'communalizing' orientation of the teacher towards the class where individual competences and responses were not sought.

Chapter 10 focuses on the third post-apartheid curriculum reform – the CAPS – showing how the curriculum marked a decisive shift towards a knowledge-based curriculum. In so doing the model of the teacher and student imagined approximated far more closely the reality of those in the system – teachers who required support in what to teach and students who required systematic induction into formal school knowledge. I go on in Chapter 11 to look at pedagogic practice subsequent to the implementation of the CAPS reform. Teachers adopted surface features of the new curriculum without effecting real change in the learning possibilities provided in their classrooms. The chapter argues that in the absence of specialized knowledge of reading and early mathematics, teachers were unable to make the appropriate judgments of students' productions to engender learning.

In concluding the book, Chapter 12 provides an overview of the central analyses, looking at the relationship between the macro societal structuring, the three curriculum reforms and the attendant pedagogic practice at the micro level of the classroom. The chapter draws together the arguments of the book and identifies some of the implications for theory, policy and research around teachers and pedagogy in particular. In relation to teachers I argue in the chapter that no reform is likely to succeed without a significant shift in the cognitive horizons of those teaching in our schools. I conclude with an argument for a relational conception of curriculum and pedagogy or knowledge *in* pedagogy in thinking about how to effect change.

Note

1 I use 'racial' categorisations – such as 'white', 'black' and 'African' – throughout the book that are rooted in generic and descriptive labels from 'racial' taxonomies generated under apartheid. Such classifications were constructed under apartheid law as part of oppressive social practices. The reason for using these is to examine the continued social inequalities impacting different groups in South African society, in particular unequal access to and experience of education.

References

Allais, S. (2014). Selling out education: National qualifications frameworks and the neglect of knowledge. Rotterdam: Sense Publishers.

Bernstein, B. (1975). Class, codes and control volume 3: Towards a theory of educational transmissions. London: Routledge & Kegan Paul.

Charlot, B. (2009). School and the pupils' work. *Sisifo Educational Sciences Journal, 10*, 87–94.

Craig, A. P. (1989). The conflict between the familiar and the unfamiliar. *South African Journal of Higher Education*, *3*(1), 166–171.

Freire, P. (1970). *Pedagogy of the oppressed.* New York: Herder & Herder.

MacDonald, C. (2002). Are the children still swimming up the waterfall? A look at literacy development in the new curriculum. *Language Matters*, *33*(1), 111–141.

Muller, J. (2000). Reclaiming knowledge: Social theory, curriculum and education policy. London: RoutledgeFalmer.

Ravich, D. (2000). *Left back: A century of battles over school reform*. New York: Simon and Schuster.

Schofield, J. W. (1993). Increasing the generalizability of qualitative research. In M. Hammersley (Ed.), *Educational research: current issues*. London: Paul Chapman Publishing, 201–232.

Spaull, N. (2013). South Africa's education crisis: the quality of education in South Africa 1994–2011. Johannesburg: The Centre for Development & Enterprise.

Spaull, N., & Kotze, J. (2015). Starting behind and staying behind in South Africa: The case of insurmountable learning deficits in mathematics. *International Journal of Educational Development*, *41*, 13–24.

Taylor, N., van der Berg, S., & Mabogoane, T. (2013). *Creating effective schools*. Cape Town: Pearson.

Taylor, N., & Vinjevold, P. (1999). Getting learning right: Report of the president's education initiative research project. Johannesburg: Joint Education Trust.

Van der Berg, S., Burger, C., Burger, R., de Vos, M., du Rand, G., Gustafsson, M., Moses, E., Shepherd, D. et al. (2011). *Low quality education as a poverty trap*. Stellenbosch: Stellenbosch University.

Van der Berg, S., Spaull, N., Wills, G., Gustaffson, M., & Kotze, J. (2016). *Identifying binding constraints in education*. Stellenbosch: Research on Socio-Economic Policy.

Venkat, H., & Spaull, N. (2015). What do we know about primary teachers' mathematical content knowledge in South Africa? An analysis of SACMEQ 2007. *International Journal of Educational Development*, *41*, 121–130.

Wyse, D., Hayward, L., Livingston, K., & Higgins, S. (2014). Creating curricula: Aims, knowledge, and control. *The Curriculum Journal*, *25*(1), 2–6.

Young, M. (2013). Overcoming the crisis in curriculum theory: A knowledge-based approach. *Journal of Curriculum Studies*, *45*(2), 101–118.

2 Curriculum and pedagogy in developing country contexts

Introduction

South Africa has a dual economy, a mix of developed and developing country features, with one of the highest levels of inequality in the world. This dual economy is reflected in a dual economy of schooling, between 'schools for the poor' and 'schools for the rich' (Van der Berg & Louw, 2006). Eighty percent of schools are no-fee and low-performing, where the vast majority of students are poor and African. Twenty percent of schools are multiracial (though formerly white), semi-privatized through user-fees, well-resourced and high-performing. With respect to dominant pedagogical forms, attempted curriculum reforms and educational outcomes, this 80% of schooling in South Africa strongly resembles education systems of other developing countries, albeit with its own particular history.

In this chapter I locate South Africa by reviewing the secondary literature on curriculum and pedagogy in developing countries. I begin by sketching what dominant forms of pedagogy look like across these contexts. I then go on to discuss some of the curriculum and pedagogy reforms that have been adopted, why they have been adopted and how they have fared. I also consider the research focused on what has worked in these contexts.

In this account of education in developing countries there is a risk of suggesting homogeneity within and between contexts that are highly heterogeneous. I want to draw attention to commonalities (of which there are many) rather than suggest that there is no difference between different contexts defined as 'developing'. The intention here is to suggest that South Africa represents a *case* of a developing country, with its particular curriculum and pedagogy reform dynamics presented in this book, being more broadly relevant.

In much of the commentary and critique of reform efforts, especially in post-colonial countries, the question of knowledge has been avoided. The mode of analysis generally is strategic, rhetorical or descriptive (Unterhalter, 2000). The problems of the dominant reform efforts – learner-centred and constructivist pedagogies and outcomes-based curricula – are often cast as problems of implementation. This book presents an epistemic account of curriculum and pedagogic change, focusing on how knowledge is positioned in curriculum and pedagogy in processes of reform. In concluding the present chapter I turn to some of the current theoretical debates around knowledge in curriculum and pedagogy that have been around for some time in the South African context.

What is the dominant pedagogic form in classrooms in developing country contexts?

A number of recent reviews of classroom practices in developing countries provide characterisations of dominant pedagogic forms across a range of contexts (for example, Nag et al., 2014 and Westbrook et al., 2013). There are also a host of country-specific studies that lend greater detail to the descriptions provided in these reviews. I draw on both the broad reviews and some of the country-specific ones (especially those based on countries in Sub-Saharan Africa) in order to describe these dominant forms. Again, the intention is not to homogenize or suggest no differences within and between contexts, but rather to identify common pedagogic and curriculum forms presented across the literature.

A ubiquitous developing country pedagogic form is identified as 'traditional' and involves rigid, teacher-dominated and lecture-driven instruction where 'chalk and talk' predominates. The pedagogy places students in a passive role and limits their activity to memorizing facts and reciting them back to the teacher. Various descriptors are attached to these practices: rote and surface learning, collective chanting, chorus, copywriting and drill. Limited curriculum coverage and exceptionally slow pacing are also features regularly cited.

Pedagogy in these contexts is also defined by bureaucratic routine, deferential ritual and whole class production of knowledge at a very low level of cognitive complexity. In these classrooms the undifferentiated pedagogy allows little scope for the evaluation of individual learner productions and the matching of instruction to meet a range of abilities and needs. Further, the classrooms are defined by ineffective use of instructional time and a lack of textbooks and texts. Discourse is predominantly oral, with limited engagement with written text for reading and writing (especially extended text).[1]

In summary, the literature shows that the pedagogic forms in classrooms in poor communities are consistent across a wide range of contexts, they have been dominant for a long time, have resisted a great deal of reform efforts and continue to dominate currently. These practices are associated with persistent low schooling outcomes (Glewwe & Muralidharan, 2015) that indicate that, despite impressive improvements in enrolments in education in developing countries, many children are receiving schooling without learning (Pritchett, 2013).

Learner-centred and outcomes-based reforms

As a result of persistent poor outcomes, there have been extensive policy debates and reform efforts around curriculum and pedagogy, regarded as key levers to address the quality of schooling (and in these developing contexts especially, improve the production of human capital). The wide series of reforms largely began in the 1980s, many coming with structural adjustment packages that, at the time, were also concerned with the structure of schooling and issues of curriculum (Chisholm & Leyendecker, 2008). In many countries changes in curriculum and teaching methods were proposed, and proposals generally were for the promotion of learner-centred (or child or student-centred) pedagogies, constructivist methods or curricula. The intention in almost all cases was to replace content-driven curricula by objectives-based, process-driven or outcomes-based curricula. In this neo-liberal shift, education market curricula were to become "more transparent and responsive to the needs of employers and learners" (Allais, 2014, p. xvii), and the requirements for economic growth and the production of human capital. The student in these curriculum types was often cast as a consumer who was able to choose, transfer and accumulate learning outcomes. Knowledge was atomized and commodified and choice was maximized.

There were other key and relatively common features of these learner-centred, outcomes-based reforms. One was that they stressed the inclusion of values, attitudes and skills as opposed to strictly content or knowledge. A second was the emphasis on relevance and the inclusion of local knowledge and ways of understanding. The third was a move towards integrated curricula, where thematic approaches were privileged (see Altinyelkin, 2010 for the Ugandan example).

Learner-centred pedagogies (LCPs) were also favoured by international aid organizations in the 1980s. The preference for these types of pedagogies was entrenched by the 1990 adoption of the 'World Declaration of Education for All' (UNESCO, 1990) as a global policy. Focusing on expanding access *and* improving quality, the document addressed the issue of quality largely through promoting revised curricula and new pedagogic regimes. Paragraph 44 of the framework reads as follows:

> Governments and all other EFA partners must work together to ensure basic education of quality for all, regardless of gender, wealth, location, language or ethnic origin. Successful education programmes require: (1) healthy, well-nourished and motivated students; (2) well-trained teachers and **active learning techniques**; (3) adequate facilities and learning materials; (4) a **relevant curriculum** that can be taught and learned in a local language and **builds upon the knowledge and experience of the teachers and learners**; (5) an environment that not only encourages learning but is welcoming, gender-sensitive, healthy and safe; (6) a clear definition and accurate assessment of **learning outcomes**, including **knowledge, skills, attitudes and values**; (7) participatory governance and management; and (8) respect for and engagement with local communities and cultures.
>
> (UNESCO, 1990, p. 16, emphasis added)

LCP, 'relevance', 'constructivism' and 'outcomes' were privileged in the construal of quality education amongst multilateral and donor agencies. Reforms with elements of these pedagogic and curriculum proposals were adopted across a wide range of developing countries throughout the 1990s and early 2000s. In 1999 the World Bank was explicit about its advocacy through the programmes it supported: "Since active learning is generally superior to learning by rote, countries that move strongly toward more participatory and individualized modes of learning will be at an advantage relative to those where teachers talk and write and students listen and read." (World Bank, 1999, p. 8). Thus, progressive pedagogic and curriculum features increasingly influenced the design of formal curricula and informed privileged pedagogies.

The progressive project

Although progressive education has meant different things to different people, most versions converge around two things: the importance attached to child development and an antagonism to the academic curriculum. In one version of progressivism, what Labaree (2012) terms 'bureaucratic progressivism', this antagonism led to an emphasis on vocational education, as well as a utilitarian approach to making schooling efficient, professionalized, bureaucratized and differentiated (Labaree, 2012). The other version, 'pedagogical progressivism' (with Dewey as the major inspiration), saw "developmentalism as a rationale for rejecting the traditional curriculum in favor of classroom processes that would harness individual student interests and abilities and would foster engaged, self-directed learning" (Labaree, 2012, p. 92).[2]

Both forms of progressivism found expression in reforms in developing country contexts over time. While pedagogical progressivism underpinned pedagogical reforms, bureaucratic progressivism was seen in curriculum frameworks. There were significant shifts toward 'outcomes-based' frameworks that focused on the specification of outcomes to be met by learners (often skills-based), rather than details of content to be covered. Barrett et al. (2007) argue that these curricula were (and largely still are) attractive to governments and international agencies because they held out a promise of producing prized '21st century skills': 'lifelong learners' with the 'flexibility' to adapt to rapidly changing work environments created by globalization and rapid technological developments. They were also appealing in that the LCP underpinning them, as well as emphasizing relevance and local knowledge, was viewed as inherently democratic.

Both strands of progressivism – bureaucratic and pedagogical – have led to knowledge dead ends. In the pedagogical sense, progressivism all too often treated knowledge as existing only to reproduce forms of social inequality, and thus subordinating it to needs and interests of the discovering, self-directed learner. In the bureaucratic strand, a utilitarian progressivism has tied education too directly to human capital development and indices of development and a consequent generic skills approach. Both lose sight of the fact that self-actualization *and* high level skills development may be epiphenomena of the learning of subject content knowledge. Be that as it may, the drive was towards measurable skill outcomes, packaged in politically palatable notions of learner-centredness.

Donor and international aid organization critique of LCP

The 2005 Global Monitoring Report (UNESCO, 2004), titled *Education for all (EFA): The Quality Imperative*, focused on the question of quality, with teaching and learning at its centre. Its approach was firmly within a school effectiveness mould, resembling earlier frameworks around quality in developing countries (for example, Lockheed & Verspoor, 1991). By this time, some criticism of LCP had begun to emerge. The report stated:

> Pedagogical renewal across sub-Saharan Africa has included many attempts to switch to learner centered, activity-oriented pedagogy and away from teacher-dominated instructional practices. These efforts may be explained in part by the current tendency of some international agencies to favour such pedagogies. In most of the countries concerned, however, attempts to institutionalise child-centered pedagogy in schools and teacher-training institutions have produced inconclusive results.
>
> (UNESCO, 2004, p. 3)

Ten years later, in the 2013/14 EFA report entitled "*Teaching and learning: Achieving quality learning for all*" (UNESCO, 2014), there is only one brief reference to learner-centred approaches, and scant reference to curriculum and pedagogy at all. The focus is on teacher quality, the recruitment, retention and training of good teachers and an even more intensive focus on inputs and outputs than in the 2013/14 report, with little attention to process. The only reference to pedagogy is a brief discussion of enduring dominant practices:

> In many low income countries, teaching relies on traditional approaches such as lecturing, rote learning and repetition, rather than fostering transferable skills such as critical thinking. A school-based teacher development programme in Kenya has shown that training can be effective in helping teachers adopt learner-centred methods.
>
> (2014, p. 40)

The curriculum emphasis throughout the 2014 document is on so-called 21st century skills, transferable skills:

> Curricula need to ensure that all children and young people learn not just foundation skills, but also transferable skills, such as critical thinking, problem-solving, advocacy and conflict-resolution, to help them become responsible global citizens. An interdisciplinary approach involving hands-on, locally relevant educational activities can also develop students' understanding of the environment and build skills to promote sustainable development.
>
> (p. 49)

Relevance and interdisciplinarity also remained part of the vocabulary, but there was less dedication to particular curriculum and pedagogy approaches beyond the very general and vague references in the above extract.

In a recent UNESCO document, 'Towards universal learning: Recommendations from the learning metrics task force' (LMTF, 2013), there is an abandonment of any form of curriculum or pedagogic prescription and a move to a preoccupation with ***measurement***. The report claims that the broader education community has reached a consensus on the skills and competencies that children need to acquire in schooling, and they are thus able to set forth "a broad, holistic framework of seven learning domains as the aspiration for all children and youth around the world by the time they reach the post-primary level" (p. 20). On the basis of this they argue that they can develop a small set of indicators to track at the global level. Given a competency frame, the framework ends up being up being predictably very generic. Rather than setting out clear common content, and with an emphasis on measurement of generic skills, the implicit assumption is that things will improve if you set out to measure – what you are measuring precisely is not, in the end, specified. Again, however, the move can be understood as part of the neo-liberal tendency of market economies to commodify and marketize knowledge and education provision, making measurement thereof essential.

Despite discernible broad trends there is contradiction and multivocality within and between international organizations. The World Bank, as a particular example, shifted from promoting LCP, to a critique of the ***implementation*** of LCP to a later critique of LCP itself (see Abadzi, 2006). The shifts in emphasis have thus not been linear, consistent or of a piece.

Why were the reforms taken up in developing countries?

A number of authors suggest that the LCP reforms were taken up in countries under pressure from multilateral and donor organizations. Many claim a hidden ideological agenda behind LCP as a prescription through educational projects and consultancies that were funded by them (Tabulawa, 2003, Altinyelkin, 2010). For some these reforms were disguised as 'better teaching' or neutral technical educational interventions, masking a form of cultural imperialism (Carney, 2008, Guthrie, 1990), echoing prior colonial encounters with their colonizing/domesticating pedagogies (Crossley & Tikly, 2004; Tabulawa, 2003). In more radical critique, the reforms "construct education and society more generally as objects of surveillance, transparent to the gaze of neo-liberal, supranational funding agencies and their conduit states" (Tamatea, 2005, p. 318).

However, not all subscribe to what is sometimes called the 'donor conspiracy' view above. Some of those focused on 'policy borrowing' argue that, in a context of globalization, nations look more broadly for education innovations, and these may be constrained *or* enabled by the international donor network (Paige et al., 2008). Chisholm and Leyendecker (2008) argue that pressure from donor networks only partially explains why LCP has readily been taken up. Importantly, for many countries, progressivist curriculum and pedagogy tenets "were not entirely new ideas and were ambiguous enough to be seen as key vehicles for achieving not so much educational, as economic, social and political goals" (Chisholm & Leyendecker, 2008, p. 2).

The argument around LCP as a vehicle for achieving extra-educational goals is confirmed in a review by Schweisfurth (2011) of 72 studies related to LCP, published in the *International Journal of Educational Development* between 1981 and 2010. These studies represented all the developing regions of the world and pertained to reforms in 39 different countries. A vast body of this research argues for LCP as an emancipatory vision for education, and LCP is set up to solve a range of educational, social and political problems. In developing countries it "enjoys an almost hegemonic position with its 'justified', 'admirable' and 'inspiring' educational ideas" (Altinyelken, 2010, p. 153), and a large scholarship supports the general position that active learning, using real-life situations, promotes students' ability to use their knowledge in a variety of contexts (Vavrus et al., 2011). In this research literature there is a *presumed* correspondence between pedagogical and political outcomes. Joel Samoff (1991) articulates this presumption: "Only education that is engaging and participatory in this sense can be empowering to non-elite students. And only where non-elites become self-conscious, self-reliant, self-confident and critical citizens can democratic society flourish" (p. 17). We will see that South Africa's first post-apartheid curriculum was a salutary lesson in relation to this elision of pedagogy and politics.

What has the impact of the reforms been?

Westbrook et al.'s (2013) review of pedagogy in developing countries found that constructivism was the most frequently cited theory underpinning pedagogy across a wide range of countries, with active learning and student-centred practices cited as the most frequently promoted pedagogies in national reforms and interventions (p. 31). In terms of curriculum models, the review found a shift from content-driven curricula to outcomes-based and competency-based curricula. Thematic and integrated curriculum designs often underpinned the promoted pedagogies. In the review the effects of these curricula and pedagogies was shown to be very thin and mixed. In general, the curricula emanating from reforms were found not to meet their goals, often being overloaded, fragmented and irrelevant. A key issue that the authors of the review draw out in relation to privileged pedagogic approaches is that the descriptions of pedagogic approaches as 'student-centred', 'child-centred' or 'active learning' lacked "details of actual practices, with the assumption that these terms were stable and the reader would know what they meant" (p. 31). Nonetheless, across the 489 studies of pedagogy in developing countries reviewed, Westbrook et al. (2013) found that child-centred, student-centred, learner-centred constructivism and social constructivism were by far the most dominant pedagogic approaches described or promoted in these studies.

Despite this espousal of dedication to LCP reforms, in large measure they have not been implemented successfully, and have failed to show effects on students' academic outcomes. In a number of cases, including South Africa, adoption of these reforms has impeded learning, especially where these 'process pedagogies' led teachers to think that content was no longer important and so was left out (Nykiel-Herbert, 2004; Balarin & Benavides, 2010, on Peru). In most cases, as the reviews above confirm, despite espousal of LCP, 'traditional' practices have persisted.

There is a wide range of reasons provided for the failure of the reforms. A number of researchers point to the superficial uptake of competence-based curriculum and LCP pedagogy reforms in local contexts, where the outward mechanics of the proposed practices were enacted without the underlying principle being observed. For example, putting students into groups but allowing interaction only between the teacher and student, or making superficial links between students' experiences and the subject content (Westbrook et al., 2013). What is seen is the 'mimicry' of outward forms of proposed pedagogy and 'ritualized' adoption of the form of policy (techniques, methods) without substantive change in the practice of teaching (for example, engaging with students' ideas and understanding).

This surface compliance to reforms is often a result of the nature of implementation. Here issues range from a lack of preparedness of the system, especially the training of teachers, to the pace of implementation, as well as the fact that many of the reforms are complex (and at times contradictory), with an unfamiliar set of concepts, methods and vocabulary. Abadzi (2006) argues that there is little common agreement on what terms mean. Active learning, child-centred learning, student-centred teaching, joyful learning, constructivism, outcome-based instruction, discovery-oriented, inquiry-based, technology-centred, project-based, group-oriented and individual-based (Abadzi, 2006, p. 73) are all contrasted to 'traditional', formal or direct instruction without much further explanation.

Another prominent account given for the failure or superficial uptake of the reforms is cultural dissonance. Altinyelkin (2010) gives a classic account of how learner-centred pedagogies contradict the cultural context of African (and many Asian) societies, particularly with respect to the adult-child relation. In the case of Uganda, he argues that "children are brought up to respect adults and those in authority . . . they are expected to be respectful, charming and smiling in the company of elders" (p. 155).

Further, some argue that teachers' conceptions of knowledge, its transmission and the purposes of schooling are often at odds with the reforms. One of the most ardent critics regarding dominant cultural models is Tabulawa (1997), who points out that shifts from traditional modes (what he calls, following Freire, the 'banking' mode) to learner-centred ones, requires teachers to fundamentally change their views of the nature of knowledge, of the learner and his/her role and of classroom organization in general. The reforms fundamentally disrupt the practitioner's taken-for-granted classroom world (Tabulawa, 1997: 192), which, he argues, is imbued with an intractable authoritarianism, stemming from missionary and colonial education as well as Tswana child-rearing practices.[3] Clarke (2003) refers to the 'cultural constructedness' of teacher thinking and teaching that resists change. In the Indian case, he shows how teachers skilfully integrate 'activity and joyful learning' into their traditional rote methods of instruction without changing the fundamental understanding of knowledge as given and to be memorized (p. 37–38).

Cultural traditions may emerge from diverse sources – indigenous practices, colonial structures, religious and racial hierarchies and particular understandings of time and of the child. What is interesting is the commonality of certain pedagogic features across different contexts, and Ensor (2015) points out that the difficulty with cultural explanations is that the specific practices in question – rote learning, collective chanting etc. – are extremely common across classrooms in poor communities in countries with very different cultural traditions. Alexander (2001) suggests that culture intersects with material conditions to produce particular pedagogic forms. In particular, very large classes and limited materials use rote learning as "a kind of cognitive blunderbuss which, if fired often enough, eventually has some kind of impact on the learning of most pupils, if not all of them" (Alexander, 2001, p. 424).

There are a number of researchers who support the argument that the pedagogy is a response to material conditions, especially large classes and lack of texts (Barrett et al., 2007; Jacklin, 2004), which are particularly acute in the context of the rapid expansion of primary schooling (Ackers & Hardman, 2001; Fuller & Snyder, 1991; Omokhodion,1989). Antiphony – whole class chorus chanting of responses to the teacher – provides a means for maintaining control and security in unpredictable and resource-constrained environments (Moloi et al., 2008; Chick, 1996). While the resource argument is important in the book, by focusing on knowledge I consider specifically the ***cognitive*** resources in the system and the ways in which these provide an explanation for enduring so-called traditional classroom practices.

What curriculum and pedagogy forms are effective?

If the LCP reforms have proven to be ineffective, what does research tell us about what works in developing country classrooms? While there are relatively robust descriptions of what classrooms look like, the evidence for pedagogic practices or curriculum forms that promote better student outcomes is meagre. There isn't a robust ***body of research*** that might inform how we address the problem of pedagogy in the context of poverty in developing country contexts. In this section I review the evidence there is and, in doing so, raise three issues in relation to this body of research: the evidence produced by this research, the role of theory and the place of knowledge in debates around curriculum and pedagogy.

The evidence

Here I report on three reviews which systematically worked through the research literature on classroom practices in developing countries in order to discern effective pedagogic practices: Abadzi (2006), Nag et al. (2014) and Glewwe and Muralidharan (2015).

Abadzi (2006), for the World Bank, considered the evidence in the effectiveness tradition that related particular classroom methodologies to improved student outcomes. The effectiveness of five dominant methodologies found in classrooms in developing countries were considered: 1) chalk and talk; 2) practice, questions, feedback and discussion; 3) independent seatwork (including copying); 4) groupwork; and 5) projects. First, in relation to chalk and talk she makes the point that the method (how) is not really problematic, but concerns rather for what chalk and talk is used. When the teacher talks and uses the board in order to introduce anecdotes, analogies, stories, hooks and links, these can be extremely conducive to learning. In relation to the second method, she argues that, although the developed world evidence around practice, questions, feedback and discussion is that it is very effective, there is insufficient evidence of these practices actually occurring in developing country classrooms to really consider effectiveness.

Abadzi also found that the third methodology considered, independent seatwork, had limited effectiveness because, all too often, a majority of children did not participate, paying less attention during routine practice exercises. In this form copying was found to be common and not effective. Fourth, groupwork, considered to be desirable across a vast range of contexts, was found to be negatively associated with achievement in developing country contexts given difficulties of controlling large classes as well as monitoring participation. Finally, projects were found to be ineffective. Thus, the only finding to emerge from this review is that classroom discussion is effective, but rare. Overall, Abadzi's review failed to find strong links between any particular classroom activity and learning outcomes.

More recently, Nag et al. (2014) undertook a comprehensive review of early language and numeracy, the empirical focus of this book. Alongside a review of qualitative and naturalistic studies of literacy and numeracy instruction, they also undertook a systematic review of randomized controlled trials (RCTs) and quasi-experimental studies (QES). They found relatively few robust evaluations of the efficacy of interventions. After excluding studies of low quality, eight RCTs and eight QED studies in early literacy and numeracy were reviewed.

Their review of RCTs found positive impacts of six different programmes for reading and/or numeracy. These were:

- A '31-day reading marathon' (Abeberese et al., 2011), and a whole-class dialogic reading intervention (Opel et al., 2009) found positive effects on reading and on expressive vocabulary development, respectively.
- For numeracy, a programme which included 'hands-on' mathematics activities (Opel et al., 2012) and a computer-assisted learning programme (Banerjee et al., 2007) were shown to be effective.
- Two programmes combining literacy and numeracy instruction showed evidence of positive effects. One was four months' exposure to an educational multimedia intervention (Borzekowski & Henry, 2011), and the other a remedial intervention using young women from the local community as teachers (Banerjee et al., 2007).

The specificity and singularity of these studies makes it difficult to draw any general lessons, however, especially given that the studies failed to systematically investigate the factors critical to the success of the interventions. Nag et al.

(2014) also point out that it is important to recognize, in resource-poor settings, that it might be relatively easy to bring about immediate gains (and, I would add, relatively low-level gains, for example in Bannerjee et al., 2007).

In a recent review of evidence around effectiveness in developing countries economists Glewwe and Muralidharan (2015) claim that "Overall, the evidence on pedagogy suggests that the quality of classroom pedagogy may be a key determinant of the extent to which increases in school inputs are translated into improvements in learning" (p. 58). But their evidence is thin and largely draws on the RCTs cited above that suffer significant threats to external validity (being singular, context-specific studies). In addition, as they themselves acknowledge, "there is a relative paucity of well-identified quantitative evidence on the critical question of how best to structure classroom instruction and pedagogy to most effectively improve learning outcomes in developing countries" (p. 48). Nonetheless, they go on to report on a very small number of 'high quality studies' that have looked at the impact of pedagogy on student outcomes in developing countries.

Most of Glewwe and Muralidharan's evidence is drawn from RCTs of the Pratham literacy non-governmental organization (NGO) in India. Further scrutiny of what the improvements entail shows that these are off a very low base and equip students with very rudimentary skills, such as letter and word recognition. Although an important first step, these children are probably as far from reading as they were prior to the intervention. These claims are a good example of how a focus on impact and measurement (here of improvements) distracts from clear thinking around what constitutes educational improvement (learning to read).

Nonetheless, the authors draw attention to four promising directions. The first is remedial interventions that teach to a targeted level and increase instructional time. The second is tracking, which helps to decrease the heterogeneity of student learning levels in a given class, a significant problem, especially in developing country classrooms (evidence is provided from a single RCT).

Third, based on a single RCT in the Philippines, the authors draw attention to one programme that provided age-appropriate reading materials and trained teachers to incorporate reading into their teaching and which reported significant gains in student outcomes in reading. Finally, their fourth pedagogic point is one that is of great interest, both in South Africa and elsewhere, where currently vast sums of money are being diverted from other programmes into ICT infrastructure. They conclude from relevant studies that the key success factor in technology-enhanced education interventions is "the extent to which careful thought goes into integrating effective pedagogical techniques with technology" (p. 56). In other words, they recognize technology as another pedagogical tool (much like a textbook) rather than a substitute for effective pedagogy.

These suggested directions and conclusions are useful, both challenging common assumptions and appealing to educational good sense. However, their evidence is too localized and thin. In general, evidence around effective classroom practice in developing countries is weak and the studies often claim too much for and of RCTs in directing what we should do (Deaton in Ogden, 2016). The studies also work with an atomized conception of pedagogy. Without a strong theory and research design to investigate pedagogy as a set of ***related*** aspects and dimensions, it is doubtful that these kinds of recommendations and suggestions advance understanding of classroom processes, how they work and how they can improve outcomes.

Alexander (2014) produces a related critique, especially of the construal of pedagogic forms in and for developing countries privileged by international aid agencies and the Global Monitoring Reports produced by UNESCO referenced above. He identifies the conflation of indicators and measurement and the lack of attention to process variables in accounts of pedagogy. He argues that this mass of research and policy work misses the "'thick description' of close-grained, cross-national and cross-cultural comparative studies of school and classroom life and the forces that shape it" (p. 9). Finally, I would argue that because there is no focus on knowledge, proposals and recommendations fail to recognize the difficulty of change in the absence of a shift in the discursive or cognitive recourses necessary to enact change, the focus of this book.

Theorizing pedagogy and knowledge

One of the problems with the specification, implementation and analysis of various reforms, including discerning 'what works', is the sparse theoretical articulation of pedagogy: what does pedagogy entail, what are its dimensions and how do these dimensions relate? In general, the lack of theory in the research reviewed for this chapter is most obvious in discussions around learner-centredness. What learner-centred in fact means varies considerably in its usage and intention. Hopkins (2002) argues that on the one hand, LCP refers to

> a particular ethos within a school or classroom that prizes individuality of the learner, that respects the current phase of their learning history, and that creates conditions within the school and classroom where the learner feels accepted and secure. In simple terms, this approach to child-centered learning refers to a caring, accepting and happy school environment
>
> (p. 280).

Bernstein (1990) would refer to this as the 'regulative discourse', or the hidden curriculum of the classroom, its social norms, culture and affective dimensions. On the other hand, Hopkins argues, LCP refers to cognitive development, the children as active learners who both respond to tasks and set tasks themselves, and who actively construct meaning. This concerns the instructional discourse (Bernstein, 1990), which refers to the transmission and acquisition of content, skills, knowledge in the pedagogy. I will return to this distinction between instructional and regulative discourse below, but for now it makes clear that different authors are not always talking about the same thing.

In their extensive reviews both Schweisfurth (2011) and Barrett (2008) call for frameworks better able to analyze pedagogy. The lack of theory is evidenced in an impatience amongst many researchers with the teacher-centred/learner-centred dichotomy, which not only lacks precise referents as indicated above, but also negates a continuum of possibilities between authoritarian teacher-led 'chalk and talk' and unstructured discovery (Barrett et al., 2007). Vavrus (2009) summarises that it is not formalism or constructivism that should be promoted but rather a 'contingent pedagogy' or 'contingent constructivism' that adapts to the material conditions, as well as local traditions, of teaching, and the cultural politics of teaching in particular contexts. This notion is similar to that of Altinyelken's (2010) description of Ugandan teachers' 'pedagogic palette' and Tikly's (2011) 'structured pedagogy', which suggest a mix of teacher-centred and learner- centred features, particularly relevant where teachers are required to graft new and very different pedagogies onto established old ones.

This book exemplifies a particular approach to 'anatomizing pedagogy' (Fitz et al., 2006), drawing predominantly on Bernstein's (1990) theorization of pedagogic discourse. The theory allows for the isolation of specific variables or dimensions that make up pedagogy without prior normative or ideological assumptions regarding 'best practice' (like learner-centredness). Bernstein's theory recognizes the structuring effects of the cultural or social discourses within which instruction is situated: for Bernstein educational processes embed a discourse of competence (instructional) in a discourse of social order (regulative) "in a way that the latter always dominates the former" (Bernstein, 1990, p. 183). Work in this tradition has already begun to tease out the lineaments of a 'mixed pedagogy', more beneficial for children schooled in poor contexts. In their review, Hoadley and Muller (2009) argue that empirical evidence from this body of work has underlined the futility of current curriculum policy debates between 'learner-centred' approaches and the 'back to basics' lobbies. What students require is a hybrid of these, varying across specific dimensions.

Sriprakash (2012) used a Bernsteinian framework in her analysis of a child-centred education reform in India. She showed how the LCP (or what she terms following Bernstein, 'competence') reform was recontextualized through an existing performance regime that emphasized ability and privileged narrowly evaluated, written outputs. In addition the regulative discourse of the classroom emphasized hierarchy and strict rules, at odds with the democratic ideals of LCP. She found that in this way both the existing instructional and regulative discourse of schooling mitigated implementation of the reform. It is this kind of theoretically nuanced study that helpfully moves beyond more blunt characterizations of learner-centred/teacher-centred pedagogy.

The Bernsteinian framework also draws attention to subject knowledge. In this schema subject knowledge is captured in particular in the concepts of classification (the organization of knowledge in curricula) and evaluation (which concerns the transmission of knowledge criteria in pedagogy). A concern with *what* is to be learnt (subject knowledge) is notably absent in the vast body of literature around curriculum and pedagogy in developing country contexts. I discuss this issue in depth below.

Knowledge

In reviewing the literature referred to above, what emerges is a silence around the issue of curriculum knowledge and its transmission, despite clear threats to knowledge that are posed by the reforms across developing country contexts. One of the few passing references to one of these threats is made by Vavrus et al. (2011), who suggest the possibility that constructivist pedagogies undermine the authority of the teacher:

> One of the principal philosophical challenges lies at the heart of learner-centered pedagogy: the notion that knowledge can be co-constructed by teachers ***and*** students. The assumption may engender hostility as it challenges the authority vested in teachers as the person in the classroom who possesses knowledge.
>
> (p. 13)

A common feature of learner-centred, constructivist or outcomes-based reforms, is that, in reaction to content-laden syllabi, much of the content is removed and replaced with themes, generic outcomes or broad competences and strategies. Alternatively, teachers are led to believe that content isn't important and curriculum is eclipsed by a strong (political) pedagogical project. South Africa's first post-apartheid curriculum provides a telling case of knowledge erasure in an LCP reform (in Chapters 6 and 7).

South Africa is somewhat unique, however, when considering the developing country literature in relation to the robust debates it has had around knowledge. These debates stem from both policy processes and research. Although elaborated further in the book, I discuss the issues of knowledge and pedagogy and debates around these in the South African context in particular, below.

Knowledge debates in the South African context

A number of aspects of the very lively debate around knowledge in the South African context have played out in interesting ways in relation to the reforms considered in this book. The issue of knowledge and the curriculum was emphasized early on in the post-apartheid reform era. Initially, in the thinking around a post-apartheid curriculum, some scholars began to reflect on some of the alternative thrusts in the anti-apartheid movements, asking questions in relation to LCP proposals that were generated there. A central concern was how to ensure that the inclusion of the proliferating 'worlds of meaning', including that of the everyday knowledge of learners, didn't deform the formal knowledge of the curriculum. "How can or should the commonsense knowledge of experience and folklore, indeed of the everyday world, relate to the codified knowledge deemed worthy of inclusion, reproduction and certification in the formal curriculum?"(Muller & Taylor, 1993, p. 317). In other words, there was a concern by some from the beginning around the relationship between formal school knowledge on the one hand and everyday knowledge and relevance on the other. In the mid-1990s these concerns were sustained in a series of papers[4] that argued that everyday knowledges, radical forms of LCP or constructivism increase the difficulties that working-class children will have in trying to acquire the formal discourses of schooling (Taylor & Vinjevold, 1999). These ideas fanned fiery debate.

The first post-apartheid reform (in 1998) was based on a radical form of LCP and an outcomes-based framework. In the review of this first curriculum, debates around knowledge were extended into questions of curriculum integration, knowledge progression and school knowledge as having an objective conceptual structure. In some ways the debate around knowledge split curriculum scholars into two 'tribes' – one focused on the knower (and constructivist epistemologies) and one on knowledge (and the forging of arguments in a realist frame) (Hoadley, 2010). In the two subsequent post-apartheid reforms in 2002 and 2012, debates around knowledge and the curriculum shaped the processes and foregrounded a set of issues: the distinction between everyday knowledge and school knowledge, the role of formal knowledge and subjects in the curriculum, the specialized and differentiated nature of knowledge and the distinction between curriculum and pedagogy. The distinctions and debates are presented in detail in the discussions on curriculum change, pedagogy and the position of knowledge in the chapters that follow. The point here is that, in South Africa as a developing country undergoing similar reforms to elsewhere, LCP and competency-based frameworks were highly contested in relation to the question of knowledge.

Pedagogical debates in the South African context

Alongside and related to issues of knowledge, pedagogy has also been the subject of intense debate. In explaining the contours of the debate, the distinction introduced earlier is useful in this regard: pedagogy entails the transaction of knowledge (instructional discourse as above), and it does so within a set of social relations or is embedded in a set of social norms or culture (regulative discourse). Both are critical to an understanding of the social form of pedagogy and the transmission of content. A review of the literature above suggests, however, that much focus (especially in discussions about teacher-centred and learner-centred pedagogies, as well as the need to acknowledge existing cultural forms) is on regulative discourse. Failure to make the distinction between regulative and instructional aspects of pedagogy has led to an interesting debate that has evolved through a series of papers (Hoadley, 2006; Hugo & Wedekind, 2013a; Zipin, 2013, Hugo & Wedekind, 2013b) and has been drawn into discussion around pedagogic forms in developing countries more broadly (Guthrie, 2015).

The debate is essentially about the place of knowledge in pedagogy, and two positions (not dissimilar to the knowledge/knower split referred to earlier) emerge. Hugo and Wedekind (2013a) argue that, without specialized knowledge driving pedagogy, there is no pedagogy (what they term 'zero pedagogy').[5] Zipin

(2013) counters that the privileging of specialized knowledge in the pedagogic relation over everyday knowledge is a 'Euro-cultural imperialism' suppressing debate around *whose* knowledge is represented. Zipin, invoking the notion of 'funds of knowledge' states that "rich cultural resources in the lives of both learners and teachers are what is un(der)valued in the prime stress on 'specialised' knowledge" (p. 162). Hugo and Wedekind argue that, while teachers do bring funds of knowledge to the classroom, this does not qualify them as teachers – their specialized, knowledge-based practice does.

Hugo and Wedekind and Zipin differ on the 'ordering principles of pedagogy'. For the former it is specialization, for Zipin 'deep everyday knowledge of a community'. While both specialized and everyday knowledge feature in pedagogy, the question Hugo and Wedekind raise is which principle does the ordering (p. 170). This is a crucial move, linking thinking around knowledge to how we think about pedagogic forms and thus delineating the crux of the debate. But arguably, they are talking about different things. Zipin's points are relevant to regulative discourse, but perhaps not instructional discourse. In instructional discourse, the proliferation of everyday knowledge to the exclusion of specialized, codified knowledge is one that has long characterized the South African and other developing country contexts, often rooted in competency-based curriculum and progressive pedagogic reforms discussed at length above.

Guthrie (2015) challenges Hugo and Wedekind's argument more directly in relation to instructional discourse, as one focused on 'disciplinary induction'. This focus, according to him, reflects "a Northern, continental European academic tradition that is highly contestable in the South and, in their version, denied indigenous culture unless filtered through Eurocentric disciplinary induction" (p. 164). The argument as to why disciplinary induction and a focus on knowledge specialization should be the preserve of Europe or the North is not made explicit.

The debate, then, has moved beyond the question of teaching styles (learner-centred/teacher-centred) to the question of knowledge and the ordering principles of pedagogy. Guthrie (and many others) dismisses the emphasis on access to specialized formal knowledge in labeling it 'Eurocentric' and arguing that it constructs a deficit model of children's knowledge. The book will argue that the subordination of the formal knowledge of schooling to particular pedagogic styles or forms has been radically experimented with in the South African case in the first apartheid curriculum, C2005, demonstrating clearly the damage of not recognizing the school as the *only* site through which *most* children will access formal knowledge. This knowledge is not the preserve of Europe or any other developed nation and the deficit lies not within the ways in which it is transmitted, but when it is not transmitted at all.

'Zero pedagogy' refers to the collapse of the instructional discourse in pedagogy. However, there remains a regulative discourse where teachers and students come with lived, everyday knowledge and experience to the classroom, with particular social norms and understanding of the relationship between adults and children. My interest in the book is the relationship between these two discourses – instructional and regulative – and the ways in which specialized knowledge shapes and changes both and their relation to each other. While Bernstein claims that regulative discourse is dominant, I will go on to suggest that in the context under study here it is possibly instructional discourse that is dominant, where knowledge shapes the moral order, social norms and relationships of the classroom.

Notes

1 See Hoadley (2012) and Adekola (2007) for reviews of South African and Nigerian classrooms that provide examples of the detailed accounts of pedagogy given of these and other specific country contexts in the literature.
2 Ravich (2000) identifies a third form of progressivism which she terms 'intellectual progressivism' which championed students' joy in learning without denying the importance of academic disciplines (promoted by people like Thomas Sizer, Howard Gardner and Deborah Meier, and arguably Dewey himself). This form of progressivism did not, however, take root in the public system, in a sense being trumped by bureaucratic progressivism. Rather by the end of the 20th century it was the preserve of elite private and small alternative schools.
3 Tabulawa (1997), however, though an ardent affirmer of traditional and local pedagogic practice, acknowledges that, in the face of a colonial history, it is difficult to determine what a local, 'authentic' pedagogy is. Mass schooling is also an invention of colonial powers and, in any case, does not stem from indigenous educational practices. Further, as Schweisfurth (2002) points out, there is also a danger in reifying culture, something that has been done time and again in relation to less salutary practices in Africa.
4 For example, Dowling 1995; Ensor 1997; Davis 1996; Muller and Taylor 1995.
5 They draw on arguments forged over time by a wide range of South Africa scholars including Yael Shalem, Joe Muller, Lynne Slonimsky, Paula Ensor and Jeanne Gamble, as well as others.

References

Abadzi, H. (2006). Efficient learning for the poor: Insights from the frontier of cognitive neuroscience. Washington: World Bank Publications.

Abeberese, A. B., Kumler, T. & Linden, L. L. (2011). Improving reading skills by encouraging children to read: A randomized evaluation of the Sa Aklat Sisikat Reading Program in the Philippines No. NBER Working Paper No. 17185.). Cambridge, MA: National Bureau of Economic Research.

Ackers, J., & Hardman, F. (2001). Classroom interaction in Kenyan primary schools. *Compare*, *31*(2), 245–261.

Adekola, O. A. (2007). Language, literacy and learning in primary schools: Implications for teacher development programs in Nigeria. Washington: World Bank Publications.

Alexander, R. (2001). Culture and pedagogy: International comparisons in primary education. Oxford: Blackwell.

Alexander, R. (2014, February). Teaching and learning: The quality imperative revisited. Paper presented at the Teaching and Learning for Development: the 2013/14 Education for All Global Monitoring Report Conference. 3 February, Oslo.

Allais, S. (2014). Selling out education: National qualifications frameworks and the neglect of knowledge. Springer.

Altinyelken, H. K. (2010). Curriculum change in Uganda: Teacher perspectives on the new thematic curriculum. *International Journal of Educational Development, 30*(2), 151–161.

Balarin, M., & Benavides, M. (2010). Curriculum reform and the displacement of knowledge in Peruvian rural secondary schools: Exploring the unintended local consequences of global education policies. *Compare, 40*(3), 311–325.

Banerjee, A., Cole, S., Duflo, E., & Linden, L. (2007). Remedying education: Evidence from two randomized experiments in India. *Quarterly Journal of Economics, 122*(3), 1235–1264.

Barrett, A., Ali, S., Clegg, J., Hinostroza, J. E., Lowe, J., Nikel, J., et al. (2007). *Initiatives to improve the quality of teaching and learning: A review of recent literature* No. EdQual Working Paper No. 11).

Barrett, A. M. (2008). Capturing the difference: Primary school teacher identity in Tanzania. *International Journal of Educational Development, 28*(5), 496–507.

Bernstein, B. (1990). Class, codes and control: The structuring of pedagogic discourse, vol. 4. London: Taylor and Frances.

Borzekowski, D. L., & Henry, H. K. (2011). The impact of jalan sesama on the educational and healthy development of Indonesian preschool children: An experimental study. *International Journal of Behavioral Development, 35*(2), 169–179.

Carney, S. (2008). Learner-centred pedagogy in Tibet: International education reform in a local context. *Comparative Education, 44*(1), 39–55.

Chick, J. K. (1996). Safe-talk: Collusion in apartheid education. *Society and the Language Classroom*, 21–39.

Chisholm, L., & Leyendecker, R. (2008). Curriculum reform in post-1990s sub-Saharan Africa. *International Journal of Educational Development, 28*(2), 195–205.

Clarke, P. (2003). Culture and classroom reform: The case of the district primary education project, India. *Comparative Education, 39*(1), 27–44.

Crossley, M., & Tikly, L. (2004). Postcolonial perspectives and comparative and international research in education: A critical introduction. *Comparative Education, 40*(2), 147–156.

Davis, Z. (1996). The problem-centred approach and the production of the vanishing pedagogue. *Kenton-at-Wilgespruit Conference, October.*

Dowling, P. (1995). Discipline and mathematise: The myth of relevance in education. *Perspectives in Education, 16*(2), 209–226.

Ensor, P. (1997). School mathematics, everyday life and the NQF: A case of non-equivalence? *Pythagorus, 41*, 36–44.

Ensor, P. (2015). Regulative discourse, ritual and the recontextualising of education policy into practice. *Learning, Culture and Social Interaction, 6*, 67–76.

Fitz, J., Davies, B., & Evans, J. (2006). Education policy and social reproduction: Class inscription & symbolic control. London: Routledge.

Fuller, B., & Snyder, C. W. (1991). Vocal teachers, silent pupils? Life in Botswana classrooms. *Comparative Education Review, 2*, 274–294.

Glewwe, P., & Muralidharan, K. (2015). Improving school education outcomes in developing countries: Evidence, knowledge gaps, and policy implications. *University of Oxford, Research on Improving Systems of Education (RISE).*

Guthrie, G. (1990). To the defense of traditional teaching in lesser developed countries. In V. D. Rust & P. Dalin (Eds.), *Teachers and teaching in the developing world* (pp. 219–232). London & New York: Garland Publishing.

Guthrie, G. (2015). Culturally grounded pedagogy and research methodology. *Compare, 45*(1), 163–168.

Hoadley, U. (2006). Analysing pedagogy: The problem of framing. *Journal of Education, 40*, 15–34.

Hoadley, U. (2010). Tribes and territory: Contestation around curriculum in South Africa. In W. Pinar (Ed.). *Curriculum studies in South Africa: Intellectual histories and present circumstances* (pp. 125–176). Palgrave MacMillan.

Hoadley, U. (2012). What do we know about teaching and learning in South African primary schools? *Education as Change, 16*(2), 187–202.

Hoadley, U., & Muller, J. (2009). Codes, pedagogy and knowledge: advances in Bernsteinian sociology of education. In M. W. Apple, S. J. Ball & L. A. Gandin (Eds.), *The Routledge international handbook of sociology of education*. London: Routledge.

Hopkins, D. (2002). The Aga Khan Foundation school improvement initiative: An international change perspective. In S. E. Anderson (Ed.), *School improvement through teacher development: Case studies of the Aga Khan Foundation projects in East Africa* (pp. 271–296). Lisse, The Netherlands: Swets & Zetlinger Publishers.

Hugo, W., & Wedekind, V. (2013a). Ordering principles and operating principles of pedagogy: A reply to Zipin. *Southern African Review of Education, 19*(1), 167–176.

Hugo, W., & Wedekind, V. (2013b). Six failures of the pedagogic imagination. *Southern African Review of Education, 19*(1), 139–158.

Jacklin, H. (2004). *Repetition and difference: A rhythmanalysis of pedagogic practice.* Unpublished PhD dissertation, University of Witwatersrand.

Labaree, D. F. (2012). *Someone has to fail.* Cambridge, MA: Harvard University Press.

LMTF (Learning Metrics Task Force). (2013). *Toward universal learning: Recommendations from the learning metrics task force.* Montreal and Washington, DC: UNESCO Institute for Statistics and Center for Universal Education at the Brookings Institution.

Lockheed, M. E., & Verspoor, A. M. (1991). *Improving primary education in developing countries.* Oxford University Press for World Bank.

Moloi, F., Morobe, N., & Urwick, J. (2008). Free but inaccessible primary education: A critique of the pedagogy of English and mathematics in Lesotho. *International Journal of Educational Development, 28*(5), 612–621.

Muller, J., & Taylor, N. (1993). Into other wor(l)ds: Curricular knowledge in the making. In N. Taylor (Ed.), *Inventing knowledge.* (pp. 145–161). Cape Town: Maskew Miller Longman.

Muller, J., & Taylor, N. (1995). Schooling and everyday life: Knowledges sacred and profane. *Social Epistemology, 9*(3), 257–275.

Nag, S., Chiat, S., Torgerson, C., & Snowling, M. J. (2014). Literacy, foundation learning and assessment in developing countries: Final report education rigorous literature review. Department for International Development.

Nykiel-Herbert, B. (2004). Mis-constructing knowledge: The case of learner-centred pedagogy in south Africa. *Prospects, 34*(3), 249–265.

Ogden, T. (2016). *Experimental conversations.* Cambridge, MA: MIT Press.

Omokhodion, J. O. (1989). Classroom observed: The hidden curriculum in Lagos, Nigeria. *International Journal of Educational Development, 9*(2), 99–110.

Opel, A., Ameer, S. S., & Aboud, F. E. (2009). The effect of preschool dialogic reading on vocabulary among rural Bangladeshi children. *International Journal of Educational Research, 48*(1), 12–20.

Opel A, Zaman SS, Khanom F, Aboud FE (2012). Evaluation of a mathematics program for preprimary children in rural Bangladesh. *International Journal of Educational*
Development 32(1): 104–110.

Paige, K., Chartres, M., & Kenyon, A. (2008). Using teacher stories to reveal quality educational practice: An Eastern Cape experience. *International Journal of Educational Development, 28*(5), 524–533.

Pritchett, L. (2013). The rebirth of education: Schooling ain't learning. Washington: Brookings Institute Press.

Ravich, D. (2000). *Left back: A century of battles over school reform.* New York: Simon and Schuster.

Samoff, J. (1991). Socialist education? *Comparative Education Review, 1*, 1–22.

Schweisfurth, M. (2002). Teachers, democratisation and educational reform in Russia and South Africa. Oxford: Symposium Books Ltd.

Schweisfurth, M. (2011). Learner-centred education in developing country contexts: From solution to problem? *International Journal of Educational Development, 31*(5), 425–432.

Sriprakash, A. (2012). Pedagogies for development: The politics and practices of child-centered education in India. *Education in the Asia-Pacific Region: Issues, Concerns and Prospects, 16*, 179–189.

Tabulawa, R. (1997). Pedagogical classroom practice and social context: The Case of Botswana. *International Journal of Educational Development, 17*(2), 189–204.

Tabulawa, R. (2003). International aid agencies, learner-centred pedagogy and political democratisation: A critique. *Comparative Education, 39*(1), 7–26.

Tamatea, L. (2005). The Dakar framework: Constructing and deconstructing the global neo-liberal matrix. *Globalisation, Societies and Education, 3*(3), 311–334.

Taylor, N., & Vinjevold, P. (1999). Getting learning right: Report of the president's education initiative research project. Johannesburg: Joint Education Trust.

Tikly, L. (2011). Towards a framework for researching the quality of education in low-income countries. *Comparative Education, 47*(1), 1–23.

UNESCO. (1990). World declaration on education for all: Meeting basic learning needs. In *World conference on education for all, Jomtien, March 1990.* Paris: UNESCO.

UNESCO. (2004). Education for all: The quality imperative: EFA global monitoring report. Paris: UNESCO.

UNESCO. (2014). Teaching and learning: Achieving quality for all: EFA global monitoring report 2013/14. Paris: UNESCO.

Unterhalter, E. (2000). Education, citizenship and difference in the South African transition: Policy, politics and practice. *Curriculum journal, 11*(1), 69–85.

Van der Berg, S., & Louw, M. (2006). *Lessons learnt from SACMEQII: South African student performance in regional context.* Paper presented at the Investment Choices for Education in Africa Conference, September 19–21, in Johannesburg, South Africa.

Vavrus, F. (2009). The cultural politics of constructivist pedagogies: Teacher education reform in the United Republic of Tanzania. *International Journal of Educational Development, 29*(3), 303–311.

Vavrus, F., Thomas, M., & Bartlett. L. (2011). Ensuring quality by attending to inquiry: Learner-centered pedagogy in sub-Saharan Africa. Addis-Ababa: UNESCO

Westbrook, J., Durrani, N., Brown, R., Orr, D., Pryor, J., & Boddy, J. (2013). Pedagogy, curriculum, teaching practices and teacher education in developing countries, EPPI education rigorous literature review. London: Institute of Education.
World Bank. (1999). ***Education sector strategy***. Washington, DC: World Bank.
Zipin, L. (2013). Starting from pedagogical zero in 'developing' contexts? Let's re-imagine! A response to Hugo and Wedekind. ***Southern African Review of Education With Education with Production***, *19*(1), 158–166.

3 From tribalism to technicism

Curriculum policy under apartheid

Introduction

This chapter traces the evolution of the national curriculum under the apartheid regime. I begin by looking briefly at the roots of segregated education in South Africa under colonial rule and then look in some detail at the apartheid period, 1948 to 1994. In this way I lay the ground for the analyses of curriculum reforms under the democratic regime, the focus of this book. In the chapter I show how curriculum under apartheid was not a unified, monolithic approach to education as it is sometimes characterized. It was reformed in relation to changes in the political economy, and it was adapted to the ideological shifts across the 46-year apartheid rule under the National Party. Consonant with the focus of the book, the chapter considers the distributive regime over time – who was given access to what knowledge. The chapter also focuses on the ways in which particular knowers were projected for schooling and how this projected (or ideal) knower shifted over time. These shifts occurred both in relation to the racial ideologies of the time, as well as in response to changes in the economy and demands for labour.

Characterizing curriculum under apartheid is difficult, as no easy generalizations can be made. By 1984 there were 19 separate education departments, divided along racial, political and geographic lines. Although curriculum remained largely a centralized state function, its implementation varied greatly across these departments, and different departments undertook some independent curriculum tinkering. In attempting to maintain the edifice that was apartheid, constant changes in the organization and structuring of education took place as the state attempted to address the economic, social and political fissures that emerged over time. In addition, the education apparatus was not entirely sealed off from broader international trends in curriculum and these were also reflected in curriculum reforms.

Throughout, however, the various curricula produced under apartheid took a determinedly traditional, content-based form with clear knowledge boundaries. While the curriculum for different race groups was very similar on paper, it differed vastly in implementation. Through a process of state neglect, extremely poor quality provision and student resistance to this provision, black learners were deprived of access to knowledge and meaningful learning. While apartheid succeeded in massifying schooling, the quality of that schooling for the majority was dire.

This chapter draws largely on secondary literature and original curriculum documents and reports in constructing an account of the shifts in the official pedagogic discourse under apartheid. Given the complexity of curriculum construction under apartheid it is difficult to do it justice in a single chapter. Nonetheless, the aim here is to draw together various accounts of curriculum under apartheid in order to establish the historical context for the studies reported in the chapters that follow.

The chapter begins by briefly tracing the origins of a traditional curriculum that was largely inherited from the colonizers of South Africa from the 17th century onwards. It shows how a progressivist orientation to curriculum was introduced in early discourse around curriculum, especially in the 1930s. A regressive form of traditional curriculum dominated the apartheid years, however, as schooling was massified. As discontent with apartheid schooling grew in the 1970s and 1980s in particular, the traditional curriculum became a strong symbol of the oppressive apartheid state. This explains some of the late apartheid state's attempts at curriculum reform, and also partly explains the nature of the first democratic curriculum that rejected entirely the structuring and organization of the traditional curriculum established in the apartheid years.

Colonial era curriculum

Soudien (2010) in his account 'What to teach the natives: a historiography of the curriculum dilemma in South Africa', argues that it was in colonial times that the basis for a segregated education system – along the lines of race and class – was established in South Africa. Dutch Reformed Church elders committed to the biblical instruction that was necessary for church confirmation established the earliest European schools in the Cape Colony in the late 17th century. The first school specifically for black children in South Africa was established around 1658 for slaves, with a strong evangelical thrust (Jansen, 1988). Over time the number of Dutch and British mission schools grew. Reading Malherbe, South Africa's major educational historian, Soudien describes how who taught, what was taught and the shape of the classroom was initially completely shaped by the Dutch experience. Not fully modern itself, Dutch education was dominated by the church. So, in the colonial environment of the Cape, education in those days was

> like in Europe, chiefly an instrument for the perpetuation of a ***religious order***" (Malherbe, 1925/1937, p. 46, emphasis in the original). It was chiefly rote learning to enable children to read the Bible. Malherbe makes the comment that "it is due to strong (Calvinist) influence that education often deteriorated into mere formalism (ibid. p. 47)".
>
> (Soudien, 2010, p. 27)

Soudien (2010) gives some examples, however, of the development of independent educational initiatives outside the "totalizing grip of the Dutch colonial experience" (p. 29). There were also differences in the curriculum emphasis of different missions, for example the Glasgow Mission Society's academic and practical training at Lovedale that would later flourish and produce an African professional class. Jansen (1990) also discusses the alternative offering of the Dutch Batavians in their rudimentary liberal arts and more academically-oriented curriculum. In these early times, however, the Dutch, almost pre-modern form, dominated as the official curriculum. The biblical schools that were established for slaves, and for some of the Khoisan people of the Cape, were separate from those for the white children of settlers. Through the 19th century, especially under subsequent British colonial rule at the Cape, there was a large expansion of secular schooling for white students, the first high school being established in Cape Town in 1829 (the South African College School).

The early 20th century and 'Native Education'

In the early part of the 20th century as Afrikaans and English-speakers[1] struggled for political and economic power there was a growing concern around the production of labour for the mines and for agriculture. 'Native education', as it came to be referred to, remained under mission control and was resource-constrained and haphazardly distributed. Education for black children was largely regarded as a charitable exercise, best performed by the church, and any state involvement was limited, uneven and grudging (Hartshorne, 1992, p. 22). The education of white children was regarded as a state responsibility.

Soudien (2010) explains the colonial authority's own ambivalence around native education at the time: "it wants useful labour for the burgeoning economy but it is not convinced yet that the "savage" in the "native" has been quelled" (p. 31). It was also suspicious of attempts within mission schools to follow white, state provision in increasing the academic nature of the curriculum. As Soudien explains, colonial authorities were concerned that, in their quest to save the souls of Africans, they were teaching them how to read and write (p. 31–32). This was regarded on the one hand as unnecessary and on the other as a potential threat to the established social hierarchy.

By the early 1900s, and especially after the South African War, the British tradition of educational administration, curriculum and pedagogy came to dominate in the Cape and Natal provinces.[2] In 1886 different curricula had been produced for different race groups in one of the provinces, Natal. The other three provinces existent at the time followed suit in 1920 (Transvaal), 1921 (the Cape) and 1924 (the Orange Free State). The emphasis of curricula for black children was explicitly on the preparation of 'the native' for work. The curricula asserted "the ultimate social place of the Native as that of efficient worker", emphasizing manual training (as a prelude to industrial training) and elementary instruction (Hartshorne, 1992, p. 26).

These curricula introduced mother tongue teaching in all classes and emphasized hygiene, handwork, gardening, agriculture, housecraft and needlework. At the high school level there was curriculum differentiation which favoured non-academic training for those few black students who managed to progress to the higher levels. Gradually, Jansen (1990) argues, a stronger emphasis on industrial training for black students pervaded all four provinces. This was driven by both industrialization and the antipathy to equal educational offerings for different race groups.

The discussion so far has shown how the segregation of schooling began long before the advent of apartheid, and race had been an underpinning category in South African education from the establishment of the first schools. From 1910 into the 1940s, there were broader international, ideological discourses around race, education and the perceived intractable colonial problem of education of the indigenous populations in the colonies. 'What to teach the natives' in the light of the production of the colonial subject became a source of significant debate in the 1930s. In 1934, the 'New Education Fellowship' (NEF), convened a conference in Johannesburg and Cape Town to bring together "the anthropologist, the missionary and the educationalist" to deal with "adaptations" needed in African society (Tiles, 1992, p. 151). The NEF was a broad church. Bronislaw Malinowski and John Dewey attended and addressed the conference. So too did the Hitler Youth, Eiselin and Verwoerd (the latter two instrumental in the evolution of the apartheid system, see below). A prominent strand of the movement was progressivist child-centred education aimed at making schooling more responsive to the psychological and spiritual needs of children. Some based this on theosophical spiritual beliefs; others had political or ideological agendas (Clews, 2009, p. 2).

The central thrust of the broader NEF movement settled around an adaptive approach for education, arguing for the production of the native colonial subject who was affirmed culturally but integrated into western education, adopting its 'scientific attitude'. Progressivism at the time was contested, and it would live on in small and marginal initiatives. In relation to mainstream provision it was not evident in curriculum shift, policy or practice.

'Native' education became increasing chaotic and inefficient during this time. In 1935–36, of all black students who were in school, 57% were in the first two grades and 80% had left school before completing their fifth year (Hartshorne, 1992, p. 28). Around 1945, there was increasing urbanization of Africans. At the same time there were increasing labour shortages and labour protest action amongst impoverished and urbanized black workers. Education for labour thus became a more pressing issue, and its poor quality was regarded by the state as a serious hindrance to the economic and social development of the country. As a result Native education progressively came under state control. The state resolved to establish a system of government schools alongside the missionary schools and provide some aid to overburdened mission schools. There was a general attempt to improve the financing, extension and improvement of primary schooling at this time, but it was far from adequate.

From 1935 to 1936 E. G. Malherbe led a commission to consider the parlous state of Native education. A strong cultural emphasis was evident in the report that issued from this commission, which recommended that every attempt should be made to avoid the 'dualism in the child's learning process' that resulted from the separation of classroom activity and 'the great and insistent life-problems of the Native outside the school'. Here the seeds of a formal policy of separate development that underpinned apartheid were sown.

The knower to be produced by the curriculum around this time was the low-skilled, disciplined worker on the one hand and the culturally distinct and localized community 'native' on the other. With regard to the worker, the expansion and increased expenditure on 'Native education' was in response to labour demands, and the curriculum was shaped in this regard, teaching both the fundamentals of early literacy and numeracy and also specific manual skills and appropriate dispositions for work.

In this period there was an increasing emphasis on cultural affirmation of the black learner as a community-located person. This stemmed partly from the international debates referred to above, but these were largely framed in crude, homogenizing terms, rendering black children as rural, simple and pliable. Mother tongue instruction was an important part of the process of circumscribing the learner culturally.

The development of curriculum under apartheid

The Eiselin commission

The cultural emphasis referred to above gained traction in relation to the separate development policies formulated in the 1940s, and was specifically applied to education and the content and form of syllabi following the Eiselin Commission of 1949–51. The purpose of the Eiselin Commission was to consider education for the native from an essentially anthropological view, and to formulate "the principles and aims for natives as an independent race, in which their past and present, their inherent racial qualities, their distinctive characteristics and aptitude, and their needs under ever-changing social conditions are taken into consideration" (RSA, 1951, cited in Soudien, 2010, p. 36). What exactly was its position on the African child? Soudien argues:

> The Commission prevaricated when it came down to deciding whether the African mind was innately inferior, but it determined that African culture, which formed that mind, limited the capacity for African children to perform on a level with White children (Soudien, 2005). It was out of this that Bantu education was born.
>
> (ibid.)

The Eiselin report of 1951 (RSA, 1951) had a strong cultural thrust, calling for curriculum emphasis on 'Bantu traditions and mental attitudes'. It affirmed the use of mother tongue instruction throughout primary school, with the understanding that English or Afrikaans be introduced primarily to teach basic communication between the black worker and the future white employer.

Bantu education

In 1948 the National Party came to power, and the racial segregation that had been in place in schooling for at least 150 years was systematized and made law. Under apartheid there were a number of major curriculum reforms. There was also considerable tinkering in between these reforms. Small reforms of parts of the system occurred within different provincial departments, by national state educational authorities and also by projects external to the state.

The Bantu Education Act was passed in 1953, and the control of Native Education was centralized in the Department of Native Affairs. Mission schools were brought under the control of the state, on very tight budgets. Quasi-independent 'reservations', 'homelands' or 'bantustans' were created from 1951 onwards.[3] These entities were theoretically able to devise their own education systems but in fact largely operated in accordance with Bantu Education. The intention behind the creation of the bantustans can be seen as mirroring the establishment of Bantu Education: "to limit and reorient African's political, economic and social aspirations away from a common political and economic life and towards a separated, rurally-oriented, ethnically-based life" (Chisholm, 2013, p. 408).

Under this new legislative regime, funding for black schools became more iniquitous, school feeding disappeared and the state largely placed the burden of the costs of the expansion of schooling on local black communities themselves. Hartshorne (1981) gives an indication of the injustice of the system. In 1969 the gap between the unit cost of black and white education reached its widest at a ratio of 20:1 white to black per capita spending on education. At the same time as financing of black education was being squeezed, the government attempted to increase enrolments, especially in light of the Eiselin commission recommendations. It did this largely by introducing a double-shift system in primary schools, later to become known as 'platooning'. Hartshorne (1992) explains:

> Under this system the woman teacher was expected to instruct two separate groups daily. Each group – on average 45–50 children – thus received just over three hours of schooling, with each teacher responsible in total for 90–100 pupils.
>
> (p. 38)

The double-shift system lasted well into the 1990s, and was evident in schools in 1998 when I began the research I report on in this book. The impact of massifying schooling in this and other ways significantly affected the abysmal quality of schooling offered to black learners.

Christian National Education

When the National Party came to power in 1948 they already had a specific set of principles for education. Partly derived from a Dutch initiative to deal with cultural and religious identity in the Netherlands after World War II, these principles had been fomented at the end of the South African War in reaction to the British attempts to impose English as the language of education. The principles were formalized in the 1948 Christian National Education (CNE) policy. Article 15 of the CNE policy of 1948 explains the understanding of education under apartheid:

> We believe that the calling and task of White South Africa with regard to the native is to Christianize him and help him on culturally, and that this calling and task has already found its nearer focusing in the principles of trusteeship, no equality and segregation. We believe besides that any system of teaching and education of natives must be based on the same principle. In accordance with these principles we believe that the teaching and education of the native must be grounded in the life and worldview of the Whites most especially those of the Boer nation as senior White trustee of the native.
>
> (cited in Vatcher, 1965, p. 104)

Although ostensibly a policy for white Afrikaans children, CNE was clear on certain curriculum features for black children, crucially mother tongue instruction and the preservation of the 'cultural identity' of the native. The development of this identity, however, entailed leading 'the native' to acceptance of Christian and National principles, and development was necessarily organized and administered by whites (Enslin, 1988, p. 141). As the policy states, the 'native' was in a state of 'cultural infancy' requiring guidance from the 'superior white culture'.

Kallaway (2002) argues that at the same time, African, Coloured and Afrikaans trainee teachers in colleges of education were indoctrinated in "religious and culture beliefs aimed at creating docile citizens, effectively sealed off from the influence of mainstream contemporary debates at a time of dramatic educational change elsewhere" (p. 11). This was partly driven by the development of a philosophical system of thought around education called 'Fundamental Pedagogics', discussed in detail in the next chapter.

In relation to the world of work, Hyslop (1988) argues that the intention of the bantu education system in the 1950s was to produce African workers, and a process of rapid expansion of African schooling began and continued through to the mid-1980s. Two tiers of workers were envisaged: the majority in the bantustans, with a minimal education, feeding the migrant labour system, and a small, urban bantustan, better-educated working-class. Education thus focused on the 'self-supporting' native, embedded in their own cultural community, but, as above, 'developed along Christian-national lines'. The ideal knower was schizoid – Christian National, but also culturally tribal, and somewhat differentiated in relation to labour.

What were the curriculum implications of the new more formalized system of Bantu Education based on the principles referred to above? The Eiselin Commission had set down the terms for culturally-determined separate development. Verwoerd, in a 1954 Senate speech, clearly stated that the previous curriculum, based on a 'European model' had not sufficiently attended to both the cultural needs and occupational possibilities of 'Natives'. He stated that this curriculum was unable to prepare Natives for 'service within their own communities'. Rather, "By blindly producing pupils trained on a European model, the vain hope was created among Natives that they could occupy posts within the European community despite the country's policy of 'apartheid'" (1954, p. 7, cited in Hartshorne, 1992, p. 40). Verwoerd asserted that, in a new, culturally appropriate curriculum, "The vehicle of instruction will be the mother tongue of the pupil. Besides the usual subjects – religious instruction, handicrafts, singing and rhythm must come into their own, that is self-evident" (1954, p. 17, opp. cit). 'Practical subjects' underpinned the notion of self-support.

The most significant shifts in the new 1956 syllabi were the extension of the use of mother tongue as language throughout the primary school,[4] and the introduction of compulsory Afrikaans instruction, as a subject on an equal footing with English. There was some ideological content added to the syllabi specifically for black learners, presenting a narrow (largely rural) and static view of 'Bantu society', and referencing some folk and historical heroes as well as contemporary apartheid arrangements and governing institutions for the black population. Despite Eiselen's intellectual sophistication as an anthropologist (Kros, 2002), the apartheid uptake of the notion of 'bantu culture' was blunt and crass, with a homogenous notion of ***a*** culture linked to ***a*** race group and educationally realized primarily through insistence on mother tongue instruction.

Critical comment on the 1956 syllabus for lower primary at the time was that although it was an improvement on the previous syllabus, "in subjects such as environmental studies and handicrafts there was far too much emphasis on the needs of rural children and the tribal environment" (Horrell, 1963, p. 64). The same commentary expressed disquiet at the too-early introduction of two official languages so that, by the second grade, black children were learning three languages.

A revised syllabus was introduced in 1968 and, although similar in many ways to the 1956 syllabi, there was growing recognition of the dominance of content-driven memorization in classrooms. In the 1968 syllabi there was some emphasis on 'understanding' rather than 'factual learning' across all subjects (Horrell, 1968, p. 65). The primary school subjects, similar to those of 1956, were: Religious Education; English; Afrikaans; Home Language; Arithmetic; Health and Physical Education; Writing; Music; Environmental Studies (which grouped History, Geography and Nature Study together); and practical subjects.

Practical subjects included arts, crafts and gardening at the lower primary level.

Alongside the language demands made by the syllabus on black teachers and learners, where three languages were still taught by the second grade, there were insidious racial biases towards whites, and the stereotyping of the black population. Textbooks communicated that:

> legitimate authorities should not be questioned; whites were superior to blacks; the Afrikaner had a special relationship with God; South Africa rightfully belonged to God; South Africa and the Afrikaner were isolated; the

> Afrikaner was a military genius and strong; the Afrikaner was threatened; South Africans were sensitive of their image abroad; South Africa was the leader in Africa; and the Afrikaner had a God-given task in Africa.
>
> (Taylor & Methula, 1993, p. 300)

Figure 3.1 is a representation of the 19 different departments of education that were eventually constituted under the apartheid state. White provincial departments of education produced the 'core' curricula for different subjects on a rotation basis. Other departments had the option to make additions (though not excisions) according to "conditions within that department" (ibid. p. 278). What often resulted were augmented syllabi in the different provincial white departments, and a watered-down or minimal or narrower curriculum for black departments. There were also different subjects on offer in white and black schools, and black children were required to take three languages while white children were required to take two. The "independent homelands" and "self-governing territories" (see Figure 3.1) were largely dependent on, and subject to the syllabi and textbooks developed within the black Department of Education and Training (DET). The exceptions were Transkei, which used the Cape Education Department syllabus and Bophuthatswana, which exercised some autonomy over curriculum making.

The inclination for curriculum development within the black departments was limited. The press of the final examination, which was under control of the white departments, also limited departures from the core syllabus. The fact that the curriculum was essentially the same was, however, one of the ways in which inequities were masked. The Minister of Bantu Education at the time proudly claimed

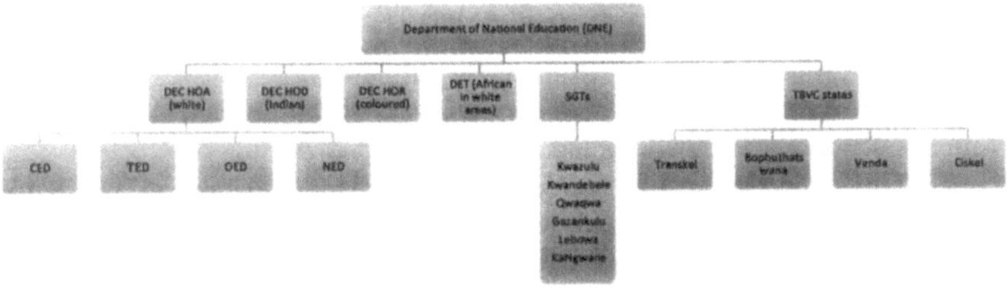

DEC	Department of Education and Culture
HOA/HOD/HOR	House of Assembly/ House of Delegates/ House of Representatives
CED/TED/OED/NED	Cape Education Department/ Transvaal Education Department/ Orange Free State Education Department/ Natal Education Department
DET	Department of Education and Training
SGTs	Self-governing territories (6)
TBVC	"Independent Homelands" – Transkei; Bophuthatswana; Venda; Ciskei

Figure 3.1 Nineteen separate apartheid education departments formalized in 1984

that his department "had not only adopted the same curricula and syllabi as were used by Whites, but Black and White students were now writing the same senior certificate and matriculation exams" (Marcum, 1982, p. 21, cited in Jansen, 1990, p. 202).

All syllabi were underpinned by the CNE which became an Act of parliament in1967, and an Afrikaner, Christian and nationalist perspective throughout the system was ensured at the level of policy. Specific cultural categories, especially those of the (superior) Afrikaner ***volk*** (people), were emphasized. The ***volk*** had a "religious duty as the caretaker and all-knowing guide over other volk" (Karlsson, 2004, p. 328).

Despite some recognition of the need to foster 'understanding', the 1968 curriculum was regressively traditional: content-driven, with little elaboration of conceptual learning or the learning of skills. The syllabi contained very strict prescriptions for the selection, sequencing and scope of content. The syllabi, especially in Religious Education, General Science and Social Studies, were also overloaded (Jansen, 1990).

Institutionalized inequality

Given that the core curriculum for all children under apartheid from the mid-1950s was similar, it was rather the institutionalized inequality experienced in black schools where the curriculum was implemented that excluded black students from accessing the curriculum. Black school children received the curriculum in the context of poorly trained teachers, overcrowded classrooms, a limited school day and poor facilities. There was an inequitable distribution of educational material (especially teacher guides and graded readers) and the quality and elaboration of teachers' guides varied drastically. Certain subjects were allocated less time in black schools (Nkondo, 1979). At the secondary level different subjects were offered in black, white and middle and working-class schools, and there was practical and academic streaming at the school level. For example, in Natal in 1968, six out of 89 'Bantu' secondary schools offered physical science and 18 out of 89 schools offered mathematics (South African Institute of Race Relations, 1969). This acute shortage of mathematics and science teachers endured across the decades. Most children did not make it through this system and continued to 'fall at the first hurdle' (Taylor, 1989) with persistently low survival rates through the early grades of primary school.

Ongoing political protest

The late 1950s and 1960s were marked by increased political protest. A State of Emergency was declared in 1960 after the Sharpeville massacre.[5] There was widespread banning of organizations and imprisonment of individuals. At the same time there were renewed efforts by the apartheid state to segregate different races with the promulgation of the Promotion of Bantu Self Governance Act in 1959. This act led to a reorientation of education policy towards the requirements of 'self-governance' and the creation of a black civil service for the homelands (Unterhalter, 1991). Education was to produce this civil service and a professional class. There was thus large-scale expansion of schooling again, but this time secondary schooling, and increased infrastructure and financing of black schooling was again concentrated in the bantustans. The apartheid state continued to severely restrict the movement of black people in non-bantustan areas, conducted forced removals from urban areas where black people had settled outside of the bantustans and redrew the boundaries of these bantustans (Simkins, 1983).

In the 1970s the entire apartheid system showed signs of failure due to internal resistance, the failure of regional security, division within the ruling party and the cost of implementing the system (Kallaway, 2002, p. 18). In 1972, responding to the crisis in African schooling, the structure of financing changed, and slowly per capita spending differences between black and white children were reduced. However, the backlog was too great to deal with. Little additional funding reached primary schools although, in some provinces, there was a significant reduction in the number of double-shift schools. Although some gains were made in the retention of children in primary school, the quality remained dire.

The teacher training system under apartheid mirrored that of schooling in relation to its rapid expansion in the 1980s and in relation to its poor quality. In the 1970s, in order to become a primary school teacher in an African school, one only needed to have completed the Grade 8 examination (written at the culmination of primary school) (Horrell, 1980). Black teacher training colleges were understaffed and the college lecturers seriously under-qualified (Hartshorne, 1992). Students entering teaching typically had very low schooling results. Hartshorne shows that in 1988, for example, 93% of the successful senior certificate group had 'F' aggregates (i.e. 33–39% of the total aggregate mark). This was the main pool from which student teachers were recruited (Hartshorne, 1992, p. 249). Freer (1993) comments that in many of these colleges the courses offered were repetitions of the three final years of an impoverished secondary programme.

Schooling was further disrupted through the late seventies in widespread student protest action. Hartshorne (1992) argues that, contrary to popular perception, it was not just secondary schools that were involved and affected by the 1976 school uprising, but primary schools were where the uprising started, and they were significantly affected. The immediate reasons for the uprising had largely to do with curriculum and, in particular, the issue of an attempt to impose Afrikaans as a medium of instruction in black schools.

With a shift to a 12-year school structure in the early 1970s, a year was eliminated from primary school. The external Standard 6 (Grade 8) examination was now moved to the end of Standard 5 (Grade 7). In addition, mother tongue instruction was shortened to the end of Standard 3 (the fifth grade). By 1975 students in black schools were required to transition to Afrikaans and English as media of instruction in Standard 4 (sixth grade). They had to write the public examination in these two languages after barely a year of instruction in them. In secondary schools the medium of instruction had previously been determined by consideration of the dominant language of the white community nearest to where the school was situated. Now all children were required to adopt a dual medium – English and Afrikaans medium – approach. For a while English had been the stronger and more dominant language of teaching and learning in these schools. The issue culminated in the 1976 Soweto riots, a key event in the struggle to end apartheid.

There were minimal changes in the next major curriculum reform that, in part, tried to address the issues of 1976. The Education and Training Act of 1979 addressed the language issues which had become so pressing after the 1976 protests. However, while committing itself to increased vocational education, it left the content of the curriculum largely unchanged. The apartheid state agreed to a single medium of instruction from Standard 5 (Grade 7) upwards, to be determined by the school. In 1978 statistics showed that over 96% of black pupils from Standard 5 (Grade 7) upwards were being taught in English (Hartshorne, 1992, p. 203). The curriculum also introduced flexibility regarding when the transition from mother tongue to English or Afrikaans as medium of instruction could be made. Hartshorne (1992) argues, however, that because the DET (overseeing schooling for black learners) was made up largely of Afrikaners, this policy – early transition to English after initial mother tongue instruction – was never given support, resourcing or development.

The 1979 Act also ushered in a more concerted focus on vocational and technical education, which was to be taken up directly in the de Lange report in 1981. This focus stemmed from changes in the mode of production in the economy, in particular an increase in mechanization of production activities on mines and farms, leading to demands for more highly skilled workers.[6] Again the response was to concentrate schooling in and for the bantustans and further limit the influx of workers now needed less in non-bantustan areas, mainly cities.

The 1980s and curriculum 'modernization'

In the 1980s, under President P.W. Botha, there was an effort to 'modernize' apartheid education, particularly in the light of a failing economy and the demand for more highly skilled workers. There was also a more generalized attempt to legitimize the nationalist, apartheid government both locally and internationally by presenting the apartheid state as reforming. An education overhaul was to be the key aspect of this strategy (Kallaway, 2002, p. 18). There were massive increases in African enrolments in both primary and secondary schools at this time, and by 1985 there were four times the number of secondary students than in 1975 and 76% of children aged 5–14 were enrolled in primary school (Unterhalter, 1991, p. 39). Enrolments, expenditure and the number of African matric passes continued to increase through the 1980s.

The de Lange Commission

Despite these 'reformist' efforts the country was experiencing widespread political turmoil and economic failure. The de Lange Commission of 1980–81 was a key lever through which the nationalist state aimed to address the crumbling apartheid system. The Cabinet-appointed commission's task was to launch an investigation into the entire provision of education in South Africa. The central curriculum thrust of the de Lange Report (Human Sciences Research Council, 1981) was to recommend a move away from a system based solely on the traditional liberal arts and an academic training for university. The report recommended a much more differentiated system, with an expanded vocational system and greater recognition of non-formal education. Differentiation was also proposed in relation to different phases of schooling – pre-basic, basic and post-basic, in relation to vocational and academic tracks and in relation to internal differentiation to cater to different learner abilities.[7] The report explicitly rejected curriculum integration (dedifferentiation), which, it argued, was "regarded in many countries as the ideal educational model" (Human Sciences Research Council (HSRC), 1981, p. 41).

The central criticism of de Lange was that it was a 'technicist' document, treating "social issues as technical problems open to technical solutions" (Buckland, 1984, p. 383). What it did do, however, was shift from orthodox Christian Nationalism and Afrikaner Nationalism toward a more instrumental approach to social policy. Hartshorne's (1999) defense of the report was that a more radical approach was not possible at the time, and that although problematic, the 'value-free', 'scientific' approach had more chance of challenging the status quo. Even so, the main principles of de Lange, which were equality of opportunity for all in relation to a common curriculum, common standards and access and a unified system of education, were summarily dismissed in the government's 1983 White Paper. Education, according to this 1983 policy, was to stay firmly within the apartheid model, with segregation reinforced by the creation of four separate ministries for the four population groups, as well as continued commitment to CNE, mother tongue instruction and separate schools. De Lange proved too radical for the time, and any curriculum reform based on the de Lange recommendations would only come much later in 1988, 1989 and 1991 with the development of the NATED syllabi and the publication of the Curriculum Model for South Africa (CUMSA).

There were, however, a number of official attempts at targeted curriculum interventions in black schools following the de Lange Commission. These included school readiness programmes, programmes for the development of 'technical study' and some language programmes involving graded readers in a range of languages. However, by this time, black schools, especially those in urban areas, had become largely dysfunctional, the material conditions deplorable and teacher morale decimated. These conditions frustrated attempts to intervene in schools or retrain teachers. Student protest action at this time also rendered many schools ungovernable and there was wide-scale rejection of apartheid schooling.

By 1984 the education system had become highly fragmented. The National Policy for General Education Act 76 of 1984 extended the racially and ethnically divided system of general administration of the apartheid state into education. As a result, 19 different departments of education were formally created. The former

Bantu Education department and its various subsequent incarnations became further split. These are represented and explained in Figure 3.1.

Alternatives to traditional curriculum forms under apartheid

There was an enduring progressivist thrust in curriculum, both inside and outside of the state, and sustained through the decades up until the transition to democracy in 1994. Official attempts at curriculum innovation in the 1970s and 1980s were largely piecemeal – often consisting of taking out contents or adding in new contents in different subjects. These micro-reforms were often influenced by trends in the United States and United Kingdom, notably ideas arising out of progressive reforms there. Galant (1997) gives the example that, between 1974 and 1984, there were at least five new syllabi introduced in South Africa following the 'new maths' movement in Europe. However, these largely had effect in white schools only.

There was also a significant amount of curriculum work being done outside of state institutions, as alternatives to the traditional curriculum forms developed during the apartheid era. The number of initiatives was vast, from 'Worker Education', drawing on the British experience, to Freirian-inspired approaches. There was extensive work by historians engaged in alternative readings of history, and alternative ways of doing history, such as Callinicos's (1981) 'people's history' and Bundy's 'history by assertion' (Bundy, 1989). The NECC produced a 'history pack' as a grassroots exercise in developing a critical understanding of the past through analysis and collective input (Witz & Hamilton, 1991). There were also broader curriculum models inspired by African projects, such as the Tanzanian Ujamaa villages and the Education with Production project in Botswana. A large number of NGOs, especially in the 1980s, and with varying relationships to the state, also produced alternative curricula. Although intellectually invigorating and breaking new ground in curriculum development, analysis and critique, the programmes were generally small-scale and under-resourced, and had limited impact on state curricula (NECC, 1992, p. 33).

The broad range of initiatives is collectively referred to as People's Education. Chisholm and Fuller (1996) argue that this was not the unified movement it is often presented as, but entailed the work of about 50,000 organizations, including some tertiary institutions. The rallying cries of the movement were 'People's education for people's power' and 'The doors of learning and culture shall be opened', with curriculum and pedagogic ideals largely based on reconceptualist theories of curriculum[8] and theorizing around critical, radical and populist pedagogies and progressive curriculum forms.

Hartshorne (1999) argues that, in much the same way as the apartheid state's attempts to reform education practice in the 1980s were largely ineffectual, so were the attempts of People's Education. They faced the same the obstacles as state programmes – limited capacity within schools, a breakdown of teaching and learning, low morale and limited resources. However, People's Education served to involve a large number of people in processes of dialogue, of curriculum and materials development, and the development of new and more radical visions of a post-apartheid education system.

The early 1990s marked a turning point in curriculum debates. A new post-apartheid, democratic state now looked imminent, and "competing social movements and political actors vehemently began to stake their curriculum positions" (Jansen, 1999, p. 4). One of the most significant groupings in opposition to apartheid schooling was the National Education Coordinating Committee (NECC), which initiated the National Educational Policy Investigation (NEPI). NEPI's task was to set out policy options for a post-apartheid state. Documents for a range of schooling domains, for example governance, financing and early childhood development, were produced, including one for curriculum. In some ways NEPI formalized some of the ideas of People's Education and suggested how they might be turned into policy realities. What is interesting is that outcomes-based education (OBE) which would become the central frame for the first post-apartheid curriculum is not mentioned at all in the documents (Jansen, 1999).

Apartheid's last gasp: NATED and CUMSA

Concurrent with the activities of NEPI, various NGOs and the private sector, the apartheid state launched its own curriculum revision as part of its Education Renewal Strategy (ERS). The ERS represented the apartheid government's final reform effort, and a curriculum model that was based on the 1988 and 1989 curriculum efforts was contained in the Curriculum Model for South Africa (CUMSA). Work on what would become CUMSA had in fact begun in 1984, following de Lange, in an attempt to develop a common curriculum for all given the fragmentation that had come to define the system. New curricula were devised and published in 1988/89 and in 1990/91. These were the so-called 'NATED' syllabi (Department of National Education, 1988, 1989a, 1989b). The guiding principles of CUMSA, following de Lange, emphasized equal opportunities for education, non-race based provision and response to economic demands. CUMSA aimed at the rationalization of the large number of subjects in the curriculum,[9] as well as a rationalization of the wide range of syllabi in operation. In 1992 there were 1,400 registered syllabi from Sub A to Standard 10 in the system (NECC, 1992, p. 15).

There are two central thrusts discernible in CUMSA, one vocational, the other progressivist. In relation to the former, the influence of de Lange in CUMSA was clear. It placed a strong emphasis on vocational education, arguing that "the number of learners receiving academically-oriented education was too high" (DNE, 1991, pp. 3–4). Three new vocationally-oriented subjects – Arts Education, Technology and Economic Education – were introduced, and the focus of 'Guidance' was on vocational orientation. 'Relevance' was emphasized, particularly to the world of work and demands of labour, where "a change of accent to vocationally-oriented or vocational education" (p. 11) entailed "schooling in the application of operations, rules, techniques and procedures required in certain occupations, and guidance in the acquisition of the required attitudes" (p. 18). Thus following a general-formative education based on subject disciplines, CUMSA proposed the final three years of secondary schooling offer a choice between academic subjects and vocationally-oriented subjects. The latter were organized into fields such as Arts, Agriculture, Engineering and Business.

Alongside the vocational emphasis was a progressivist thrust. 'Relevance' was defined in the documents as "highlighting and emphasizing the application value of the content of all teaching programmes in the learners' everyday life" (DNE, 1991, p. 11). Constructivist tenets appear in a number of statements, such as "the learning content of a school curriculum should take the learner's phase of development into account" (p. 9) and the aim was expressed as "the development of the inherent ***potential*** of learners to enable them to realize their full potential through the development of all their physical and intellectual abilities" (p. 12, emphasis in the original). Reference is also made to the development of critical thinking, good moral character and responsible citizenship. The 'Aims of junior primary education' focus on the development of learners' confidence and self-worth, an awareness of their abilities, interests and personal and community convictions and a range of social and cognitive skills, as well as "a feeling of love, belonging, security and safety in the school" (p. 15).

There is a strong emphasis on the individual and the recognition of a range of 'areas of experience' that should be encompassed in the curriculum: aesthetic, creative, social, economic, linguistic, literary, mathematical, ethical, etc. (p. 8).

The constructivist influence on the mathematics curriculum was clear in the mathematics CUMSA 1991 draft core syllabus:

> The pupil learning mathematics is conceptualized as an active mathematical thinker who tries to construct meaning of what he is doing on the basis of personal experience, and who is developing his way of thinking as his experience broadens, always building on the knowledge which he has already constructed.
>
> (DEC, 1991, p. 1, in Adler, 1992, p. 29)

In relation to knowledge, however, CUMSA asserts at a number of points the importance of the acquisition of the "structured knowledge possessed by humankind" (16) or the "mastering of knowledge of reality as structured by humankind" (p. 17); to help learners in "mastering the structured knowledge humankind commands" (p. 67). This departs from more constructivist tenets expressed elsewhere in the document. What came to prevail were the NATED curricula that were detailed, content-driven syllabi, widely argued to be overloaded (NECC, 1992, p. 43).

The CUMSA document does, however, suggest shifts towards the establishment of 'fields of study', a proto-integration move. 'Social studies' replaced history and geography. A new subject, 'Technology' integrated traditional subjects like writing, technical orientation, home economics and wood-/metalwork.

Technology, environmental education and vocational education were introduced as cross curricular themes, to be integrated into all subjects. Finally, CUMSA foregrounded the importance of skills (as opposed to prior curricula that had been fundamentally content-driven), and lists sets of different kinds of skills. These resonate with the generic skills set out in the 'critical' and 'developmental outcomes' of the first post-apartheid curriculum (in Chapter 6), and can be seen as a precursor to these.

There is no evidence of CNE in the CUMSA document. The only references to religion in the document are that learners should develop "an awareness of the beauty and wonder of Creation" (p. 14), and one of the aims was to orient learners to "various religions and cultures" (p. 17). The statement of purpose is very different to the projection of learners in previous syllabi produced under apartheid: "Pre-tertiary education is concerned with the preparation of learners for life. It is therefore important that learners enjoy learning experiences covering various aspects of reality" (p. 19). This is a far cry from the 'native' requiring development in manual skills and work-appropriate behaviours.

The purpose of pointing out some of these progressive curriculum features, such as a focus on the development of the whole child, relevance and integration, is to suggest that the first post-apartheid curriculum, Curriculum 2005 (C2005), was less of a radical break with the past than is often suggested. The NATED syllabi and CUMSA introduced these progressive principles in a concrete and substantive way (much more so than the NEPI proposals, which were vague and broad in the main). Similarly, the emphasis on the world of work and a skills emphasis in some ways pre-figure the outcomes-based framework that would be adopted for C2005. In this way a more direct line can be drawn from the final curriculum reform under apartheid to C2005. Arguably, the 'radical break' that is often claimed for the first post-apartheid curriculum came with de Lange, which pulled away from CNE and introduced progressive features in its pedagogy, as well as a skills focus and integration in the setting of content.

CUMSA was an obvious attempt to reorient education towards principles of equal opportunity and equal standards for all South African learners, irrespective of race. The reasons for doing so are more ambiguous. On the one hand there was a need to modernize the curriculum, but it also appears that the last apartheid government seized the opportunity to shape the direction of curriculum into the post-apartheid period.

Around transition, in 1995, the NATED and CUMSA curricula that had been implemented in white schools for some time were adopted as interim curricula. A civic body, the National Education and Training Forum (NETF), was set up to generate new societal and general aims of teaching and learning for the NATED documents and to cleanse syllabi and textbooks of racial stereotypes and offensive language. Fataar (2006) argues that NETF's role was to run the process with the intention of undercutting influence of the apartheid era bureaucrats. The outcome was, however, that in 1996 everybody was intended to follow a core syllabus that white teachers and students had been following since at least 1991, and for which textbooks had already been produced. Thus, these first 'new' curricula, prior to C2005, were effectively only new to black schools. The differences between the white curriculum of 1988/89 and 1990/91 and the implemented curricula of 1995/96/97 were minimal and the last, still-functioning, curriculum under apartheid became de facto the first curriculum of the democratic era.

Conclusion

Through the course of the history of racially differentiated curricula in South Africa we see a shifting vision of the knower: initially one who was to be converted, the heathen indigene, a view prevalent especially under mission and colonial education. With the shift to industrialization, the subject becomes potential labour, at first for unskilled labour on farms and mines and so developing both manual skills and docility ('moral' and 'industrious'). In the thirties, in the light of international debates, the notion of the (indigenous) colonial subject becomes tied up in issues of cultural specificity and questions of the mind of the 'native'. Here strong culturalist notions of the subject, whose language and traditions should be preserved through education, provide the platform for bantu education and its ideology of separate development. Under CNE this particular knower, who must be the 'ward' of the superior white race, reaches its apogee. With changes in the economy in the 1960s towards greater mechanization in farming and mining, higher skills for fewer workers were needed. With the establishment of bantustans at the same time, the knower of the curriculum shifts to the self-governing African, and education seeks to produce a civil service and professional class for specifically demarcated ethnic groups.

The cultural particularity and apartness of black learners and their requirements remains until a series of reforms in the 1980s, beginning with de Lange. De Lange raises the principle of equality of opportunity and a South African knower not defined by race. Though concerns around the demands of labour and a deepening focus on vocational education remained, the knower of the later 1980s and early 1990s curriculum became something quite different – the individual learner of no determinate race on the one hand, and a worker for a growing and diversifying economy on the other.

Although clear and radical shifts are discernible in the knower projected in the curriculum, the shifts in knowledge are fewer and more subtle. From early on different knowledge was distributed to different race groups, accomplished less through different syllabi and more through different institutionalized forms of provision and material and symbolic deprivation in schools for black learners.

Curricula constructed during apartheid were subject-based and content-driven, a regressive traditional form, and until CUMSA, with minimal explicit conceptual-content-skill relationships made. Knowledge across curriculum reforms was regarded as 'given' and strong boundaries were maintained between different subjects. In the CUMSA there were contradictory shifts in relation to knowledge. Subject disciplines were asserted on the one hand – "structured knowledge possessed by humankind" (DNE, 1991, p. 16). On the other hand there was a movement towards integration, an emphasis on skills and more progressively-oriented weakening of boundaries between curriculum knowledge and the world of work and curriculum knowledge and the everyday knowledge of learners. There was also patchy incorporation of constructivist ideas.

In brief, the shift can broadly be described as a move from a culturally-oriented curriculum, with a strong emphasis on content and education for the rural, racially distinct native and manual labourer, to a progressively more technicist orientation, an emphasis on higher skills for the modern workplace and some regard for the whole person and citizen to be educated. Knowledge throughout remains given, with a specific purpose driving selection at different times – either around religious conversion, ideological conditioning, vocational preparation or, vaguely, some sense of a liberal education for self-realization. The chapter has mapped these shifts in relation to the broader ideological discourses and shifting economic context of the rising and declining apartheid state. The legacy, however, to the changing system described in the chapters that follow, was a broken down and iniquitous system of schooling especially for black South Africans.

Notes

1 Afrikaners (translated "people of Africa") were a community that had evolved from the Dutch settlers, as well as French Huguenots and some Germans. As the Dutch colonial influence waned, the settlers developed a simplified form of the Dutch language that came to be known as Afrikaans. The English referred to here were generally settlers of British origin.

2 There were, however, also other strong influences within the Union, such as the "Du Toit-Mansveld" regime developed for Dutch citizens in the North and the Orange Free State.

3 Four of the South African bantustans -Transkei, Bophuthatswana, Venda and Ciskei (the so-called "TBVC States") were declared independent, though this was not officially recognized outside of South Africa. Other South African bantustans (like KwaZulu, Lebowa and QwaQwa) received partial autonomy but were never granted independence.

4 There was widespread resistance to this decision, many arguing that this would restrict African learners to the narrow bounds of tribal society and diminish their broader communication opportunities. There was also a lack of appropriate subject terminology in the different languages as well as a paucity of books in different African languages. On the other hand, Hartshorne (1987) drew attention to the fact that there was also very poor quality of English instruction and, where it was taught, it was almost completely by non-mother-tongue speakers of English.

5 Sixty-nine people protesting again the 'pass laws' were fatally shot by police and 180 seriously injured. Pass laws were a form of internal passport system designed to control the movement of African and Coloured people.

6 While many argue that apartheid education served to reproduce the needs of capitalism and white supremacy (for example the volume edited by Kallaway, 1984), Wolpe and Unterhalter argue that de Lange saw education as an instrument for the transformation of South Africa *into* a dynamic capitalist economy (Wolpe & Unterhalter, 1991, p. 7)

7 Interestingly, the de Lange report recommends a modularized system of education, attempting a structure of different levels suggesting 'outlets' and 'links' between formal and non-formal education and between these and the world of work. Discussion of horizontal and vertical flow and openness in the structure presages the

principles of transferability, access and equivalence introduced later in the National Qualifications Framework discussed in Chapter 6.

8 In response to traditional curriculum studies' focus on design, implementation, and evaluation of curricular materials, the reconceptualists in the US from the 1970s onwards focused on the political and sociological dimensions of curriculum and issues of personal authenticity and social justice. The British counterpart to this movement was the 'New Sociology of Education'. Both versions had influence in South Africa, particularly through those who had spent some time in the apartheid years studying abroad.

9 There were five subjects in the Junior Primary (Foundation Phase): Languages (1 or 2 in Grade 1; 2 from thereon); Mathematics; Environmental Studies (including social sciences and natural science); Arts Education; Technology; and Lifestyle Education (including Religious instruction, Guidance, Economic Education and Physical Education). Up to 1992, the compulsory subjects at this level were First Language, Second Language, Third language (DET), Bible Ed./Religious Ed./ Right Living, Mathematics, Environmental Studies, Class music, Handwriting. There were an additional 13 optional subjects, of which four could be selected. They included: Art, Needlework, Youth preparedness, Library and Gardening. (NECC, 1992, p. 20)

References

Adler, J. (1992). What is new and different in the draft core syllabus for mathematics: std 2–4? *Pythagoras*, *28*, 26–32.

Buckland, P (1984). Technicism and de Lange: Reflections on the process of the HSRC investigation. In P. Kallaway (Ed.), *Apartheid and education*. Johannesburg: Ravan.

Bundy, C. (1989). History then and now. *Mentor*, *71*(3), 371–386.

Callinicos, L. (1981). *A people's history of South Africa, Vol. I: Gold and workers 1886–1924*. Johannesburg: Ravan Press.

Chisholm, L. (2013). Bantustan education history: The 'progressivism' of Bophuthatswana's Primary Education Upgrade Programme (PEUP), 1979–1988. *South African Historical Journal*, *65*(3), 403–420.

Chisholm, L., & Fuller, B. (1996). Remember people's education? Shifting alliances, state-building and South Africa's narrowing policy agenda. *Journal of Education Policy*, *11*(6), 693–716.

Clews, C. (2009). The new education fellowship and the reconstruction of education: 1945 to 1966. PhD thesis, Institute of Education, University of London.

Department of National Education. (1988). Educational programmes for pre-tertiary education in South Africa: NATED 02-124. (88/06). Pretoria: Department of National Education.

Department of National Education. (1989a). Instructional programmes in public ordinary schools of the various departments of state responsible for education (89/09): NATE 02-501. Pretoria: Department of National Education.

Department of National Education. (1989b). *Instructional programmes in public ordinary schools: NATED 02–550. (89/03)*. Pretoria: Department of National Education.

Department of National Education. (1991). *A curriculum model for education in South Africa: Discussion document*. Pretoria: Department of National Education.

Enslin, P. (1988). The state of pedagogics. *Perspectives in Education*, *10*(1), 67–74.

Fataar, A. (2006). Policy networks in recalibrated political terrain: The case of school curriculum policy and politics in South Africa. *Journal of Education Policy, 21*(6), 641–659.

Freer, D. (1993). The residuals of apartheid: Impediments to teacher development in South Africa. In G. K. Verma (Ed.), *Inequality and teacher education* (pp. 23–46). London: Falmer.

Galant, J. (1997). Teachers, learners and mathematics: An analysis of HSRC research reports on mathematics education 1970–1980. Unpublished MEd thesis, University of Cape Town.

Hartshorne, K. (1981). Private sector involvement in education, 1960–1986. In C. Millar, S. A. Raynham & A. Schaeffer (Eds.), *Breaking the formal frame: Readings in South African education in the eighties*. Cape Town: Oxford University Press.

Hartshorne, K. (1987). Language policy in African education in South Africa, 1910–1985, with particular reference to the medium of instruction. In D. Young (Ed.), *Bridging the gap between theory and practice in English Second Language teaching* (pp. 62–81). Cape Town: Maskew Miller Longman.

Hartshorne, K. (1999). *The making of education policy in South Africa*. Cape Town: Oxford University Press.

Hartshorne, K. B. (1992). *Crisis and challenge: Black education 1910–1990*. Cape Town: Oxford University Press.

Horrell, M. (1963). *African education: Some origins, and development until 1953*. Johannesburg: South African Institute of Race Relations.

Horrell, M. (1968). *Bantu education to 1968*. Johannesburg: South African Institute of Race Relations.

Horrell, M. (1980). *The race relations survey, 1980*. Johannesburg: South African Institute for Race Relations.

Human Sciences Research Council. (1981). Provision of education in the RSA, July 1981: Report of the main committee of the HSRC investigation into education. Pretoria: Human Sciences Research Council.

Hyslop, J. (1988). State education policy and the social reproduction of the urban Africa working class: The case of the southern Transvaal 1955–1976. *Journal of Southern African Studies, 14*(3), 446–476.

Jansen, J. (1988). Curriculum change and contextual realities: An analysis of recent trends in black South Africa education. *International Review of Education, 34*(3), 378–387.

Jansen, J. D. (1990). Curriculum as a political phenomenon: Historical reflections on black South Africa education. *The Journal of Negro Education, 59*(2), 195–206.

Jansen, J. (1999) The school curriculum since apartheid: Intersections of politics and policy in the South African transition. *Journal of Curriculum Studies, 31*(1), 57–67.

Kallaway, P. (1984). Apartheid and education: The education of black South Africans. Johannesburg: Ravan Press.

Kallaway, P. (2002). The history of education under apartheid, 1948–1994: The doors of learning and culture shall be opened. Cape Town: Pearson South Africa.

Karlsson, J. (2004). Schooling space: Where South Africans learnt to position themselves within the hierarchy of apartheid society. *Pedagogy, Culture and Society, 12*(3), 327–346.

Kros, C. (2002). W.W.M. Eiselen: Architect of apartheid education. In P. Kallaway (Ed.), *The history of education under apartheid, 1948–1994: The doors of learning and culture shall be opened* (pp. 53–73). Cape Town: Pearson South Africa.

National Education Co-ordinating Committee. National Education Policy Investigation. (1992). ***Curriculum: Report.*** Cape Town: Oxford University Press.

Nkondo, C. (1979). Comparison of the syllabus of the bantu education department with that of the Transvaal Education Department and other related matters. ***Reality***, *11*(4), 17–19.

Republic of South Africa. (1951). Report of the commission of enquiry into native education, 1949–51, UG53/1951. (Eiselin report). Pretoria: Government Printer.

Simkins, C. (1983). Four essays on the past, present and possible future of the distribution of the black population of South Africa. Cape Town: SALDRU.

Soudien, C. (2010). What to teach the natives: A historiography of the curriculum dilemma in South Africa. In W. Pinar (Ed.), ***Curriculum studies in South Africa: Intellectual histories and present circumstances*** (pp. 19–49). New York: Palgrave Macmillan.

South African Institute of Race Relations. (1969). ***The 1969 conference on Bantu Education.*** Johannesburg: South African Institute of Race Relations.

Taylor, N. (1989). Falling at the first hurdle: Initial encounters with the formal system of African education in South Africa. Johannesburg: University of the Witwatersrand, Education Policy Unit.

Taylor, N., & Methula, P. (1993). Shifting relations of authority: Public administration and curriculum policy in South Africa. In N. Taylor (Ed.), ***Inventing knowledge: Contests in curriculum construction*** (pp. 292–311). Cape Town: Maskew Miller Longman.

Tiles, J. E. (1992). John Dewey: Political theory and social practice. London: Taylor & Francis.

Unterhalter, E. (1991). Changing aspects of reformism in Bantu education 1953–1989. In E. Unterhalter, H. Wolpe, T. Botha, S. Badet, T. Diamini & B. Khotseng (Eds.), ***Apartheid education and popular struggles*** (pp. 53–72). South Africa: Ravan Press Johannesburg.

Vatcher, W. H. (1965). White laager: The rise of Afrikaner nationalism. New York: Praeger.

Witz, L., & Hamilton, C. (1991). Reaping the whirlwind: The reader's digest illustrated history of South Africa and changing popular perceptions of history. ***South African Historical Journal***, *24*, 186.

Wolpe, H., & Unterhalter, E. (1991). Introduction: Reproduction, reform and transformation: Approaches to the analysis of education in South Africa. In E. Unterhalter, H. Wolpe, T. Botha, S. Badet, T. Diamini & B. Khotseng (Eds.), ***Apartheid education and popular struggles*** (pp. 1–17). Johannesburg: Ravan Press.

4 The formal frame

Pedagogy under apartheid

Introduction

In 1992 the NEPI Report (NECC, 1992) characterized classrooms in South Africa as follows:

> South African teachers work in authoritarian and bureaucratic departments which largely exclude them from curriculum decision-making. The teachers are the receivers, not the creators, of the curriculum. Overloaded syllabuses and prescribed texts further restrict their autonomy. This in turn has discouraged classroom initiatives. Black teachers in particular work in a highly politicized environment, and face large classes with poor resources. Authority relations have broken down in many schools, with the result that relations between teachers and students are often hostile. Visible indicators of success (or failure), such as examination results, offer little encouragement to teachers and their students. Other indicators of assessing effective learning and teaching have not developed under these circumstances. Such a situation means that teacher-centred classroom activities predominate. Though there are, of course, exceptions, South African classrooms show strict adherence to prescribed syllabuses, a heavy reliance on textbooks and other forms of 'received knowledge', and an emphasis on factual information and rote learning. These trends are exacerbated by assessment practices which are geared towards selection rather than progression through the system, and by the 'backwash' effects of the matriculation examination on the senior school curriculum
>
> (NECC, 1992, pp. 24–25)

The report synthesized the broad understanding of classroom practices under apartheid at the time. It emphasized the poor material conditions under which teachers worked, as well as the highly politicized context of their work. 'Factual information', 'received knowledge' and a 'reliance on textbooks' were identified as restricting teacher autonomy. 'Teacher-centred classrooms' where 'rote learning' predominated characterized classrooms. Although perhaps overgeneralizing, given the limited empirical evidence available to support the descriptions, the NEPI characterization reflected dominant understandings of classroom conditions in black schooling at the time. In this chapter I discuss two very divergent attempts to shape pedagogy under apartheid and attempt to understand why particular forms came to dominate and be sustained in classrooms.

Like Chapter 3, this chapter locates the research presented in the book in its historical context, and describes some of the evidence available on how education was delivered in classrooms in black schools under apartheid. When looking at accounts of teaching and learning at the time, classrooms (as in the description above) are often characterized as bound by very authoritarian relations between teachers and students, and rote learning devoid of meaningful participation and critical engagement on the part of learners. Often this is attributed to the dominant philosophies underpinning apartheid education – Christian National Education (CNE) discussed in the previous chapter and the philosophy of 'fundamental pedagogics'. There were also, as outlined in Chapter 3, several progressively-oriented reforms and initiatives within the system which may have shaped what went on in classrooms. I consider both fundamental pedagogics and progressivism as potentially shaping or changing pedagogy at the time. Looking at a small number of empirical studies, I suggest that dominant classroom practices can be explained in relation to structural, material and cognitive resource constraints facing black schools at the time which rendered policy programmes ineffective.

Fundamental pedagogics

Fundamental pedagogics (FP) was a particular philosophy and 'science' of education, prevalent in teacher education under apartheid in the former Afrikaans and black universities and their associated colleges. It is often presented as a monolithic programme, indoctrinating trainee teachers into particular understandings of pedagogical practice and outlook, influencing syllabi and filtering down to produce certain practices in classrooms.

Fundamental pedagogics (FP) was a recontextualization of a range of German and Dutch theoretical sources: Langeveld's phenomenological method as applied to education, Warink's Calvinism, and in some institutions, the German/Dutch Didaktik tradition. From a review of the literature around FP, and in particular in more recent debates (Kruger and Yonge, 2008; Le Grange, 2008; Yonge, 2008), it is clear that didactics was differently interpreted and recontextualized across different universities. Suransky's (1998) political history of Fundamental Pedagogics (FP) elucidates it as an adaptation, arguably a distortion, of Dutch education theory. She shows how the divergent meanings of Langeveld's education theory were developed in the context of post-World War II Holland and were used as an attempt to foster new modernist and social democratic identities through education in that country. In its recontextualized form in the South African context – called 'fundamental pedagogics', its use and purpose was debated, with some arguing that it was bent to serve a context defined by ethnic-nationalism and racist divisions.

Put simply and summarily, fundamental pedagogicians argued that the 'scientific method' was the only authentic method of studying education. Taking a phenomenological approach, the fundamental pedagogician would come to understand the 'essences' of education through 'radical reflection' on the educational situation. Advocates of fundamental pedagogics argued that practising pedagogics as science freed it from metaphysics, dogmatics and ideology. Viljoen and Pienaar (1971) in their textbook distinguished three stages or moments in the process of this scientific research:

- the pre-scientific (pre-reflective) life-world in which the original phenomena reveal themselves, and which arouse the wonderment of the scientist;
- the scientific reflection on the phenomenon and the universal, verifiable, logically systematized body of knowledge offered by such reflection; and
- the post-scientific meaningful implementation of this body of knowledge in society.

A crucial feature was the epoche (bracketing) at the scientific stage of extrinsic aims and beliefs, or politics. In the pre-scientific and post-scientific stages values or life-views played a prominent role, but the scientific reflection stage gave priority to the knowledge being taught and its relation to a broader 'systematized body of knowledge'.

The theory and conceptual underpinnings of FP were thoroughly critiqued. It was argued that it was inaccessible and mystifying (Reagan, 1990); not amenable to rational challenges and critical scrutiny (Parker, 1981; Morrow, 1989); and inarticulate, conceptually confused and contradictory (Morrow, 1981; Enslin, 1988). The most prominent critique, however, was political, the objection to the presentation of FP as a 'science', a "theoretical discourse from which the political has been exorcised" (Enslin, 1990, p. 86). It was argued to promulgate a pedagogy devoid of analysis and critique (Taylor & Vinjevold, 1999) which at the time was unpalatable to those seeking political shift, and looking in part to the education system to support this. Enslin critiqued the notion of bracketing or epoche: "By excluding the political as a legitimate dimension of theoretical discourse, fundamental pedagogics offers neither a language of critique nor a language of possibility" (1990, p. 78).

FP was also strongly tied to and seen as symbiotic with Christian National Education (CNE). Some argued that it was an attempt to make CNE academically respectable (Enslin, 1984), others that it was an "outgrowth of the educational ideology of Christian National Education" (Reagan, 1990, p. 66).

But the academic (and scientific or 'quasi-scientific') arguments were frequently backgrounded in the critique. FP was often portrayed (and indeed caricatured) by a selective rendering of the philosophy drawn from particular theorists. For example, de Vries (cited in Enslin, 1990) was often cited and critiqued for FP's construction of the child as:

> still dependent, in need of help and seeking help because he is incompetent, ignorant, unskillful, irresponsible and undisciplined . . . Because the child is

not good by nature and as a fallen being is inclined to evil, he will not of his own accord find the way that leads to truth and persist on it.

(de Vries, cited in Enslin, 1990, p. 85)

But Van der Stoep (1969), one of the key figures in South African FP, emphasized in children 'anticipation':

A child is in the world as an anticipating being; however, awakened and practised anticipation is the fruit of successful teaching – and thus, anticipation can be nothing less than a didactical category or building block of a didactic theory.

(p. 28)

It is clear here that two very different knowers were projected by different recontextualizations of the theory. The dominant critique at the time, however, focused on the FP ontology which "produces docile and useful students and teachers" (Enslin, 1990, p. 87), where the teachers' moral authority was to be delegated from God.

Unstable meanings

More recently there have been alternative views of FP, its conceptualization of the child and knowledge. Yonge (2008) convincingly argues that there was no necessary connection between FP and Christianity, or any other worldview. Further, Kruger and Yonge (2008) present a conceptualization of the child or learner in a very different way to those who critiqued FP:

Teaching and learning are inalienably part and parcel of being human. To a child there is no other way to a meaningful life other than the urgent, and at times demanding, mastery of life-contents. Hence, didactic pedagogics advances the establishment of didactic situations with a view to the imaginative unlocking of contents as the only way along which children's forming, educating, and becoming can be actualized.

(pp. 247–248)

Enslin's interpretation of the learner in her reading was that education was, universally, the leading of the helpless dependent child to adulthood by the adult pedagogue. And out of this claim emerged the justification for authoritarian practices (1990, p. 87). These contradictory understandings perhaps account for why FP became an enduring ideological battleground between academics in English liberal universities and Afrikaans universities (see Beard & Morrow, 1981).

At least part of the problem in debates around FP was that its definition is variable. Different authors and different universities that invoked the term emphasized different meanings and orientations (Beard & Morrow, 1981, p. 13). But it is not clear how the following definition, for example, is derived from the various articulations set forth:

> Teaching and learning in this theory of education is structured by the understanding that knowledge is given to the learner by experience, for the learner is a 'tabular rasa'. Learning is possible through reinforcement, 'banking' or talk and chalk. Assessment is based on the ability to reproduce uncritically the information transmitted to the learner.
>
> (Flanagan, 1992: p. 29)

These kinds of over-simplifications of the theory were also found in the Journal of Bantu Education, (later called Educamus). These were monthly publications issued to administrators and teachers by the Department of Bantu Education and later DET. The journal offered teachers explanations of a range of subject content, articles on various aspects of teaching-learning and issues related to conditions of service, as well as advice on methodology. It was often written by bureaucrats recontextualizing the high (and in places definitely confused) theory emerging from the Afrikaans universities.

If one sets aside the dominant political critique (that treated the political as central to critically understanding education and its future possibilities in South Africa), it is possible to interpret FP in a different way. More didactically-oriented explanations of FP might be seen as a distinct method of inserting knowledge in pedagogy. One version which draws strongly on the work of Wolfgang Klafki, theorizes the necessity of bracketing of the social and political in order that fundamental contents of subjects, learning matter or concepts, can be 'reduced' to make complicated contents or concepts available to children, and to consider the ways in which the reduced contents (essence) may appear. Eliminating the political from the process of scientific consideration may arguably make subsequent reflection on the life-world, and political and social action more meaningful. Muller and Hoadley (2017) explain:

> the ***didaktik*** tradition distinguishes between ***bildungsinhalt*** (subject content) and ***bildungsgehalt*** (content substance). Subject content is the disciplinary knowledge, 'the subject with reference to its knowledge structure' (Künzli, 2013, 672; see also Hopmann, 2007); content 'substance' is a reduced form of subject content, 'reduced' in the culinary sense, less summary than a reduction to its idealized essence in a form appropriate for pedagogic induction. In the ***didaktik*** tradition, teachers would be trained to do the reduction in the interests of their learners, a process called 'didactic analysis' by Klafki, a major ***didaktik*** theorist (see Klafki, 1995). Having reduced the knowledge-to-be-taught to a digestible learning bite, the teacher shows how the reduction can be 'unlocked' to expand the range of its generalisabilty, and inducts the learner into 'unlocking' it him or herself, a process called 'double unlocking'.

The understanding of knowledge or content in relation to FP may in some ways explain its rejection on political grounds – it left out 'real', contextual, everyday knowledge, and was thus construed as a-political, conservative and socially-blind. Under apartheid, amongst liberal academics in a highly politicized environment where education was seen as key to liberation, this was anathema. Further FP was in many ways conflated with CNE, rather than seen as infused but separable from CNE (see the following section).

What effect did FP have in classrooms?

Although across the literature there are widespread claims about the devastating effects of FP on teachers' thinking and practice, in their careful analysis Beard and Morrow (1981) show how it was 'almost impossible' to demonstrate the effects of FP on policymaking for "persons of colour" (p. 14), and that even were it to have influence at higher levels of the system (as a dominant discourse in policymaking arenas), the question of its impact at grassroots level was open. Its actual influence on teacher education, and classroom practices by extension, was difficult to determine, likely very variable (Beard & Morrow, 1981) and I would argue, probably negligible.

I argue negligible from the descriptions of teacher education provided of the time. Freer (1993) shows how in many of the colleges, the courses offered for secondary teachers were repetitions of the three final years of an impoverished secondary programme. Students in these courses mainly used school textbooks for study, and courses entailed very little and generally no content that could be identified as challenging or insightful.

Further, the educational qualifications of the 26 465 teachers employed by the Department of Education and Training (DET), in 1961 are shown in Table 4.1.

Some 57.2% of teachers had only a Standard 6 (Grade 8) in 1964. Low levels of qualification were especially acute in the bantustans. Horrell (1980) reported that in Transkei in 1979 11,182 or 93.7% of primary school teachers had qualifications lower than matric. Up until the era of democracy it remained possible for students in the black schooling sector to qualify as teachers with a Standard 8 (Grade 10) school-leaving certificate. Hartshorne (1992) explains how particularly in the 1980s, black teacher training colleges were understaffed and the college lecturers under-qualified. Students entering teaching had very low schooling

Table 4.1 Educational qualifications of DET teachers, 1961 (adapted from Horrell, 1964, p. 113)

Educational qualification	*Number of teachers*	*Percentage of teachers*
8th grade (Standard 6)	15,149	57.2
10th grade (Standard 8)	9,515	36
12th grade (Standard 10)	905	3.4
University degree	896	3.4

results. The quality of training received in black colleges, as a result of these various factors, was severely compromised. Finally, for lower primary teachers in particular, in the 1970s the entrance requirement for teacher training was a pass in the Standard 6 (Grade 8) exam (Chisholm, 2013, p. 409).

FP was a highly theoretical and complex 'science of education', based on phenomenology as described above. That there was some exposure, particularly in the Afrikaans universities, is probably correct. But the nature of that exposure and its variability is not known. Given the quality of college staff especially in black colleges, it is unlikely that they would have grasped and transmitted a coherent or stable version of the theory, if transmitting any theory at all.

It is doubtful then that FP fundamentally shaped and defined pedagogic practice under apartheid. Even in relation to teacher education, the more ideological aspects are likely to have inhered in Christian National Education, rather than FP, and it could be the tight coupling of the two that generated more heat towards FP than perhaps it warranted. In terms of the CNE policy, education departments at the white Afrikaans and many black universities and colleges were dominated by an ideology that propagated a fundamentalist view of Christianity and forms of school discipline and authority designed to encourage unquestioning compliance and acquiescence to the state and the Dutch Reformed Church. It was only in the four white English-speaking universities and one coloured university, and in colleges of education linked to them, that this dominant discourse was challenged and alternative offerings became possible (see Ensor, 1999 for an illuminating discussion of alternative discourses within mathematics teacher education produced in these institutions, both liberal and radical).

However, I argue below that the main alternative to FP in the form of progressive initiatives in the system which were set up to counter its supposed negative effects also likely had limited impact on teaching and learning. I address this progressive thrust briefly below.

The influence of progressivism

The influence of international progressive movements was raised in Chapter 3, showing how developments especially in the United States and Britain began to filter into curriculum development, both outside of and later within formal, state curriculum-making domains. Many of the progressivist initiatives, especially those outside of the state, aimed to challenge what was construed as the very authoritarian pedagogies with a strong emphasis on rote memorization found in classrooms at the time.

Many of the progressive interventions targeted white schools and the very small number of private schools only. One of the more well-known progressivist alternatives for black schooling was the Primary Education Upgrading Programme (PEUP), operating in the 'bantustan' of Bophutatswana. The project was an attempt to introduce more child-centred and discovery-learning methods in classrooms, aiming to counter the passivity of learners. By 1985, 760 schools, the vast majority of the bantustan's primary schools, were involved in the project

(Chisholm, 2013). The non-profit organization Molteno also led a literacy programme within the PEUP that attempted to break with the common practice of teaching literacy via the chanting of words by rote from chalkboards, and introducing children to readers and other whole language approaches to teaching literacy (MacDonald, 1990, p. 71). Evaluations of the programme showed limited impact. Very few child-centred methods were found in classrooms subsequent to the programme's implementation. Failure of the programme was attributed to the design of the programme itself, as well as the context of its implementation that was defined by extreme household poverty and poorly resourced school contexts. Jansen's (1988) fundamental critique of PEUP and other progressive initiatives in black schools was the fact that they were ultimately technical exercises which failed to adequately take into account the contextual realities and structural constraints to teachers' real participation.

There were many such progressive pedagogical interventions, generally on a much smaller scale, driven by NGOs. '*Projects Speak for Themselves*' (Levy, 1994) provides an interesting description of the type of work being undertaken, especially in science, mathematics and environmental studies. Galant (1997) also details a number of initiatives in relation to mathematics teaching, and the uptake of 'People's Mathematics', 'Critical mathematics education' and 'ethnomathematics'. '*Breaking the formal frame*' (Millar et al., 1991) was another significant collection of papers spanning 1981 to 1988 focused on non-formal and alternative ways of reconstructing pedagogy outside the traditional frames of schooling and tertiary education.

Within the state there were also progressive experiments. Flanagan (1992) reviews a sample of official policy documentation from the 1970s, showing how progressivist discourse had filtered into public policy. A substantial critique of child-centredness had also emerged early on, and 'Rote versus meaningful learning' became an object of study and debate amongst bureaucrats and academics aligned with Bantu Education and committed to its 'improvement' (Duminy, 1967).

The progressivist influence can be seen in a number of guides to practice, such as teachers' guides and also in the aforementioned 'Educamus'. As well as elucidating aspects of fundamental pedagogics, the journal also, especially in the 1980s, suggested a range of progressive approaches. For example in the 1982 editions, tips on how to do groupwork, as well as 'The teaching-learning conversation as a teaching method' gave teachers suggestions of how to implement new pedagogic techniques in their classrooms.

In departmentally produced official documentation strands of progressive pedagogies were also evident. For example, in a 1978 teachers' guide for primary mathematics teachers in House of Representatives (or 'coloured') schools in the Cape province, the 'teaching method' for mathematics was stipulated as follows:

> There is often more than one method of tackling and solving a problem. In addition, pupils often learn more effectively from one another than from their teacher. A good approach is to give the pupil the first opportunity to

> try and solve a problem, before the teacher gives an explanation. Pupils may individually or in groups attempt to solve the problem. It is worthwhile to follow this approach even if only one pupil finds the solution. The pupil should then explain to the group how he arrived at the solution. He should also try to give a written explanation on the writing board.
>
> (House of Representatives Department of Education and Culture, 1978, p. 15)

As indicated already, these progressive attempts to shift pedagogic practice were much more common in white schools and even there were limited. Nonetheless, exposure of white teachers to more progressive pedagogical tenets was well established, especially through teacher education in the liberal white universities. The vast majority of black schools were not influenced by the initiatives. This was evident in the failure of PEUP, but also in descriptions of dominant practices in black classrooms at the time in a small number of empirical research studies.

Classroom pedagogy in black classrooms under apartheid

A tradition of empirical classroom-based research in education in South Africa under apartheid was almost non-existent, and research at the school level was limited and superficial. This was partly explained by hostility towards educational researchers on the part of education departments and school management. Further, teachers were hostile to outsiders entering their classrooms given the highly autocratic and bureaucratic system of inspection, often used punitively and vindictively against teachers (Chisholm et al., 2005). Muller's (1996) review confirmed that there was a paucity of empirical, school-based sociological enquiry prior to 1996. Of the relatively insubstantial work in the sociology of education in South Africa up until this time, most were policy studies.

Insights around classroom practices prior to the 1990s are available largely from accounts from in-service teacher education projects, gleaned from reports of school inspectors (Bot & Schlemmer, 1986; Thembela, 1986) or from the very few research studies that were conducted at the time. These early studies were able to characterize prevalent teaching styles and forms of interaction in black classrooms, summarized as "teachers adopting authoritarian roles and doing most of the talking, with few pupil initiations, and with most of the pupil responses taking the form of group chorusing" (Chick, 1996, p. 21). Below I discuss four studies that provide a description of dominant practices as well as explanations for the observed practices. These are the Threshold Project, reported by MacDonald (1990) and three smaller studies by Muller (1989), Chick (1996) and Walker (1989).

Crossing the threshold

The Threshold Project was a three-year project that followed a 1985 pilot study examining the nature of the language and learning difficulties that black

Standard 3 (Grade 5) children in South Africa experienced when they changed from their mother tongue of Sepedi to English as a medium of instruction and learning. The study focused on the demands and problems entailed as children crossed this 'threshold', where they were suddenly expected to learn all their subjects through the medium of English. The study was conducted as part of the PEUP described above. MacDonald (1990), who evaluated the programme, showed how Grade 5 learners had about 700 words at most in English but that the curriculum required at least 7,000, making it difficult for them to understand text even if they could decode it. However, what also made it difficult for students to read with meaning or learn effectively was that they did not have a sufficient grasp of the linguistic structure of the English language. The sudden transition to English as medium of instruction resulted in most learners resorting to rote learning content that they did not understand. MacDonald argued that students experienced a loss of meaning – "The children are likely to be alienated by what they have to learn, and only dimly perceive the implications and linkages between the concepts they are presented with" (p. 143). The study made connections between this pedagogical experience of learners and the very high dropout rate of learners at this level at the time.

In relation to actual pedagogic practices, MacDonald also visited a number of classrooms that had undergone the PEUP reforms, as well as conventional DET classrooms. She found traditional teaching styles with little initiation on the part of the pupil in learning activities. Almost none of the progressive features of the programme had been sustainably incorporated into classrooms. In particular she found a predominance of memory, practice and rote. The pedagogy largely consisted of oral input and oral answers, very slow pace and weak coverage (attributed to very low expectations of pupils on the part of teachers). Classrooms were frequently interrupted. She argued that many of the progressive features of the programme were at odds with local conditions and understandings. Groupwork, as suggested by the project, and differentiated teaching, were not possible, especially given large class sizes. Teachers' competence in the pedagogic forms was very restricted:

> the teacher uses up much time essentially repeating the same exercise. She tells a story, two children repeat it, and then she repeats it again with the reader in her hand, with extra details. The story is treated as an undifferentiated whole, and the teacher is not able to make use of oral language development strategies, such as prediction, alternative endings etc.
>
> (MacDonald, 1990, p. 33)

A key progressive tenet of teaching is to generate positive affect in order to facilitate learning. On this issue MacDonald summarizes:

> In practice teachers have a very pragmatic approach to their children's affect; they think that they have a job to get done; they are not entertainers, they do not need specific affirmation from their pupils, but they have particular

> expectations about what good learning behavior entails. It entails doing what is expected of you, and not attempting more than that unless it is explicitly asked.
>
> (p. 40)

There are a number of other features of classrooms that MacDonald (1990) identifies, drawing on her research, that gives a clear picture of classrooms in the mid-1980s, and focuses more explicitly on the nature of the social relation and knowledge in the classroom. She found that ***role division was marked***. Children were not expected to solve problems independently and the teacher was regarded as the one who knows. The focus was on the ***outward appearance of the task***, possibly because "the forms of learning and knowledge construction would be opaque to teachers, and therefore they themselves can only mimic surface characteristics of the task" (MacDonald, 1990, p. 81).

The central teaching strategy was identified as ***example and demonstration***, and the parallel learning mode ***observation and imitation***. In this version children received very little feedback on their answers, confronted rather with repetitions of previous examples (often woefully inadequate). Instructions were often piecemeal and incomplete, again focusing on the ***surface features of the task*** rather than on its structuring and purpose. The teacher generated a ***synchrony*** between herself and the learners, and demanded attention from them through a cue of 'ne?' (meaning, not so?] which was followed by a chorused affirmative. The teacher sought responses from children that corresponded closely with what she had said or intended. "Evidence of independent thought – difficult for them to express in English – would be sufficient to startle the teacher" (p. 84). In terms of the social relation, MacDonald identifies a caring and accepting environment for children early on, which diminished as children proceeded through the grades so that by the end of the junior primary phase discipline was largely punitive and authoritarian.

The reason for reporting on this study in detail is that it was one of the few studies to go into classrooms under apartheid, and report in detail on observations of pedagogic practices.

Safe-talk

Another early socio-linguistic study by Chick (1996) made the argument that the chorusing and rhythmic chanting in classroom, and absence of individual, evaluated performances, what he terms 'safe-talk', was a strategy to mask both the teacher's and students' poor command of English and their lack of understanding of academic content. The safety sought was from the "oppressive and demeaning effects of apartheid ideology and structures" (p. 24). Chick argues that teachers resisted innovation because they had vested interests in the maintenance of this 'safe-talk'. Through safe-talk they were able to "avoid the loss of face associated with displays of incompetence. This is because they ensure that the lesson develops along predetermined lines, and that the opportunities for students to raise issues and problems that teachers may not be competent to handle are few" (p. 30).

Knowledge out there

Muller (1989) also related communicative routines or classroom interaction to social arrangements. In his analysis of two science classrooms, one catering to white learners and the other to black learners, he eschewed the notion that drill and rote procedures in classrooms are rooted in culture or personal preference, but rather that these related to the former restricted learning of teachers. Black teachers, he argued, had little opportunity to 'internalise the grammar of science' to teach it appropriately. Thus, rote-learning routines were an "exigency resorted to by people operating within a particular communicative contract" (p. 320). Muller linked authority relations in the classroom to particular ways in which knowledge was treated in those classrooms, and which derived in part from an analysis of the social set up under apartheid.

He argued that in the white classroom analyzed, control by the teacher is channeled through personal and privatized tests of knowledge of the students. In the black classroom control is achieved through a joint class accession to understanding between teacher and students that knowledge is 'out there'. In the black classroom studied, the teacher was not authoritative and did not display competence. But both the teacher's and the students' lack of understanding of science knowledge was ascribed to the social arrangement (of apartheid), denying them any agency: "as far as they are concerned, the causes for their failure lie outside of them. By the same token, this view also tends to block any sense that failure could be for reasons of personal shortcoming" (p. 325).

Synchrony and the absence of knowledge

MacDonald and Chick point to classroom interactions that mask an absence of knowledge, creating a safe space and a synchrony in the classroom. This is safety from the 'volatile possibilities of talk' (Alexander, 2001, p. 566) that may expose linguistic or cognitive inadequacies on the part of students or teachers. Similarly, Muller emphasizes the complicity that develops between teachers and students in avoiding explanations by focusing on a ritualistic exchange of facts and definitions. Muller argues that by fulfilling the social requirements of classroom interaction and participation the cognitive or knowledge requirements of the lesson are eclipsed (p. 336).

Walker (1989) conducted a significant amount of action research in classrooms at the time, relating teaching practices to teachers' own schooling and training and their socialization into their practice. On the basis of her research she argued that

> African teachers will have internalised a particular understanding of teacher behaviour which they then act out themselves in their own classrooms. So

> the dominance of transmission teaching with its concomitant emphasis on teacher-talk, drill and practice and rote learning continues to hold sway and few questions are consciously posed by teachers regarding what and how they teach, and in whose interests.
>
> (1989, p. 20)

MacDonald, Chick, Muller and Walker all veer away from culturalist arguments to more structural accounts which draw attention to the dearth of both cognitive and symbolic resources in classrooms at the time. Chick, MacDonald and Muller argue in slightly different ways, that the 'synchrony' established between teachers and students in the class and call and response communicative patterns of classrooms was a masking of the fact that there was little substantive knowledge being transmitted. Muller and Walker draw attention to how the pedagogy is reproduced – teachers have been socialized into these practices through their own restricted schooling and training, with ongoing structural inequality denying teacher agency.

While I have focused on the arguments related to knowledge presented in the studies reviewed here, Soudien (2010) argues that the rite of rote probably began with mission schooling, which consisted mainly of rote learning to enable children to read the Bible. The strong Calvinist influence in much of mission education contributed to this formalism (p. 27).

Explaining the persistence of these pedagogic forms over a long period of time, however, is more complex. Ensor (2015) argues that particular ritualized practices such as chorusing are often deployed as mechanisms for control in difficult circumstances and contexts of material deprivation and large classes. She argues that these practices become "habituated over time, as part of the regulative discourse of classrooms, so that even when resource constraints are eased, historical practices live on and are difficult to change" (p.74). Jacklin (2004) brings these diverse explanations for habituated practices together when she argues that it is not just material conditions that require change in order to shift practice, but also "the discourse or underpinning knowledge, the social relations and interactions and the material aspects (space/time and technology use) that constitute the practice" (p. 86).

Conclusion

This chapter has outlined what we know from limited research about the forms of pedagogy under apartheid. Of course these are generalizations, masking greater variety that is likely to have made up teaching and learning in different classrooms at the time. Barrett (2007) points out, "Efforts to construct 'purified' histories of pedagogies, from whatever angle, are bound to caricature and hide the complexity and diversity of educational practice" (p. 292). The chapter argues, however, that neither FP nor the progressive agenda in education disrupted the dominant pedagogic forms. Rather, resource constraint, especially cognitive resources, provides an explanation for practices at the time that were impervious to policy programmes.

What we do know about pedagogic forms under apartheid accords with much of the characterization of developing country pedagogies offered in in Chapter 2: rote memorization of a low level of subject content with collective chorusing and chanting a common feature. Given the establishment of a traditional curriculum and rote pedagogy under apartheid sketched in this chapter and the preceding, the interest in the chapters that follow is what shifts and what endures in the face of the post-apartheid reforms. But first I turn to the theoretical framing for the analyses in the next chapter.

References

Alexander, R. (2001). *Culture and Pedagogy: International Comparisons in Primary Education*. Oxford: Blackwell Publishing.

Barrett, A. (2007). Beyond the polarization of pedagogy: Models of classroom practice in Tanzanian primary schools. *Comparative Education*, *43*(2), 273–294.

Beard, P., & Morrow, W. (1981). *Problems of pedagogics*. Pretoria: Butterworths.

Bot, M., & Schlemmer, L. (1986). *The classroom crisis: Black demands and white responses*. Durban: Centre for Applied Social Sciences, University of Natal.

Chick, J. K. (1996). Safe-talk: Collusion in apartheid education. In H. Coleman (Ed.), *Society and the Language Classroom* (pp. 21–39). Cambridge: Cambridge University Press.

Chisholm, L. (2013). Bantustan education history: The 'progressivism' of Bophutatswana's primary education upgrade programme (PEUP), 1979–1988. *South African Historical Journal*, *65*(3), 403–420.

Chisholm, L., Hoadley, U., & Kivilu, M. (2005). Educator workload in South Africa. final report prepared for the education labour relations council. Pretoria: Human Sciences Research Council.

Duminy, P. (1967). Trends and challenges in the education of the South African bantu. Pretoria: Van Schaik.

Enslin, P. (1984). The role of fundamental pedagogics in the formulation of educational policy in South Africa. In P. Kallaway (Ed.), *Apartheid and education: The education of black South Africans* (pp. 139–147). Johannesburg: Ravan Press.

Enslin, P. (1988). The state of pedagogics. *Perspectives in Education*, *10*(1), 67–74.

Enslin, P. (1990). Science and doctrine: Theoretical discourse in South African teacher education. In M. Nkomo (Ed.), *Pedagogy of domination: Toward a democratic education in South Africa* (pp. 77–92). Trenton, NJ: Africa World Press.

Ensor, M. P. (1999). A study of the recontextualising of pedagogic practices from a South African university preservice mathematics teacher education course by seven beginning secondary mathematics teachers. University of London.

Ensor, P. (2015). Regulative discourse, ritual and the recontextualising of education policy into practice. *Learning, Culture and Social Interaction*, *6*, 67–76.

Flanagan, W. (1992). Pedagogical discourse, teacher education programmes and social transformation in South Africa. *International Journal of Educational Development*, *12*(1), 27–35.

Freer, D. (1993). The residuals of apartheid: Impediments to teacher development in South Africa. In G. K. Verma (Ed.), ***Inequality and teacher education*** (pp. 23–46). London: Falmer.

Galant, J. (1997). Teachers, learners and mathematics: An analysis of HSRC research reports on mathematics education 1970–1980. Unpublished MEd thesis, University of Cape Town.

Hartshorne, K. B. (1992). ***Crisis and challenge: Black education 1910–1990.*** Oxford University Press.

Horrell, M. (1964). ***A decade of bantu education.*** Johannesburg: South African Institute of Race Relations.

Horrell, M. (1980). ***The race relations survey, 1980.*** Johannesburg: South African Institute for Race Relations.

House of representatives Department of Education and Culture. (1978). ***Teacher's guide for mathematics: Senior primary phase (standards 2, 3 and 4).*** Cape Town: Cape and Transvaal Printers Pty Ltd.

Jacklin, H. (2004). ***Repetition and difference: A rhythm analysis of pedagogic practice.*** Unpublished PhD dissertation, University of Witwatersrand.

Jansen, J. (1988). Curriculum change and contextual realities: An analysis of recent trends in black South African education. ***International Review of Education, 34***(3), 378–387.

Krüger, R. A., & Yonge, G. D. (2008). The significance of the concepts 'elemental' and 'fundamental' in didactic theory and practice. ***Journal of Curriculum Studies, 40***(2), 215–250.

Le Grange, L. (2008). The didactics tradition in South Africa: A reply to Richard Krüger. ***Journal of Curriculum Studies, 40***(3), 399–407.

Levy, S. (1994). Projects speak for themselves: Science and mathematics education in the transition. Pietermaritzburg: Shooter & Shooter.

MacDonald, C. A. (1990). Swimming up the waterfall: A study of school-based learning experiences. Pretoria: Human Sciences Research Council.

Millar, C., Raynham, S., & Schaeffer, A. (1991). ***Breaking the formal frame: Readings in South African education in the eighties.*** Cape Town: Oxford University Press.

Morrow, W. (1981). The 'inner' and the 'outer' aspects of learning and knowledge. In P. Beard & W. Morrow (Eds.), ***Problems of pedagogics: Pedagogics and the study of education in South Africa*** (pp. 159–180). Durban & Pretoria: Butterworths.

Morrow, W. (1989). Chains of thought: Philosophical essays in South African education. Johannesburg: Southern.

Muller, J. (1989). 'Out of their minds': An analysis of discourse in two South African science classrooms. In D. A. Roger (Ed.), ***Conversation: An interdisciplinary approach*** (pp. 313–337). Clevedon, Philadelphia: Multilingual Matters.

Muller, J. (1996). Dreams of wholeness and loss: Critical sociology of education in south Africa. ***British Journal of Sociology of Education, 17***(2), 177–195.

Muller, J., & Hoadley, U. (2017, forthcoming). Pedagogic modality and structure in the recontextualising field of curriculum studies: A South African case. In B. Barrett, U. Hoadley & J. Morgan (Eds.), ***Knowledge, curriculum and equity: social realist perspectives.*** New York: Routledge.

National Education Co-ordinating Committee. National Education Policy Investigation. (1992). ***Curriculum: Report.*** Oxford University Press/NECC.

Parker, B. (1981). Freedom and authority in fundamental pedagogics. In P. N. G. Beard & W. Morrow (Eds.), ***Problems of pedagogics: Pedagogics and the study of education in South Africa*** (pp. 97–109). Durban: Butterworths.

Reagan, T. (1990). Philosophy of education in the service of apartheid: The role of fundamental pedagogics in South African education. ***Educational Foundations***, *4*(2), 59–71.

Soudien, C. (2010). What to teach the natives: A historiography of the curriculum dilemma in South Africa. In W. Pinar (Ed.), ***Curriculum studies in South Africa: Intellectual histories and present circumstances*** (pp. 19–49). New York: Palgrave Macmillan.

Suransky-Dekker, C. (1998). A liberating breeze of Western civilisation'? A political history of Fundamental Pedagogics as an expression of Dutch-Afrikaner relationships. Unpublished D.Ed dissertation, University of Durban-Westville, Durban.

Taylor, N., & Vinjevold, P. (1999). Getting learning right: Report of the president's education initiative research project. Johannesburg: Joint Education Trust.

Thembela, A. (1986). Some cultural factors which affect school education for blacks in South Africa. In G. Kendall (Ed.), ***Education and diversity of cultures*** (pp. 37–43). Pietermaritzburg: University of Natal.

Van der Stoep, F. (1969). ***Didaktiese grondvorme***. Pretoria: Academica.

Viljoen, T. A., & Pienaar, J. J. (1971). ***Fundamental pedagogics***. Durban: Butterworth-Heinemann Ltd.

Walker, M. (1989). ***Action research as a project***. Cape Town: Primary Education Project.

Yonge, G. D. (2008). Ideological alchemy: The transmutation of South African didactics (and fundamental pedagogics) into 'apartheid education'. ***Journal of Curriculum Studies***, *40*(3), 409–415.

5 Knowledge, curriculum, pedagogy

Theoretical framings

Introduction

Having sketched curriculum and pedagogic forms under apartheid in the previous two chapters, in the next six chapters I discuss the three post-apartheid curriculum reforms and pedagogic practices in classrooms where the reforms were implemented. Because I am interested in looking at change over time and in a comparison of curriculum and pedagogy under the three post-apartheid policy regimes, I use a similar theoretical framework across the chapters. I present that theoretical framework in this chapter, with an elaboration of how the theory was used in analysis in Appendix B.

The pedagogic device

Any act that is educational, say between a teacher and a learner, a doctor and a patient, a mother and a small child, involves a selection from the universe of knowledge (be it academic, community or other knowledge). This selected knowledge is refocused and changed for the purposes of teaching it, sometimes in the form of a curriculum. The knowledge is then actually transmitted through communication between a transmitter (often a teacher) and an acquirer or learner. A mother, taking her child to a family wedding, will make a selection from all the community knowledge available about wedding rituals, dress and behaviours. She will refocus this selection in relation to the age of the child to whom she wishes to teach these traditions, the social norms to which she subscribes and particular theories of how her child will understand the knowledge. She will communicate the community knowledge in a way that gives the child access to the criteria for what a wedding is, what its rituals entail and how to recognize and realize appropriate behaviours at a wedding. A primary school mathematics curriculum is a selection of particular concepts around number concept development from the field of mathematics. This mathematical knowledge is refocused, sequenced and paced in ways that accord with certain theories around early number concept acquisition. The teacher transmits this knowledge in the classroom, in different ways making the criteria for the recognition and realization of appropriate concepts and operations around number available.

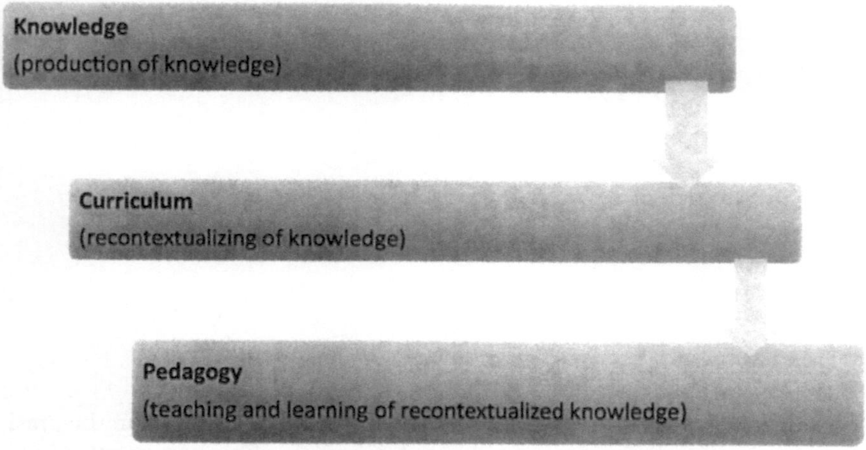

Figure 5.1 The process of transmission of educational knowledge

Bernstein, in his development of the notion of the pedagogic device, draws attention to the regularity of this process of the transformation of knowledge into pedagogic communication across all contexts that are educational. Bernstein's interest is in how at each level – the production of the knowledge (the field of mathematics, knowledge about weddings), its transformation into knowledge that is pedagogical (the curriculum, local community lores), and its actual transmission (teacher to student, mother to child) – the processes are deeply social and political, regulated by broader societal configurations of power and control.

In this chapter I discuss the pedagogic device as the central theoretical resource used in the analyses in the book. The pedagogic device is a relational set of principles to describe the process of how any knowledge – disciplinary, community, local – is transformed into educational knowledge, and communicated in pedagogy. In introducing the device, Bernstein is centrally concerned with how in the very structuring of pedagogy, from producing knowledge, to making selections around what to teach, to the actual teaching and learning processes, there are processes of differentiation, where who gets access to what educational knowledge, and how, is unevenly distributed across groups in society.

A sociological understanding of the transmission of educational knowledge

The pedagogic device is not a thing, but rather, like grammar, it is a set of rules that operates in the background, generative of particular processes and forms, in this case the process of knowledge becoming pedagogic communication. These processes and hence the device are social and political, and historically located. The device offers a way of describing the ways in which broader social norms or the moral order established by the state, the economy and the political arena as well as the field of education itself, inform decisions around what knowledge is to be distributed, to whom and how.

The device is unique in the sociology of education in that it provides a theoretical model of the ***structuring*** of the process of education, or of knowledge transformed into pedagogic communication. Conventional accounts, and in particular social reproduction theories, focus on the relations between what goes on in educational settings and external social categories, such as race, class and gender (or any other discriminating attribute) and how these bias the messages that are communicated. The focus is on the messages that are ***relayed***. Bernstein acknowledged the importance of this way of looking at the reproduction of unequal relations through education, but asserted that it told only part of the story: "it is crucial for students to know and to feel that they, the experiences that have shaped them, and their modes of showing are recognised, respected and valued. But this does not mean that this exhausts the pedagogic encounter" (Bernstein, 2000, p. 174). What the pedagogic device does is describe the grammar which makes the message in the pedagogic encounter possible. The focus is thus on how differentiation is produced in the structure of the pedagogic 'grammar' itself, the *relay*. He uses the analogy of the hi-fi to explain the distinction between the relay and the relayed:

> Think of a hi-fi (assuming you have a hi-fi system). When the tuner is activated what is heard is a function of the system carrying the signal: the system carrying the signal has already regulated the signal. What of pedagogic communication? We know what it carries, but what is the structure that allows, enables it to be carried? This is very similar to a distinction between language and speech. It is as if when we study pedagogic communication we study only the surface features, only its message, not that structure which makes the message possible.
>
> (Bernstein, 1990, p. 146)

To take the very simple example of the learning of number concept again from above, differentiation in the messages or learning around number is not carried only in what the teacher may communicate to boys and girls about mathematics, or what she might leave out for slower learners or learners from poorer homes, or other gendered or cultural biases that exert influence on what she communicates from outside. But differentiation is also carried in the actual rules established around what knowledge specific learners are given access to, how the knowledge to be transmitted is refocused and organized in the particular curriculum in use, and how the criteria are actually made available when the knowledge is transmitted in the classroom. It is this social *relay* to which Bernstein draws attention. He does this because in making the structuring of pedagogic discourse visible, he opens up the possibilities for interruption and not just reproduction of differential access. "Whatever comes into education from the outside interacts with something that is already there on the inside and pupils can engage with this 'something' in ways that are to varying degrees independent from external relations to education" (Moore, 2013, p. 103). In other words considering internal relations opens up the possibilities for resistance, challenge and change of the discourse. In this way, as Moore (2013) has it, "Bernstein stands out from the established orthodoxies that in various ways are preoccupied with how forces from outside education construct its voices only in ways that reproduce existing inequalities" (p. 2). Bernstein's radical assertion and core proposition is that there is a discretionary space when considering the relations internal to education, the structuring of pedagogic discourse itself:

> In a fundamental sense, as pedagogic communication, of both transmitter and acquirer cannot be programmed (and therefore has some autonomy) and is a specialized language, it is not possible for that communication to be effectively policed and made uniform. Further, the basis of the hierarchy of pedagogic (school/university) discourse cannot always be derived from class hierarchies or their dominant cultures except with reference to a simple mental/manual division. In these two senses there is a potential discretionary space.
>
> (1990, p. 151)

Bernstein considers the structure of pedagogic processes themselves (through the pedagogic device and the principles of classification and framing specifically which I address below) and how this structuring produces different pedagogic modalities with differential class effects. He does not dismiss the reproduction thesis, but addresses a crucial 'blind spot' (Moore, 2013) in the sociology of education: an awareness of the autonomy and possible transformative power of pedagogy itself.

The rules of the pedagogic device

The device consists of three sets of rules, ***hierarchically related***, that describe the process of the transformation of knowledge into pedagogic communication. They are hierarchical in that one set is derived from the level above. The rules are ***the distributive rules, the recontextualizing rules and the evaluative rules***, and they refer to different fields. Each set of rules is discussed in more detail below.

The distributive rules – who gets what

The distributive rule generates the field of production, where academic knowledge is produced. Bernstein distinguishes between two fundamental types of knowledge – mundane or esoteric, commonsense or uncommonsense knowledge. The distinction also refers to that between education and production, or between mental and manual, reaching back to Durkheim's original distinction between sacred and profane knowledge. The distinction takes on different expression in different historical periods (Bernstein, 1977, p. 190).

Distributive rules concern not just the production of these discourses, but also regulate what knowledge is distributed to whom, or to put it more prosaically, who gets access to specialized knowledge (and the potential to think things other than how they are) and who gets access to mundane (or commonsense) or manual knowledge. Distributive rules are therefore about power: "distributive rules specialize forms of knowledge, forms of consciousness and forms of practice to social groups" (Bernstein, 1990, p. 28). And Bernstein understood that this distribution was unequal, particularly in relation to social class. The more privileged in society gain access to specialized knowledge, carrying with it the potential for innovation and intellectual change; the socially marginalized are denied such access or gain restricted forms.

The distributive rules are historically-specific and are derived from the political economy. The moral order or dominant societal principles are generated by the state's interaction with the economy and politics of the particular historical context. This occurs within the global political economy, and so is to a greater or lesser extent influenced by the international field.

Extracts from two official statements are reproduced below. They exemplify very simply the relationship between the moral order and distributive rules. One extract is from apartheid Prime Minister Verwoerd's infamous speech to parliament in 1954. The other is from A Policy Framework for Education and Training, developed by the African National Congress, just months before the 1994 democratic elections.

> There is no place for [the Bantu] in the European community above the level of certain forms of labour . . . What is the use of teaching the Bantu child mathematics when it cannot use it in practice? That is quite absurd. Education must train people in accordance with their opportunities in life, according to the sphere in which they live.
>
> (Dr Hendrik Verwoerd, South African Minister for Native Affairs, and Prime Minister from 1958 to 66, speaking about his government's education policies in the 1950s. As quoted in Apartheid – A History by Brian Lapping, 1987)

> We believe that the curriculum must promote unity and the common citizenship and destiny of all South Africans irrespective of race, class, gender and ethnic background. It must be relevant to the needs of the individual as well as the social and economic needs of society. The curriculum must promote independent and self-critical learning and respect the equality of all forms of knowledge. And more importantly, the process of curriculum development must be democratised through the participation of all stakeholders.
>
> (African National Congress, 1994, p. 68)

It is obvious from these two extracts how differently power is enacted in the two cases. Both cases are idealized, of course. Under apartheid, with its rigid categories of persons (predominantly determined in terms of race) as well as knowledge, the distributive rules very explicitly distributed different forms of knowledge to different groups, and legitimized the construction of separate and unequal educational institutions to give effect to this distribution. In the second extract, published just before the first democratic elections, the boundaries between education, production and civil society are dissolved, as are distinctions between different kinds of knowledge. The distributive rule in this case generates an official pedagogic discourse around universal, equal access to different forms of knowledge that are equally valued.

Here we see how the distribution of power in society establishes a regulative discourse on the basis of which curriculum selections will be made (recontextualizing rules) and classroom practice will be framed (evaluative rules).

The recontextualizing rules

Specialized knowledge issues from the field of production (in universities and research laboratories, for example) at the level of distributive rules, from whence the school curriculum is derived at the next level – the recontextualizing rules.

At the level of recontextualization, Bernstein describes the movement of discursive content from the field of production into a pedagogic context. The recontextualizing rules regulate the constitution of educational (in our case school) knowledge and how it should be transmitted. School knowledge is always a selection, a refocusing and a reordering of disciplinary knowledge produced in universities, research laboratories and other knowledge-producing sites. As knowledge moves from the field of production to become pedagogized, it changes fundamentally, so that the physics of the university research laboratory is very different to the physics taught in school. In a physics curriculum, Bernstein argues,

> The rules of relation, selection, sequencing, and pacing [. . .] cannot themselves be derived from some logic internal to physics nor from the practices of those who produce physics. The rules of the reproduction of physics are social, not logical, facts.
>
> (Bernstein, 1990, pp. 184–185)

What then informs the selection? In the process of moving from the field of production, knowledge passes through 'ideological screens' (Bernstein, 2000, p. 115) as it becomes educational knowledge. Bernstein describes what he terms 'pedagogic discourse' as the principle for embedding an instructional discourse (the content to be mastered) into a regulative discourse (moral order of the institution; rules of order, relation and identity, of conduct, behaviour etcetera). He established the regulative discourse as dominant, as regulating how recontextualizing happens. Regulative discourse entails political, social and psychological considerations. The norms that inhere in regulative discourse are derived from the dominant principles of society. Curriculum is influenced in degree and direction by these sociological messages issuing from the socio-political context (Morais & Neves, 2001).

But this is not determinative. There is "no necessary relationship between changing the social basis of relations in the economic field and changing the social basis of the principles of the reproduction of the cultural field" (Bernstein, 1990, p. 147). There is not a direct relationship between education and the economy. Formal schooling especially has substantial relative autonomy[1] from the demands of the economy, or polity. Regulative discourse at the level of recontextualizing contains a particular model of the teacher and the learner and the relation between them. "The model of the learner is never wholly utilitarian" (Bernstein, 2000, p. 35). However, there are always ideological elements that inform the model of the learner, the theory of instruction and the moral purpose of education expressed through the curriculum at this level.

The recontextualizing field

Recontextualization takes place within a recontextualizing field that has two distinct arenas. The Official Recontextualizing Field (ORF), consisting of bureaucrats and specialized departments and sub-agencies of the state; and the Pedagogic Recontextualizing Field (PRF) which includes all interested educational actors (other than officials) with an interest in the circulation and reproduction of educational knowledge. It includes professional teacher organizations, unions, academics and specialized media of education, like journals, schools and school teachers. Bernstein's interest is in the interplay between these two fields in the recontextualizing of pedagogic discourses, in the struggle between these two fields for control over the processes of determining the what and how of schooling.

In the book, curriculum policy at different points in history is considered in terms of how knowledge is recontextualized to form curriculum prescriptions for reading and mathematics at the Foundation Phase level (Grades 1 to 3) specifically. The analyses in the relevant chapters focus on curriculum formation and also consider the interplay between the ORF and the PRF.

Evaluative rules

The evaluative rules regulate pedagogic practice at the classroom level, in the field of reproduction. This level refers to the transmission and acquisition of criteria in the classroom. Evaluative rules transform pedagogic discourse into pedagogic practice. Evaluative criteria at the level of the classroom, lecture theatre or other pedagogical setting establish what is deemed valuable and important to know, do, say and think. For Bernstein, 'Any specific pedagogic practice is there for one purpose: to transmit *criteria*' (2000, p. 28).

At the level of the evaluative rules, or pedagogic practice, we also find the distinction between instructional and regulative discourse, where instructional discourse is concerned with the transmission/acquisition of skills, knowledge and competences, and regulative discourse is about the social order and relations, norms of conduct, character and manner in the pedagogy. As two of the structural components of pedagogy, the two discourses allow for an analytical separation between the transmission of knowledge and skills on the one hand and the moral order, social norms and forms of relationship that underpin and structure this on the other. In the book the evaluative rules (or pedagogic practices) are tracked through ethnographic studies of the teaching of mathematics and reading in Foundation Phase classrooms in reference to the three curriculum reforms.

Instructional and regulative discourse

The preceding discussion makes it clear that regulative discourse operates across the different levels of the pedagogic device. At the level of the distributive rules, regulative discourse concerns the moral order. Here it is not completely divorced from the instructional order, but Muller and Hoadley (2010) argue, is ***in*** the instructional order "marking out symbolic forms, legitimate from illegitimate texts, the sacred from the profane" (p. 168).

At the level of recontextualizing rules, and the constitution of curriculum, regulative discourse regulates the selection of knowledge in this process, and here Bernstein stresses that regulative discourse is dominant:

> regulative discourse produces the order in the instructional discourse. There is no instructional discourse which is not regulated by the regulative discourse. If this is so, the whole order within pedagogic discourse is constituted by the regulative discourse.
>
> (Bernstein, 1996, p. 48)

Muller and Hoadley (2010) argue that the dominance may be overstated, and that the formulation denies or renders invisible the ways in which instructional discourse directs the logic of selection of knowledge for inclusion in curriculum. What is not raised and is pertinent to the studies here is that the operation of regulative discourse in relation to instructional discourse may vary over the course of schooling. In the earlier years the pedagogical (regulative) trumps the disciplinary (instructional), but this relationship may well be inverted in the later stages of schooling.

Finally, at the level of evaluative rules or pedagogic practice Bernstein in one formulation reverses the order of dominance: 'Rules of social order, relation, and identity are embedded in rules of discursive order (selection, sequence, pace, and criteria). The first we have called regulative and the second instructional discourse' (Bernstein, 1990, p. 92). Here regulative discourse is embedded in instructional discourse. He goes on to make two further points relevant to research in this book. One is that "It may well be the case that in some circumstances the school's instructional discourse is suspended and the discourse then is wholly regulative" (zero pedagogy referred to at the end of Chapter 2). The other crucial point that he makes is that the nature of the instructional and regulative discourse in terms of patterns of control (framing, see following discussion) may vary independently of one another.

These points are important in relation to the conclusions of the book. The data presented questions the priority of regulative discourse in establishing the mode of interaction in the classroom, or at least questions attempts to shift the instructional discourse through changes in the forms of regulative discourse. At its most specific the book considers whether the form of social relation drives the transmission of knowledge or whether the transmission of knowledge defines the form of social relation. Somewhat cryptic here, the arguments presented in the chapters that follow will hopefully make this clearer.

Classification and framing

My enduring research interest has been in the reproduction of social class inequalities through schooling, and their potential interruption. The key resource that I have deployed to investigate these processes has been Bernstein's concepts of classification and framing. These concepts work across different levels of analysis, from macro, broad societal patterning to micro practices in the classroom. At the macro level (or at the level of distributive rules) classification generates categories of agents and discourses: the categories or insulations are instantiations of power. At the micro level, classification is about the organizational or structural aspects of pedagogic practice. Classification is about ***relations between*** (subjects, spaces, agents), and the degree of maintenance between these categories.

Classification is expressed as being strong (where boundaries are explicit and categories are insulated from one another), or weak, where there is integration, or where the boundary is weak or blurred. In the context of schooling and the analyses of this book I also consider the relations between different subject areas (interdisciplinary relations); between school knowledge and everyday knowledge (inter-discursive relations); and between knowledge (or topics) within a particular subject area (intra-discursive). A simple example of a strongly classified curriculum would be the kind of traditional curriculum constructed under apartheid – clear divisions between subjects, clear demarcation of school knowledge from the everyday, experiential knowledge of the learners.

At the micro level of pedagogic practice, 'Framing refers to the degree of control teacher and pupil possess over the selection, sequencing, pacing and evaluation of the knowledge transmitted and received in the pedagogical relationship' (Bernstein, 1975, p. 88). Framing has to do with the relationship between the teacher and the learner. Strong framing refers to limited control over the pedagogy for students, and weak framing implies more 'apparent'[2] control by learners. Framing is expressed in terms of its strength or degree of control: strong framing implies students have a limited degree of control over the sequencing, pacing, selection and evaluation of the knowledge transmitted. Weak framing means that learners have more control or are able to intervene in the pedagogy. For example, learner-centred pedagogy is weakly framed – students have discretion over how the lesson proceeds. The sequence, pacing and determination of what counts or is valued is to greater or lesser extent in their control. It should be apparent 'strong' and 'weak' do not denote 'good' and 'bad'.

Framing refers to ***relations within*** (within boundaries). Framing, in a sense, supports classification, it produces 'the animation of the power grid' (Hasan, 2002), but it also opens up the potential for the change of boundaries, the contesting of power relations. It is through interaction (framing) that boundaries between discourses, spaces and subjects are defined, maintained and changed. Here lies the potential for interruption alluded to earlier.

Classification and framing are relational concepts in pedagogy. Framing is the mechanism whereby the boundary (classification) is achieved. Further, for Bernstein framing or control is "double faced for it carries both the power of reproduction and the potential for its change" (Bernstein, 1996, p. 19). This distinction between power and control is unique in sociology, and allows for a description of the nature of structures and how they are changed.

Bernstein (2000, p. 100) provides a taut formula for classifying codes in terms of the different dimensions and values outlined above:

$$\frac{E}{^{+-}C/^{+-}F}$$

Here E stands for 'elaborating orientation to meaning' or in shorthand, a 'school code', where the world is treated as an object of thought not of experience (Charlot, 2009). The line stands for the embedding of the orientation in classification and framing values. Variation in these classification and framing values gives rise to different ***modalities of pedagogic practice*** and hence different ways in which school codes or orientations are produced.

The broader sociological interest is in the differential distribution of power and control relations across different social classes, and how these produce different practices and forms of consciousness. Codes allow for the description of the differential positioning of subjects of different social class groupings, dominant and dominated.

Distinctive forms of knowledge are distributed through curriculum and different forms of communication through pedagogy. In the book I am concerned with the ways in which knowledge is constituted in curriculum and projects particular learners, teachers and relations between them. In pedagogy, I focus on different modalities that differentially distribute knowledge and establish communication so that learners are positioned in particular ways in relation to the privileged school code.

Dowling's strategies and domains

Classification and framing produces a specific and limited description of pedagogy. Bernstein is concerned with the *relay*, described earlier. In the studies reported in the book I have also been interested in the ***relayed***. In other words, I have been concerned with not only the structure of the pedagogic message, but also its semantic content. Progressively, researchers working in the Bernsteinian frame have come up against the problem of the 'emptiness' of the classification. In other words it elucidates the structure of the knowledge but not the substance of the knowledge itself, and have drawn on different resources in order to describe that which is relayed (for example, Hugo et al., 2004).

In a number of the studies I have undertaken I have drawn selectively on the work of Paul Dowling to address this issue. Dowling is also concerned with the operation of the relay, but in deriving his categories of strategies and domains he also enables an analysis of the relayed. He offers a set of concepts at a lower level of abstraction than classification and framing. For Dowling, forms of consciousness (with which Bernstein is concerned) are seen in what teachers and learners do in the classroom. Dowling allows for an analysis of interaction and how different knowledge is distributed. He describes different types of knowledge as contained in ***domains***. Knowledge is distributed through ***strategies***. Sociologically, he too is interested in the differential distribution of knowledge along class lines.

Dowling allows for an analysis of interaction. Through Bernstein and Dowling, we have a means for talking about the relay and a means for analyzing what is relayed. The significance of Dowling's conceptualizing of knowledge forms and strategies will become clearer in several of the chapters in the book where I draw on his theory to elaborate my analyses of pedagogy beyond the classification and framing schema. Appendix B shows how his concepts were operationalized in the research.

Dowling's concern is with the ways in which activity (by which he means ideology) specializes practices and regulates what can be said or done. Activities also interpellate positions, and are constitutive of human subjectivity. Dowling works with classification and not framing (Dowling, 1999). Unlike Bernstein, Dowling (1999, p. 11) argues that specializing takes place, not at boundaries, but always within. In a sense he is concerned to develop the classifications within classification – to elaborate a taxonomy of classification. In the analyses of pedagogy in the book I draw on Dowling selectively, and focus in particular on specializing and localizing strategies. 'Specializing is the construction of abstract messages with respect to a specific topic or setting' (Dowling, 1998, p. 147). I attribute a slightly different meaning to localizing than Dowling, defining these strategies as those that distribute context-dependent messages.

Defining curriculum and pedagogy

Curriculum in the book is defined as the knowledge that is recontextualized from disciplines and codified and organized into school knowledge to be learnt (in this case in syllabus documents). The production of curriculum occurs within the recontextualizing field and is regulated by pedagogic discourse. Interestingly, and I will return to this in the final chapters of the book, Bernstein does not use the term curriculum in this way. He refers only to 'pedagogic discourse'. Beyond his earlier papers his preferred term is pedagogy and he does not make the distinction that has been asserted by some within the social realist frame between curriculum and pedagogy (see Young, 2005).

Pedagogy in the book refers to classroom practice, the process of teaching and learning. You cannot teach someone something that they already know, therefore in pedagogy there are always criteria to be transmitted and acquired. These criteria are essentially evaluative; in the pedagogic relation

> there is a purposeful intention to initiate, modify, develop or change knowledge, conduct or practice by someone or something which already possesses, or has access to, the necessary resources and the means of evaluating the acquisition.
>
> (Bernstein, 1999, p. 267)

Pedagogy therefore consists of a social relation of a transmitter and an acquirer, where the rules for evaluation lie with the transmitter. The pedagogic relation is therefore hierarchical and pedagogy consists of a process of constant evaluation. For Bernstein, social relations are always relations of control, and "the social relation of pedagogy is asymmetrical: teacher and acquirer are always unequal" (Dooley, 2001, p. 52).

Summary of the pedagogic device

In Chapter 1 I explained the purpose of education privileged in this book: to provide access to formal school knowledge, and in so doing to specialize student consciousness to treat the world as an object of thought (Charlot, 2009). How does the process of constituting educational knowledge and the specialization of consciousness happen? Through the pedagogic device Bernstein provides a conceptual framework that describes the process whereby knowledge is transformed into curriculum and enters the classroom to shape the consciousness of students. The pedagogic device establishes general principles for the transformation of knowledge into pedagogic communication and the specialization of consciousness – a "symbolic ruler of consciousness" (Bernstein, 2000, p. 36), ruler in the sense of having power over consciousness and in the sense of measuring legitimate realizations of that consciousness. No wonder then that there is always struggle for control of the device, seeing as "Those who own the device own the means of perpetuating their power through discursive means and establishing, or attempting to establish, their own ideological representations" (Bernstein, 2000, p. 114). Figure 5.2 summarizes both the discussion of the device, as well the way in which classification and framing can be understood in relation to this.

In the summary diagram we gain a clearer understanding of what Bernstein meant when he stated "Evaluation condenses the meaning of the whole device" (p. 36). It is at this level that we can see whether the work of classification and framing of the device (the knowledge and its transformation through pedagogic

Level of pedagogic device	*Central object*	*Theoretical referent*	
Distributive rules	Knowledge	Classification	Power
Recontextualizing	Curriculum	Framing	Control
Evaluative rules	Pedagogic practice	Classification and framing	Power and control

Figure 5.2 The levels of the pedagogic device

discourse, as well as its transmission), has been done. At this level then, the concern is with both classification and framing.

Stated in terms of power and control, and in reference to the earlier brief discussion of the distributive rules under apartheid and in the initial rethinking of education in the democratic era, Davis (2005) explains what the pedagogic device enables us to consider. This is that a change in the principle of power produces changes at three moments of the education system: at the moment of State education policy, the moment of curriculum planning, design and delivery, and the moment of the pedagogic practices of the classroom.

> Stated differently, the dominant principle concerned with the distribution of power is transformed into policies of the State, including education policy; from the education policy State agencies derive principles for the design of curriculum and the structuring of schooling; finally, from the curriculum principles and prescriptions, principles for actual pedagogic practice are derived.
>
> (p. 41)

However, power is not realized simply on the basis of its assertion or enunciation. It requires control (of activities of agents, curriculum, pedagogic prescriptions) to ensure its realization. Davis (2005) argues that this is why these aspects, the technologizing of education, are subject to heavy policing by the State – in monitoring, inspection and testing. Power and control are always simultaneously present in educational encounters, at the level of evaluative rules in the practice of the classroom.

In the three rules of the pedagogic device and the embedding of the instructional discourse within a regulative order, we find the intrinsic form of pedagogic discourse. This form is always present, it is what pedagogy is (Moore, 2013, p. 165). The modalities of pedagogy however differ, and classification and framing provide conceptual tools to describe the different nature of power and control operating across levels and contexts and the different modalities that are produced in pedagogic discourse. The rules of the device are not determinative, however. Framing (the exercise of control) holds the potential for changing the power relation (classification).

What I attempt to do in this book is make visible the processes of the constitution of official pedagogic discourse, the formation of curriculum and its realization in classrooms over time. In other words I delineate a historical sociology of curriculum and pedagogy in South Africa in terms of the pedagogic device, uncovering the structuring of educational knowledge and its transmission in a particular social, political and economic context. The similar theoretical frame used across the study of the three reforms facilitates a comparison of curriculum and pedagogy across time. It does this in relation to the changing position of knowledge in the series of reforms and the model of the teacher and the student that is projected. What we see in the South African case is a fundamental shift in society's classifications and frames as the moral order shifts from apartheid and into the democratic era. The question is how these shifts shape the classification and frames of official macro education discourse, curriculum policy and the micro interactions in the classroom across time.

Notes

1 The concept of relative autonomy derives originally from Durkheim (1938) but is recontextualized essentially by reproduction and cultural theorists to denote a space of relative independence of the educational system which is said to give its agents some autonomy over the contexts, contents and processes (151). It counters the determinism inherent in some of this theorizing.

2 Bernstein defines pedagogy as essentially ***hierarchical***. It is the transmitter who holds the rules for evaluation. It follows that the acquirer's control is 'apparent'. This also explains why the rule describing the relation/conduct between transmitters and acquirers is the 'hierarchical' rule (Dooley, 2001:61).

References

ANC. (1994). ***A policy framework for education and training.*** Johannesburg: African National Congress.

Bernstein, B. (1975). Class, codes and control volume 3: Towards a theory of educational transmissions. London: Routledge & Kegan Paul.

Bernstein, B. (1977). Class, codes and control volume 3: Towards a theory of educational transmissions. Second edition. London: Routledge & Kegan Paul.

Bernstein, B. (1990). Class, codes and control, volume 4: The structuring of pedagogic discourse. London: Routledge.

Bernstein, B. (1996). Pedagogy symbolic control and identity: Theory, research, critique. London: Taylor & Francis.

Bernstein, B. (1999). Official knowledge and pedagogic identities. In F. Christie (Ed.), ***Pedagogy and the shaping of consciousness*** (pp. 246–261). London & New York: Continuum.

Bernstein, B. (2000). Pedagogy, symbolic control and identity: Theory, research and critique. Revised edition. Oxford: Rowman & Littlefield.

Charlot, B. (2009). School and the pupils' work. ***Sisifo Educational Sciences Journal, 10***, 87–94.

Davis, Z. (2005). Pleasure and pedagogic discourse in school mathematics: A case study of a problem-centred pedagogic modality. Unpublished PhD, University of Cape Town, Cape Town.

Dooley, K. T. (2001). *Adapting to diversity: Pedagogy for Taiwanese students in mainstream Australian secondary school classes.* Unpublished PhD thesis, Brisbane, Griffith University. Retrieved from www4.gu.edu.au:8080/adt-root/uploads/approved/adt-QGU20030102.105906/public/02Whole.pdf

Dowling, P. (1998). The sociology of mathematics education: Mathematical myths/pedagogic texts. London: Falmer.

Dowling, P. (1999). *Basil Bernstein in frame: "Oh dear, is this a structuralist analysis?"* Retrieved from www.ioe.ac.uk/ccs/dowling/kings1999/index.html

Hasan, R. (2002). Ways of meaning. Ways of learning: Code as an explanatory concept. *British Journal of Sociology of Education*, *23*(4), 537–548.

Hugo, W., Bertram, C., Green, W., & Naidoo, D. (2008). Bernstein, Bloom and the analysis of pedagogy in South African schools. *Journal of Education*, *43*, 31–56.

Lapping, B. (1987). *Apartheid: A history.* London: Paladin.

Moore, R. (2013). Basil Bernstein: The thinker and the field. London: Routledge.

Morais, A., & Neves, I. (2001). Pedagogical social contexts: Studies for a sociology of learning. In A. Morais, I. Neves, B. Davies & H. Daniels. (Eds.), *Towards a sociology of pedagogy: The contribution of Basil Bernstein to research* (pp. 185–222). New York: Peter Lang.

Muller, J., & Hoadley, U. (2010). Pedagogy and moral order. In P. Singh & A. Sadovnik (Eds.), *Knowledge, knowers and pedagogic modes: Building on the sociology of Basil Bernstein* (pp. 161–176). New York: Peter Lang.

Young, M. (2005). The knowledge question and the future of education in South Africa: A reply to Michelson's 'On trust, desire and the sacred: A response to Johan Muller's 'Reclaiming Knowledge'. *Journal of Education*, *36*, 7–18.

6 Curriculum 2005 and the dissolution of boundaries[1]

Introduction

South Africa held its first democratic elections in 1994, and in the years that followed embarked on the massive task of transforming every aspect of society. The new post-apartheid curriculum, Curriculum 2005 (C2005),[2] released four years on from the first elections, set out to construct a new social order – a democratic country located within a global economy. The curriculum aims encompassed broad social and political ambitions for what schools could accomplish. C2005 was an ambitious and radical curriculum experiment on a national scale in line with the widespread learner-centred/outcomes-based reforms elsewhere, described in Chapter 2.

C2005 tested out in an extreme form many of the progressive and constructivist pedagogic principles that had come to dominate education discourse at the time. It entailed a total eschewal of academic, subject-based knowledge, the traditional teacher 'vanished' (Davis, 1996) in the face of the enquiring, self-directed learner and the boundaries between school knowledge and everyday knowledge were dissolved. At the same time unions and the Ministry of Labour asserted outcomes (or measurable skills) as the organizing structure of this new curriculum. The skills emphasis came from broader competency movements that saw education as an instrument of economic development through skills training.

In this chapter I analyze how this first curriculum was structured, focusing on the curriculum for reading and for number in the Foundation Phase. The chapter considers the strong political project of C2005, and the attempt to devolve knowledge decisions to the teacher and learner in the classroom. I show how this radical constructivist project coupled with a shift to a competency-based form of curriculum at the school level subordinated the specification of formal knowledge to the description of generic outcomes. The imagined learner that had been defined progressively in the apartheid curriculum in relation to skills is sustained in this curriculum, but is also defined in relation to the democratic project. The model of the teacher reflects perhaps what the new democracy held as its ideal, but couldn't have been further from the reality of teachers emerging from the personal and professional degradation of apartheid schooling.

The transition to democracy

The election manifesto with which the ANC came to power in 1994 was the Reconstruction and Development Programme (RDP) (RSA, 1994), a programme committing the first democratic government to prioritize poverty alleviation. The RDP aimed to empower the poor to seize opportunities 'to develop their full potential' and to 'sustain themselves through productive activity'. The state would also improve access to health, education and social services such that all could enjoy "a decent living standard and economic security" (ANC, 1994, p. 15, 16, 79). At the same time, however, the RDP suggested strong fiscal discipline given the huge debt inherited from the apartheid government. So although the RDP was viewed as the cornerstone of the new government's development policy, it was soon criticized for too strong a focus on fiscal discipline with insufficient attention to stimulating growth. The latter was seen as the key way to generate resources to implement the new social policies.

Consequently, not two years later, a new macroeconomic policy framework called the Growth, Employment and Redistribution (GEAR) (RSA, 1996) strategy, was introduced in 1996. Its aim was to stimulate faster economic growth, with the aim of meeting the social objectives of the RDP. GEAR was described as a kind of home-grown structural adjustment programme, emphasizing fiscal restraint and trade liberalization to stimulate growth. Davis (2005) comments of the subject created in the process, "just as capital cannot countenance the imposition of external boundaries that would inhibit its flow, so the subject is persuaded not to countenance the imposition of boundaries" (p. 44). His argument is that the economic requirement that boundaries be dissolved to facilitate the flow of capital also structures the form of social relations and conceptions of identity. Boundaries and their operation are key to understanding C2005, as we shall see below, reflecting these social arrangements.

Many commentators portray the shift from the RDP to GEAR as a 'revolution betrayed' by the institution of 'neo-liberal' policies (Hart, 2008). Seekings and Nattrass (2015) argue that this is overstated, that policies incorporated both capitalist principles ***and*** strong social welfare programmes. In summary, around the time of the production of the first democratic national curriculum, the broader economic environment was defined by both a concern with the rescue of the economy from its decimation under apartheid, primarily through stimulating growth and encouraging global capital flows, but also with social welfare and processes of democratization and redress, especially for the poor.

The political context was defined by discourses of transformation, redress and reconciliation realized through the negotiated settlement. The negotiated settlement[3] was established in order to circumvent revolution, facilitate peaceful transition and power sharing, and to prevent a (largely white) middle class skills flight from the new postcolonial state.[4] The negotiated settlement can be argued to have had direct impact on the process of curriculum formation in that it made it difficult for the state to define a national curriculum and specify whose knowledge should count most. Also, what was politically required was a curriculum that showed a significant shift from the content-heavy, apartheid-tainted NATED.[5] Negotiated settlement, economic demands and the demands of transitioning to democracy created tensions in decision-making and contestation over the distributive rules.

Official pedagogic discourse: equivalence, outcomes and transformation

Through the RDP and GEAR, reskilling and skills upgrading were regarded as pivotal to competing in the global economy, and it was this skills agenda that drove the idea of an integrated system of education and training (Fataar, 2006). A National Qualifications Framework (NQF) was launched in 1996 as an attempt to create equivalencies between education and workplace learning by placing all qualifications on the same grid, and breaking them down into unit standards which could interchangeably make up different qualifications. The strong influence of labour, and the demand that schooling meet economic demands was also seen in an emphasis on the recognition of prior learning, access and portability which were the key ideas underpinning the creation of qualifications. This was in the context of a system with a large number of inherited disparate qualifications and unequal institutional capacity. Thus, labour's needs, and their demands for a skills-based curriculum linked to an NQF loomed large in official pedagogic discourse.

At the heart of the notion of skill was the *outcome*, a discrete, generic, demonstrable performance required of the learner. The credit accumulation and transfer approach of the NQF rested upon the fundamental assumption of *equivalence*. The idea was that knowledge and skills gained in different contexts (schools, workplaces, for example) could be regarded as equivalent within a single framework (see Ensor, 2003). Hence prior learning could be recognized and placed in a relationship of equivalence with 'similar' outcomes achieved on the job and/or learning in the home. Integration (or weak classification) thus became a key principle in official pedagogic discourse. Integration involved the collapsing not only of knowledge boundaries, but of political and economic boundaries as well:

> An integrated approach implies a view of learning which rejects the rigid division between 'academic' and 'applied', 'theory' and 'practice', 'knowledge' and 'skills', 'head' and 'hand'. Such divisions have characterised the organisation of curricula and the distribution of educational opportunity in many countries of the world, including South Africa. They have grown out of, and helped to reproduce, very old occupational and social class distinctions. In South Africa such distinctions in curriculum and career choice have also been closely associated in the past with the ethnic structure of economic opportunity and power.
>
> (Department of Education, 1995a, p. 15)

Ensor (1997) points out that this erosion of knowledge boundaries was expected to result in the collapse of social boundaries between groups based on race and class. The strong political project of creating a new nation and a new citizenry meant that pedagogical and epistemological questions were subordinated to strong ideological notions around the kinds of persons and the ideal society to be formed for the new democratic era. This democratizing impulse alongside priority given to the skilled worker in the global economy dominated at the level of official pedagogic discourse.

The recontextualizing field

The White Paper for Education and Training (DOE, 1995b) called for the development of a new school curriculum and the establishment of democratic structures to develop this curriculum. The post-apartheid administration declared that curriculum development would be a 'fully participatory process' (DOE, 1997). The emphasis on stakeholder representation and process in development was coupled with the explicit idea that the curriculum should 'emerge' or 'evolve' and should not be designed as a finished package for implementation by teachers (DOE, 2000, p. 31). Partly because of this, C2005 was never actually completed, despite being implemented for four years in schools.

The result of the strong emphasis on stakeholderism, and the view of curriculum development as an ongoing process, was that many different people were for the first time included in these processes. It also meant, however, that many subject experts and academics were marginalized in favour of union representatives. Curriculum expertise was consequently thin on the ground. As Fataar (2006) argues:

> The position of stakeholders in education policy processes has its roots in the anti-authoritarian logic of the liberation movements, which was suspicious of the role of academic 'experts' disconnected from practice (Allais, 2003, p. 315). The entire educational architecture during the office of the first Minister (1994–1999) was 'over-determined' by stakeholder groups, mainly the unions in close collaboration with sections of business.
>
> (Fataar, 2006, p. 646)

There was a lack of continuity in the involvement of different actors over time and across different committees. At the same time there was an urgency and pressure to produce a new curriculum that represented a decisive break from the past. As a result quality was compromised, and there were many instances of inconsistency and incoherence across the curriculum documents that were produced. In Bernstein's (1996) terms, there was little expertise in the Official Recontextualizing Field (ORF) or bureaucracy and the politically dominant players in the Pedagogic Recontextualizing Field (PRF), notably the unions, controlled the discourse. Ultimately, academics and subject specialists were sidelined in the development, training and implementation for and of the new curriculum. Although the school curriculum eventually prised itself apart from the NQF, under pressure from unions it remained framed within the discourse of generic skills (outcomes), integration and equivalence.[6]

Recontextualizing rules – the formation of C2005 policy

The emphasis on equivalence meant that in order to recognize the similarity and the transferability of skills, expected learning had to be specified at a high level of generality. In other words generic skills or competences had to be distilled from various activities and areas of learning. Consequently, outcomes – representing atomized, generic statements of the outcomes of learning – were the favoured curriculum organizing device in C2005 and learning objectives or outcomes were given primacy over specifying any particular content knowledge. Teachers were given a broader scope to specify what they wanted to do in the classroom and to select what contents to focus on in order to achieve the broadly stated outcomes. Under the influence of labour, the curriculum also could not prioritize outcomes for the school as a particular site of learning but rather had to allow for a proliferation of sites for learning. And to avoid explicit prioritizing of knowledge distribution to any particular group the curriculum eschewed the specification of content altogether. The category of school student, now a more generalized 'learner', was an open one, without particular requirements set to a particular level of learning. The learner was anyone, anywhere. The envisioned teacher was able to match appropriate learning to that anyone, in any site, guided by very broad, generic outcomes.

'Transformational OBE': marrying outcomes and a learner-centred education

Some have argued that C2005 was underpinned by a tension or 'conceptual unease' (Fataar, 2006) between its progressive features – learner-centredness, integration and relevance – on the one hand and the skills focus in the outcomes-based education (OBE) organizing frame on the other. But the two impetuses were compatible. Muller (1998) explains:

> it is remarkable to what degree outcomes-based education rhetoric converges around the social aim of individual empowerment. What is brought well to the fore in the outcomes-based approaches that the South African documents draw on is the social project of maximising the citizen/learner's flexibility, opportunities, mobility and access (see Department of Education, 1997a). Outcomes-based learning programmes are 'learner-paced and learner-centred' (Human Science Research Council, 1995, p. 21): the learner determining their own educational pace, maximizing their occupational opportunities and becoming a fully participating citizen in all spheres of social, political and economic life is the guiding ideal.
>
> (p. 178)

In this view outcomes and progressive features such as learner-centredness are compatible. The very generic statement of learning outcomes also left the choice of content wide open. The skills orientation of C2005 was thus fused with discourses around transformation and democracy and C2005 claimed a particular type of outcomes-based education – one it termed 'transformational OBE'. The focus was explicitly on the creation of 'critical citizens', and consequently on the critical outcomes which specified a range of socially desirable characteristics. Given the moment in history, it is easy to retrieve the thinking behind the move. As educationally unsound as it proved to be, it presented a strong political argument for a curriculum for rapid social transformation. Transformational OBE was defined in official documentation thus:

> No thought is given to the existing curriculum. Instead schools (or local districts) are told they can choose any content and use a wide range of teaching methods as long as these develop citizens who display the agreed-upon critical outcomes.
>
> (DOE, 1998b, p. 19)

Relevance was emphasized as a benefit of the approach: "This allows educators to relate teaching direct [sic] to their local contexts and also to change syllabus content rapidly" (ibid.). The critical outcomes referred to here are interesting in their lack of direct reference to broader social competences such as the understanding and negotiation of race, gender and class differences (especially given the recent emergence from apartheid). The developmental outcomes focus on the entrepreneurial subject, developing skills consonant with broader global educational discourse around generic '21st century skills' prized in the forming of appropriate global citizens and workers:

Critical outcomes

1 Identify and solve problems and make decisions using **critical** and **creative thinking**.
2 Work effectively with others as members of a team, group, organization and community.
3 Organize and **manage themselves** and their activities responsibly and effectively.
4 Collect, analyze, organize and critically evaluate information.
5 Communicate effectively using visual, symbolic and/or language skills in various modes.
6 Use **science and technology** effectively and critically showing responsibility towards the environments and the health of others.
7 Demonstrate an understanding of the world as a set of related systems by recognizing that **problem-solving** contexts do not exist in isolation.

Developmental outcomes

8 Reflect on and explore a variety of strategies to learn more effectively.
9 Participate as a responsible citizen in the life of local, national and global communities.
10 Be culturally and aesthetically sensitive across a range of social contexts.

11 Explore education and career opportunities.
12 Develop **entrepreneurial** opportunities. (DOE, 1997, p. 10, emphasis added)

The outcomes represent the 'mobile', entrepreneurial subject, networked, connected and highly skilled in generic competences like problem-solving and critical thinking. The absence in the outcomes of explicit reference to developing in learners an awareness of class, race and gender underscores the projection of the unbridled subject.

In C2005 eight learning areas were established to "replace the traditional subject divisions used under apartheid" (DOE, 2000). In fact, it was the same bureaucrat who had been instrumental in designing CUMSA who provided the organizational and conceptual basis for the eight learning areas (Fataar, 2006). As shown in the Table 6.1, the only real difference in the 'new' learning areas of C2005 from CUMSA was that Religious Instruction, Guidance and Physical Education were subsumed under Life Orientation in C2005.

Learning area committees formulated outcomes for each of these learning areas, generating a total of 500 learning outcomes across Grades 1 to 9. These were rationalized by an NQF technical committee (that included foreign experts), reducing them to 66 specific learning outcomes. The highly generic nature of these outcomes, devoid of any specific content or skills for the different subjects (now learning areas) is clear (see Appendix A). Nonetheless, on the basis of these specific outcomes learning programmes were developed that expanded them in relation to 'performance indicators' and 'range statements' (more on these as follows).

Anything goes: learner-centred pedagogy and the progressivist thrust

Alongside this skills emphasis was the democratizing impulse and a focus on transformation. Consonant with global and especially African trends, learner-centredness became another key feature of C2005. The teacher (now termed

Table 6.1 Learning areas as defined in CUMSA (1991) and in C2005 (1998)

CUMSA	*Curriculum 2005*
Language subjects	Language, learning and literacy
Mathematics	Mathematical Literacy and Mathematics
General Science	Natural Sciences
Social Science	Human and Social Sciences
Technology	Technology
Arts Education	Arts and Culture
Economic education	Economic and Management Sciences
Religious Instruction	Life Orientation
Guidance	
Physical Education	

'educator') was to 'facilitate' learning through the selection of appropriate knowledge, including that of the learners' own local cultures. This approach to knowledge was based on a reading of constructivist and progressive principles, as a direct challenge to the restrictive high specification of syllabi under apartheid.

Those formulating the new curriculum generally missed the continuity of many of the progressive features of the pedagogy with later apartheid curriculum reforms (especially CUMSA, see Chapter 3). Rather, the continuity of these pedagogical reforms with many of the tenets of People's Education was recognized and foregrounded. The curriculum thus had strong political purchase. A well-known table at the time (see Table 6.2), explained the desired shifts.

The table indicates another progressive feature to C2005 in its approach to **assessment**. There were initially no progression requirements until Grade 9, and there was a strong emphasis on competence, or identifying knowledge already acquired by learners:

> Assessment should take place in an authentic context in a caring, non-judgmental environment. It should serve as a positive affirmation of the learner, acknowledging whatever competencies and outcomes learners have

Table 6.2 Shift from traditional to constructivist classroom (adapted from South African Department of Education, 2000, p. 12)

Traditional classroom	*Constructivist*
Curriculum is presented part to whole, with emphasis on basic skills	Curriculum is presented whole to part with emphasis on big concepts
Strict adherence to fixed curriculum is highly valued	Pursuit of learner questions is highly valued
Curricular activities rely heavily on textbooks and workbooks	Curricular activities rely heavily on primary sources of data and manipulative materials
Students are viewed as 'blank slates' onto which information is etched by the teacher	Learners are viewed as thinkers with emerging theories about the world
Teachers generally behave in a didactic manner, disseminating information to students	Educators generally behave in an interactive manner, mediating the environment with learners
Teachers seek the correct answer to validate student learning	Educators seek the learner's points of view in order to understand learners' present conceptions for use in subsequent lessons
Assessment of student learning is viewed as separate from teaching and occurs almost entirely through testing	Assessment of learner learning is interwoven with teaching and occurs through educator observations of learners, learner observation of learners at work and through learner exhibitions and portfolios
Students primarily work alone	Learners work primarily in groups

> attained to date, and taking into account previous performance levels . . . under no circumstances should any form of assessment be detrimental to the development of the learner e.g. no learner should fail but should progress to the next level with their age group.
>
> (DOE, 1998c, p. 20)

Tests and examinations in particular were de-emphasised, and regarded as less fair and useful forms of assessment. The reference to the past and the punitive use of summative assessment under apartheid is clear.

Constructivism, the dominant theory of learning fostered in the curriculum, is a theory of the construction of knowledge by learners themselves, in relation to their prior knowledge and immediate context. Outcomes were fundamentally open-ended, requiring that inputs (or learning contents) be 'designed down' from the outcomes. This in theory allowed for assessment to be moulded to the individuals' own level of growth and development.

Integration

Integration, a key feature of progressivism, was one of the central organizing principles of C2005:

> South Africa has embarked on transformational OBE. This involves the most radical form of an integrated curriculum. There are several forms of integration . . . The outcome of this form of integration will be a profound transferability of knowledge in real life.
>
> (DOE, 1997, p. 23)

In the context of the prevailing ideology of boundary dissolution, integration referred to the dispensing of boundaries between different knowledge contents of subjects, between school and everyday, local knowledge, and between school knowledge and knowledge in the workplace. The incorporation of everyday knowledge and a focus on the relevance of educational activity to everyday local life and work contexts was privileged.

Integration in C2005 was achieved through a number of design features. Learning areas, which were clusters of subjects, were introduced to support integration. 'Learning programmes' facilitated integration between these learning areas. 'Phase organizers' were themes that were meant to direct programmes of learning across different learning areas in specific phases (these themes included society, communication, entrepreneurship, environment, health and safety and personal development). 'Programme Organizers', an additional design feature, were themes chosen by teachers from everyday life to reflect local social priorities as the starting point for the planning of lessons. Finally, the critical outcomes were expected to 'infuse' all learning, and thus create a cross-cutting focus to learning in different areas.

Although there were some features that paid attention to progression (such as range statements, performance indicators and expected levels of performance), these were generally vague and were overshadowed by the powerful emphasis on integration. The complexity of design features, especially around integration is clear from the description above. The design was to create high levels of confusion; however, there was also confusion around the integration of education and training. While the NQF originated largely in competency debates within labour and focused on the integration of education and training, OBE as configured and understood in schooling made no reference to this. Jansen (1999, p. 8) argued at the time that OBE concepts in schools were gradually developed in isolation of these broader frameworks, adding to the confusion because there was a claim to an integrated approach to education and training, but no evidence of it in the curriculum.

Texts and language

Finally, another feature of C2005 evident from the Tables 6.1 and 6.2 was the marginalizing of textbooks as key pedagogic tools, also in reaction to the apartheid past. Textbooks as a pedagogical tool in the apartheid curriculum generally followed a strict, uniform and didactic structure of instructions, worked example and extensive practice. This was viewed in relation to the new pedagogical principals of C2005 as antithetical to a child-centred approach. C2005 designers also derided teachers' use of textbooks as having been over-dependent and uncritical. C2005 called for the development of locally relevant and contextually responsive materials that reflected the needs and interests of specific groups of students.

There was a paucity of material available in African languages. MacDonald (2002) argues that one of the few successful text-based reading courses available in different languages (Molteno's 'Breakthrough to literacy') was thrown out because it did not have 'programme organizers' built into the programme.[7] The state provided no African language graded readers in schools, and no texts written specifically for multilingual environments, nor written with second language learners in mind. C2005 was thus a curriculum with a weak textual base, relying heavily on the teacher as mediator of the curriculum.

Language policy was not specified in C2005, but rather was contained in the broad Language-in-Education Policy (LiEP) of 1997 (RSA, 1997). Accordingly, and given the invidious policy of mother tongue instruction under apartheid, the responsibility for determining issues of mother tongue instruction and the language of teaching and learning was devolved to the school level. Most schools did not have access to the linguistic, conceptual and literacy expertise to make decisions around these issues and so by and large existing practices remained. Language became a school governance issue and attention to the pedagogical implications of certain language choices, whether straight for English or additive bilingualism or more multilingual approaches, was deferred.

The constitution of mathematics and reading in the curriculum

An analysis of the Curriculum 2005 documents for reading and numeracy at the Foundation Phase level specifically gives a more detailed picture of C2005 and how it was constructed. The interest is both in how curricular knowledge (instructional discourse) is structured and in the model of the teacher and the learner and the relation between them projected through the curriculum (regulative discourse). The categories for analysis that were introduced in Chapter 5 and Appendix B are represented in Table 6.3, and briefly discussed below:

The external framing of curricular knowledge considers how explicit the specification of the selection, sequencing and pacing of educational knowledge is. It also considers the framing of the evaluative criteria, in other words, how clearly the curriculum specifies the criteria to be transmitted and acquired. Framing here is 'external' to the teacher. In other words, the framing or control relation is between the curriculum and the teacher. Strong framing refers to strong control exerted by the curriculum; weak framing implies the teacher has control over selection, sequence, pace and evaluative dimensions of pedagogy. Classification is concerned with how bounded the particular subject is from other curriculum subjects, and how the particular areas dealt with here – reading and number – are insulated from other topics within the subject (or learning area as is the case here). Classification also refers to the boundary between school knowledge and everyday knowledge. Classification varies from strong where boundaries are clearly demarcated to weak where there is integration and a blurring of boundaries. These categories describe the way in which instructional discourse is constituted in the curriculum document.

The regulative discourse concerns the model of the teacher and the learner inferred from the curriculum documents and refers to the degree of control or specification the curriculum asserts around the expected relation between teacher and learner

While the outcome of much of this analysis can be anticipated by the preceding discussion of the curriculum, what follows provides detail and substance to the broader descriptions.

As C2005 proceeded, more and more documentation was produced. This was both in relation to the notion that the curriculum was a 'process' as described

Table 6.3 Categories for the analysis of the curriculum documents

Instructional	External framing of curricular knowledge (evaluative criteria, sequence, pace)	$F^{e+/-}$
	Classification between subject and other subjects	$C^{+/-}$
	Classification between subject and everyday knowledge	$C^{+/-}$
	Classification between areas/topics within subject	$C^{+/-}$
Regulative	External framing of social relation (hierarchical rules)	$F^{e+/-}$
	Model of the teacher	
	Model of the learner	

above, but it was also a response to the confusion that soon became apparent among teachers. Provinces developed their own versions of the curriculum, often attempting to add more specification and clarity for teachers. As a focus for this analysis, the central, nationally-produced document that set out the curriculum for the Foundation Phase for the learning areas Language, Learning and Literacy and Mathematical Literacy, Mathematics and Mathematical Sciences was selected (DOE, 1997), as well as a series of official, national documents that elaborated various aspects of C2005 (DOE, 1998a, 1998b, 1998c).

For the Foundation Phase the 66 specific outcomes referred to above were clustered into three 'learning programmes': Literacy, Numeracy and Life Skills. Foundation Phase teachers were given three draft learning programme documents for these learning areas, and a Foundation Phase draft policy document to generate lesson plans.

Already literate: reading in C2005

Reading fell within the learning area 'Language, Learning and Literacy' for which there were seven specific outcomes:

1 Learners make and negotiate meaning and understanding
2 Learners show critical awareness of language usage
3 Learners respond to the aesthetic, affective, cultural and social values in texts
4 Learners access, process and use information form a variety of sources and situations
5 Learners understand, know and apply language structures and conventions in context
6 Learners use language for learning
7 Learners use appropriate communication strategies for specific purposes and situations

For each of these specific outcomes, the teacher had to develop (or select from documentation) assessment criteria, performance indicators and range statements at each level and for each activity. She also had to connect these to the phase organizers for the Foundation Phase to facilitate integration with broader social goals (expressed as the themes of personal development, health and safety, environment, entrepreneurship, society and communication). Teachers were also required to connect the critical outcomes to the "learning experiences" they developed for their class (DOE, 1997, p. 17). Teachers were required to make careful record (in their planning) of the different specific outcomes, assessment criteria and phase organizers that were being addressed in each activity of each unit, a process MacDonald describes as "technicism run riot" (2002, p. 117). Thus, the administrative and technical aspects of recording outcomes were strongly controlled whilst the selection of actual criteria for learning was left to the teacher to determine.

Delineation of the curriculum requirements was set out in C2005 through four components. 'Range statements' state what is required at the level of learning (the three grades of Foundation Phase). 'Assessment criteria' state what the learners need to demonstrate. 'Performance indicators' suggest how teachers will know whether the aspect of the outcome specified in the assessment criterion has been achieved. An example of the first outcome for Language, Learning and Literacy at the Foundation Phase level is given below.

Specific outcome:	Learners make and negotiate meaning and understanding
Range statement:	At this level learners are guided to create a wide range of texts. Learners also interact with and respond to a wide range of texts, interaction with other language users takes place with the emphasis on audiences from immediate and familiar contexts.
Assessment criteria:	The learners demonstrate the following: Original meaning is created through personal texts.
Performance indicator:	This will be evident when learners: create a personal text and communicate it orally and visually (DOE, 1997, p. 33).

I will refer to this particular example on a number of occasions in the discussion which follows; however, I analyzed the full set of seven specific outcomes and their range statements as well as the 37 assessment criteria and their associated performance indicators linked to the specific outcomes. These were considered in relation to how reading and writing as a specific area of learning was classified; how evaluative criteria relevant to reading and writing were framed; and how selection, sequencing and pace of learning content were set out.

The generic nature of the outcomes, range statements, assessment criteria and performance indicators is exemplified in the extract above. No information is provided as to what precisely should be taught, how, or how it develops the ability to read, write and comprehend text. Teachers decide "what content, what teaching methods, and what assessment they will use to guide their particular learners to meet the outcomes" (DoE, 1998a, p. 13). The terms 'text' and 'communicate' are used throughout generically. It is not clear whether 'texts' are written, oral, visual or otherwise, or what form the communication takes – i.e. reading, speaking or writing.

Nowhere is it stated in the documents and notably in the specific outcomes that one of the outcomes at this level is learning to read. In fact the curriculum explicitly states in the definition of the subject that:

> Initially 'literacy' was seen as a cognitive process that enables reading, writing and numeracy. In this document 'literacy' has expanded to include several kinds of literacies across all Learning Areas. 'Literacies' stress the issue of access to the world and to knowledge through the development of multiple capacities within all of us to make sense of our worlds through whatever means we have, not only texts and books.
>
> (DOE, 1997, p. 17)

A focus on written text is subordinated to a concern with general communication and meaning-making or sense-making, the semantic aspects of literacy and multiple literacies. No fundamental or basic skills regarding learning to read and write are specified. There are no direct instructions or stipulations for the teaching of phonics, grammar, language structures, comprehension and vocabulary, and no handwriting or writing formats are stipulated. One may assume, reading the document, that learners following this curriculum already know how to read. Evaluative criteria are weakly framed and implicit.

The specific outcomes refer to all Grades 1 to 9. The assessment criteria and performance indicators are developed specifically for the particular phase (in this case the Foundation Phase), although not specific to particular grades (in this instance Grade 1, 2 or 3). Teachers thus determine the pace at which instruction should proceed based on the level, need and requirements of the learners:

> The kind of learning advocated by the outcomes – developing competence as opposed to memorizing information – takes time. And it takes different learners different amounts of time . . . Classes must therefore be organized so that learners have time to practice what they are learning and be flexible enough to allow those who demonstrate competence quickly to move on to more challenging tasks.
>
> (DOE, 1997, p. 23)

C2005 expressed weak framing over the pacing of curricular knowledge, as well as an ***individualizing*** of pacing with respect to the learner.

The focus in the document is on the socio-political aspects of language learning, as evidenced in the performance indicator that states learners should "demonstrate ways in which language is used to transmit and shape socio-cultural ideas and values" (DOE, 1997, p. 38) and the specific outcome that points to developing learners' understanding of language "as a powerful instrument to reflect, shape and manipulate people's belief, actions and relationships" (DOE, 1997, p. 37). The focus is also on the affective aspects of language in reference to particular, localized, multilingual knowers that can, as expressed in a performance indicator, "engage in and respond to artistic effects of various texts (including social and cultural), relating them to personal life" (DOE, 1997. p. 42).

The classification of the topic reading within the learning area is weak; the learning area is defined by a generalized notion of 'meaning-making'. The learning area itself is weakly specified (framed) and weakly classified. What constitutes knowledge for Language, Learning and Literacy is left open, and the teacher is required to control selection of content, sequence it and decide what constitutes an appropriate production at different levels. The approach to reading in C2005 can be described as a radical form of a whole language approach, where the ability to read is 'caught' in the handling of written texts in an integrated whole language classroom (Christie, 2005, p. 90).

This orientation to literacy also formed part of the training of teachers. MacDonald (2002) describes how when teachers in training asked questions about specifically teaching reading and writing, the response was based on the convenient fiction that teachers "underestimate the ability of [their] learners; they can learn to read and write by themselves. You don't have to explicitly teach this – they will pick this up incidentally" (2002, p. 131).

A human activity: number in C2005

The definition for mathematics at the Foundation Phase level is given in the curriculum document as follows:

> Mathematics is the construction of knowledge that deals with qualitative relationships of space and time. It is a human activity that deals with patterns, problem-solving, logical thinking etc., in an attempt to understand the world and make use of that understanding. This understanding is expressed and contested through language, symbols and social interaction.
>
> (DOE, 1997, p. 115)

Mathematics in this definition is not a predetermined body of knowledge, but rather a ***construction*** of knowledge. The emphasis is on human interaction and the relation of mathematics to experience. This largely constructivist view of mathematics precludes the specification of particular contents and skills conventionally understood to constitute mathematics at this level. According to Ensor et al. (2009), there are three interlinked aspects to mastery of number in the Foundation Phase: progression in acquiring the number concept, the shift from concrete to abstract reasoning, and relatedly, the move from counting to calculating. None of these are referenced here. The socio-affective, experiential orientation to mathematics of the curriculum definition is further reflected in the 10 specific outcomes for school mathematics, applicable from Grades 1 to 9:

- Demonstrate understanding about ways of working with numbers
- Manipulate number patterns in different ways
- Demonstrate an understanding of the historic development of mathematics in various social and cultural contexts
- Critically analyze how mathematical relationships are used in social, political and economic relations
- Measure with competence and confidence in a variety of contexts
- Use data from various contexts to make informed judgments
- Describe and represent experiences with shape, space, time and motion, using all available senses
- Analyze natural forms, cultural products and processes in representations of shape, space and time
- Use mathematical language to communicate mathematical ideas, concepts and generalizations and thought processes
- Use various logical processes to formulate, test and justify conjectures (DOE, 1997, p. 116).

It is intended that these specific outcomes be read together with range statements and performance indicators as per Language. The specific outcomes for mathematics broaden the scope of mathematics through radical integration – both with everyday knowledge and with other subjects. Thus, mathematics as expressed in C2005 appears largely as a vehicle for developing social and political competences rather than mathematical ones. The explanation for specific outcome 4 (learners access, process and use information form a variety of sources and situations) demonstrates this well:

> Mathematics is used as an instrument to express ideas from a wide range of other fields. The use of mathematics in these fields often creates problems. This outcome aims to foster a critical outlook to enable learners to engage with issues that concern their lives individually, in their communities and beyond. A critical mathematics curriculum should develop critical thinking, including how social inequalities, particularly concerning race, gender and class are created and perpetuated.
>
> (DOE, 1997, p. 124)

I elaborate on the difficulties inherent in achieving these kinds of outcomes at the Foundation Phase level as well as what happens to the mathematical knowledge and learning in the process below.

The 10 specific outcomes for mathematics are each associated with a number of range statements (a total of 56 range statements). Each range statement then has one to two assessment criteria and these assessment criteria have a number of performance indicators. The number of statements across these different features, however, does not greatly strengthen specification, which is weak across the specific outcomes, range statements and performance indicators in the mathematics document. For example, the first specific outcome and its associated aspects are expressed as follows:

Specific outcome:	Demonstrate understanding about ways of working with numbers
Range statement:	1 Use personal experience to show the significance of number 2 Express numbers in symbols or words
Assessment criteria:	Evidence of heuristics to understand number concept
Performance indicator:	1 Identify situations in their environment where numbers are used; count a collection of objects, maintaining order in numbers; write symbols and number names 2 Skip-count forwards and backwards from a given number; use number knowledge to develop strategies to solve problems involving number (DOE, 1997, p. 117).

The curriculum does not differentiate between acceptable and non-acceptable achievements in relation to these outcomes (i.e. weak framing of evaluative criteria). In the example above, "count a collection of objects, maintaining order in numbers" could be achieved by counting on one's fingers from 1 to 10, or engaging in acoustic counting from 100 to 200. No number range is specified, nor is the particular form of counting required suggested. Sequencing, selection and pacing decisions are weakly framed.

Similarly, range statements for other specific outcomes such as "add and subtract positive whole numbers" or "Multiply and divide positive whole numbers" could be achieved by manipulating numbers between one and ten, or two digit or three digit numbers. Depending on number range and counting strategy, this performance may be more or less acceptable in Grade 1 in comparison to Grade 3, but the curriculum provides no guidelines for differentiating acceptable performance. In short, no progression is stipulated.

The three interlinked aspects to mastering number concept in the Foundation Phase referenced above – progression in acquiring the number concept, the shift from concrete to abstract reasoning, and relatedly, the move from counting to calculating – are not reflected in the curriculum. It is not underpinned by an explicit developmental conception of learning number. There is very little emphasis on counting and calculating – the two rudimentary and essential skills related to developing numeracy at this level. The shift from concrete to abstract understanding of numbers and understanding the symbolic system of mathematics, and its manipulation is not referenced. And the development from more simple representations and manipulation of numbers to more complex ones is not spelt out. The word "count" or "counting" is used only three times in all of the performance indicators – the word "calculate" or "calculation", or 'computation" only six times. In contrast, action verbs such as "give examples" "show a knowledge of" "identify" "demonstrate an awareness" "describe situations" "compare" are much more common. Again no guidance is provided on how these are to be achieved, or the level of specificity required.

These action verbs all entail some kind of 'mathematization' of everyday life and the document is saturated by reference to the everyday as a resource for understanding mathematics. The words 'home', 'everyday', 'personal', 'real life' and 'community' signifying everyday understandings appear 32 times across the document. At several points everyday understandings expresses its purpose: "The view that mathematics is a European product must be challenged. Learners must be able to understand the historical background of their communities' use of mathematics" (DOE, 1997, p. 123).

This emphasis on everyday knowledge is coupled with a radical form of integration of different subject areas. For example, specific outcome 3 is expressed as follows:

Specific outcome:	Demonstrate an understanding of the historical development of mathematics in various social and cultural contexts
Range statement:	1 Demonstrate counting and measurement in everyday life; illustrate at least two mathematical activities in a home 2 Show the link between mathematics and technology

Assessment criteria:	Evidence that mathematics is understood as a human activity
Performance indicator:	1 Give examples about counting and measuring at home; give examples about counting and measuring from other environments 2 Give examples that show the use of mathematics in technology; give examples that show the use of technology in mathematics (DOE, 1997, p. 123).

Here the teacher is expected to put together a learning experience that incorporates history of mathematics, mathematics in the home and mathematics and technology. The logic of the development of the statement from specific outcome to performance indicator is not driven by mathematical knowledge, but rather by the broad, generic statements about mathematics as a 'human activity'. There is a clear intention to integrate mathematics with other subjects. It is difficult to imagine the nature and amount of content that would be needed to meet the outcome as well as how points of contact between the other subjects referenced and mathematics might be made, particularly at this level.

Like language, the area of number concept, within the broader subject of school mathematics, is weakly classified. It is also very weakly classified in relation to everyday knowledge. There is also is weak framing of evaluative criteria and pacing, and weak framing over the sequence for the introduction of different skills and concepts relevant to learning number. The curriculum offers limited guidance to teachers around ***what*** to teach and ***how*** to teach it.

Framing of the social relation

While there is weak external framing over the instructional discourse in C2005, the curriculum is very clear on the form that the social relation should take in the classroom and makes constant and direct reference to the regulative discourse. There is a clear emphasis on individualization, and this is related to the inculcation of particular skills. The most prominent is 'critical thinking' which is contrasted with memorization, repetition and rote. The argument is made that for learners to acquire various skills

> individual reading, group discussions and research will be the most appropriate classroom organization [sic]. Individual attention will also have to be given because learners work in different ways and at different paces.
>
> (DOE, 1998b)

The conflation of methods, skills and classroom organization is obvious from this extract. However, the expected social relation between teacher and student is clear: learners are not to be treated as an undifferentiated group. Further, the document is explicit about the nature of hierarchy in the classroom: "if a classroom is organized with a dominant educator and rows of passive learners, the learners are likely to 'learn' that knowledge cannot be developed by them and

Figure 6.1 Promotional poster for C20005: preferred pedagogy

that they must accept authority uncritically" (DOE, 1998b, p. 9). The nature of the relationship (as well as the model of the teacher and learner) were powerfully captured and widely communicated through a series of posters, examples of which are reproduced in Figures 6.1–6.3.

Model of the learner

For C2005 to translate successfully into an implemented curriculum the assumption must be made that children come into school with an ability to read and a knowledge of number that will reveal itself over time. The action words referred

Figure 6.2 Promotional poster for C2005: a new teach identity

to above suggest a process of eliciting a mathematical gaze and a grasp of text (at a simple level) that is pre-existent. There is constant reference throughout the document to learners' own (existing) understandings and personal solutions.

There is no age identification of the learner. No differentiation is provided in terms of what a Grade 1, 2 or 3 child should be able to do in relation to reading or number. There is also no language identifier. Here is the free-floating, unmoored subject, without boundaries but consequently without an academic identity. Through an emphasis on local, everyday knowledge the curriculum focuses on learners' cultural, local, community locatedness and in many of the specific and critical outcomes their social mission and responsibility. The knower

Figure 6.3 Promotional poster for C2005: changes in student identity

projected by the curriculum includes the malleable global citizen, the responsible citizen and the community-oriented individual.

Model of the teacher

The model of the teacher in C2005 is one who has an extensive and well-developed understanding of their subject, able to construct programmes of learning on the basis of this expertise, and to differentiate their teaching according to the individual needs and levels of different learners: "educators are recognized as professionals who can make curriculum decisions in the best interests of learners and who do not have to rely on the dictates of a centrally devised syllabus" (DOE, 1998b, p. 27).

Teachers also work together, as the integrated curriculum demands: "Educators, previously separated by the need to cover discrete syllabus material, will now begin to work collaboratively in the preparation of materials and in the facilitation and assessment of learning" (DOE, 1998b, p. 29).

The curriculum also assumes a teacher who is able to adjust to vastly different pedagogical practices and arrangements, in particular instituting a child-centred pedagogy that changes the social relation between teacher and student and allows instruction to be driven by the interests of the child and the priorities of the local context.

The marginalizing of textbooks and the celebration of "preferred methods" in C2005 constitutes a highly localized form of recontextualizing, with teachers functioning as the primary recontextualizing agents. For such an intended curriculum to translate into a successful implemented curriculum, teachers would need to have powerfully developed theories of reading children. In other words, they would need to have a confident grasp of early school mathematics and literacy, and also of how children learn to read and learn number. In addition, given the extent of integration, they would also need a broad knowledge of a number of subject areas (history, technology, etc.) in order to realize the curriculum aims.

Table 6.4 summarizes the analysis of C2005 in relation to reading and number:

Table 6.4 Summary of the structuring of pedagogic discourse in the curriculum

Instructional	External framing of curricular knowledge	F^{e-}	Very weak – knowledge criteria not specified, no set pace, grade level specification or sequence, weak evaluative criteria
	Classification between subject, other subjects and everyday knowledge	C^{-}	Very weak. Everyday as a resource for mathematics. Curriculum design requires radical integration. Literacy emphasis on local meanings
	Classification between areas/topics within subject	C^{-}	Very weak. Reading, number not demarcated as specialized areas
Regulative	External framing of social relation (hierarchical rules)	F^{e++}	Very strong specification of child-centred, constructivist pedagogy
	Model of the teacher	Very competent, in whole language and mathematics, how to collaborate, how to conduct child-centred pedagogy.	
	Model of the learner	Already competent, can read/count, calculate. individualized, culturally located.	

The knowledge (or the what) that forms part of teaching reading and number is very weakly specified in the curriculum. There is a stronger emphasis on the how, spelt out in ideological rather than pedagogical terms. Progression is weak, and the model of the teacher and the learner in terms of the instructional dimension assumes competence on the part of both. The response in C2005 to the extreme emphasis on difference under apartheid is clear: there is a reluctance to make any kinds of distinctions between learners on the basis of language, age, level or competence. Dedifferentiation is consequently extensive, and the curriculum as a result is extremely underspecified, dealing in the generalities of new pedagogic forms rather than the specificities of particular knowledge requirements for specific learners at determined levels in the system. The curriculum fails to specify the site, agent or knowledge for learning.

The new curriculum was piloted in 30 schools for six months in 1997 and was implemented in 1998. The pilot was compromised by a very poor design, and Jansen argues that it was largely a public relations exercise that set out to *prove* that OBE worked (1999, p. 13). Implementation of Curriculum 2005 was rushed and chaotic. Given the very short time between finalization of the curriculum and its implementation, the national Department of Education and its various provincial counterparts had no choice but to provide crash-course training for teachers. The model adopted was one that sought to cascade the training down through the system.

Because of lack of capacity, aspects of this training were sub-contracted to a range of consultants and NGOs and the quality of the training was uneven. The cascade model itself was problematic since many of the teachers trained at the top of the cascade were not sufficiently equipped to replicate the training within their districts and schools. Thus, the complex (and confusing) new curriculum quickly became associated with a few obvious dimensions that provided teachers with a simple pegs on which to hang their understanding. Despite confusion about the implications for their practice (Jansen & Christie, 1999), learner-centredness became one of the defining features of the new curriculum for teachers. Groupwork became the major identifier of the new curriculum, and for many teachers, implementing groupwork was the core pedagogical shift required of them by C2005. C2005 was in essence a pedagogical reform where school subject knowledge all but disappeared from view. Above all, both the model of the teacher and that of the learner of the new pedagogy bore no resemblance to the reality of teachers and learners participating in schooling at the time who had just emerged from the apartheid schooling system.

Conclusion

Curriculum 2005 was ***defined in relation to the past and the future (modal) citizen***, ignoring the present and its sedimented inequities. It was referred to as a paradigm shift in curriculum, from the traditional apartheid curriculum to a new outcomes-based system. As Soudien (2010) argues, what C2005 did was "effectively, to misread the South African social landscape and to address it as if it was ***already*** the society they wanted to be, a largely middle class one" (p. 43). Or as

Harley and Parker put it, "The new system of OBE attempts to produce the kinds of consciousness and identity on which its operationalization, workability and success actually depend" (1999, p. 193). In the specific case here, a child who can already read, count and calculate.

Given the fact that OBE focused on outputs, or the end point of learning leaving open the content or inputs to arrive there, its success depended centrally on the quality of the teachers – their content knowledge, their facility with different teaching methods and their access to appropriate teaching materials. In short, it depended on high levels of cognitive resource in the system – notably texts and teachers. C2005 assumed both were well-developed, a blind spot that is startling given the history from which the system had just emerged. When generic skills replaced formal knowledge, the rules of the schooling game were hidden from those teachers and learners most needing to access them.

Notes

1 The analysis of curriculum in this chapter and in Chapter 8 stems from a research paper I originally wrote with Paula Ensor, presented at the Third IAACS World Curriculum Studies Conference, Stellenbosch, 7–10 September 2009. Although the ideas and analysis have taken a different direction in relation to the concerns of the book, some of the ideas, theoretical framing and interpretations of the original paper are reflected here and so I acknowledge Paula's contribution in the paper as well as the productive conversations we had around the issues.

2 The name of the reform is confusing, given that it was developed and implemented in 1997 and 1998, and was revised and replaced by 2002. The original intention was that full implementation of the entire new curriculum be completed by 2005, hence the title of the reform.

3 Probably marked as beginning with the 1991 signing of the National Peace Accord (NPA) between the apartheid government and 18 other organizations, including trade unions, political organizations and churches.

4 It was of course much more complex than this. See Spitz & Chaskalson (2000) for a fuller account.

5 See Chapter 3. NATED was the final curriculum developed at the end of apartheid; 'cleansed' of offensive and outdated aspects, it became the de facto curriculum in the first years of the democratic regime.

6 The DOE invoked their legislated 'power of curriculum co-ordination', and while making some show of compliance with the NQF and SAQA (the qualification accreditation body of the NQF), they did not register C2005 as a qualification through them. One of the reasons for doing this was that it would have slowed implementation down considerably (Sieborger, 2013, personal comment).

7 MacDonald (2002) argues this programme – Breakthrough to Literacy – was the most successful language experience method in sub-Saharan Africa at the time, available in 20 African languages and still widely used today.

References

African National Congress. (1994). *The reconstruction and development programme: A policy framework.* Pretoria: Government Printer.

Bernstein, B. (1996). Pedagogy symbolic control and identity: Theory, research, critique. London: Taylor & Francis.

Christie, F. (2005). *Language education in the primary years.* Sydney: NSW Press.

Davis, Z. (1996). The problem-centred approach and the production of the vanishing pedagogue. Paper presented at Kenton-at-Wilgespruit Conference, Johannesburg, South Africa.

Davis, Z. (2005). Pleasure and pedagogic discourse in school mathematics: A case study of a problem-centred pedagogic modality. Unpublished PhD, University of Cape Town, Cape Town.

Department of Education. (1995a). *Curriculum framework for general and further education document*. Pretoria: South African Department of Education.

Department of Education. (1995b). *White paper on education and training*. Department of Education. Pretoria: Government Printer.

Department of Education. (1997). *Curriculum 2005: Lifelong learning for the 21st century*. Pretoria: South African Department of Education.

Department of Education. (1998a). *Curriculum 2005: Implementing OBE – 1. classroom practice*. Pretoria: Department of Education.

Department of Education. (1998b). *Curriculum 2005: Implementing OBE – 4. philosophy*. Pretoria: Department of Education.

Department of Education. (1998c). *Curriculum 2005: Implementing OBE – 2. assessment*. Pretoria: Department of Education.

Department of Education. (2000). A South African curriculum for the twenty-first century: Report of the review committee on Curriculum 2005. Pretoria: South African Department of Education.

Ensor, P. (1997). School mathematics, everyday life and the NQF: A case of non-equivalence? *Pythagorus*, *41*, 36–44.

Ensor, P. (2003). The national qualifications framework and higher education in South Africa: Some epistemological issues. *Journal of Education and Work*, *16*(3), 325–346.

Ensor, P., Hoadley, U., Jacklin, H., Khune, C., Schmitt, E., Lombard, A., & van den Heuvel-Panhuizen, M. (2009). Specializing pedagogic text and time in foundation phase classrooms. *Journal of Education*, *47*, 5–30.

Fataar, A. (2006). Policy networks in recalibrated political terrain: The case of school curriculum policy and politics in South Africa. *Journal of Education Policy*, *21*(6), 641–659.

Harley, K., & Parker, B. (1999). Integrating differences: Implications of an outcomes-based national qualifications framework for the roles and competencies of teachers. In J. Jansen & P. Christie (Eds.), *Changing curriculum: Studies on outcomes-based education in South Africa* (pp. 181–202). Cape Town: Juta & Co.

Hart, G. (2008). The provocations of neoliberalism: Contesting the nation and liberation after apartheid. *Antipode*, *40*(4), 678–705.

Jansen, J. (1999). Introduction. In J. Jansen & P. Christie (Eds.), *Changing curriculum: Studies on outcomes-based education in South Africa* (pp. 1–18). Cape Town: Juta & Co.

Jansen, J. D., & Christie, P. (Eds.) (1999). *Changing curriculum: Studies on outcomes-based education in South Africa*. Cape Town: Juta and Company Ltd.

MacDonald, C. (2002). Are the children still swimming up the waterfall? A look at literacy development in the new curriculum. *Language Matters*, *33*(1), 111–141.

Muller, J. (1998). The well-tempered learner: Self-regulation, pedagogical models and teacher education policy. *Comparative Education*, *34*(2), 177–193.

Republic of South Africa. (1994). *Reconstruction and development plan (RDP)*. Pretoria: Government Printer.

Republic of South Africa. (1996). *Growth, employment and redistribution strategy (GEAR)*. Pretoria: Government Printer.

Republic of South Africa. (1997). *Language in education policy*. Retrieved from www.education.gov.za/LinkClick.aspx?fileticket=XpJ7gz4rPT0%3D.

Seekings, J., & Nattrass, N. (2015). *Policy, politics and poverty in South Africa*. London: Palgrave Macmillan.

Sieborger, R. (2013, May 19). Lecture. Masters in Education programme, School of Education, University of Cape Town.

Soudien, C. (2010). What to teach the natives: A historiography of the curriculum dilemma in South Africa. In W. Pinar (Ed.), *Curriculum studies in South Africa: Intellectual histories and present circumstances* (pp. 19–49). New York: Palgrave Macmillan.

Spitz, R., with Chaskalson, M. (2000). *The politics of transition: A hidden history of South Africa's negotiated settlement*. Johannesburg: Witwatersrand University Press.

7 Waiting to learn

Pedagogy under Curriculum 2005

Introduction

On a clear summer morning in November 1998, in the township of Khayelitsha, a group of 55 Grade 1 students line up and go out quietly to a sandy area in the playground of their school. The playground is dusty, with no sign of trees or grass. The teacher tells the children to write 'ihagu' [pig] in the sand. They are distracted. There is not enough space for all of them to write. Some jump around and play amongst themselves. Five children write the word, the rest are playing. After a while the teacher leads the children in a recitation. Over and over, as they file back to class, the children chant:

> Education is light
> When I first came to school
> It was dark
> The teacher taught me
> And I started to see.
> I said 'vula'. [open]

Having spent weeks in this school as part of a research project, the irony of the chorused chant at the time was unsettling. This chapter details why. The chapter is based on a study[1] of classrooms shortly after the implementation of C2005. Four case studies of Grade 1 classrooms focus in detail on the nature of the pedagogic form that emerged in the early days of the first post-apartheid curriculum regime. The chapter presents an analysis of those classrooms, showing some of the consequences of the new reforms, especially the particular interpretation of learner-centred pedagogy observed in the classrooms and consequences of the abandonment of knowledge signaling in the curriculum described in Chapter 6.

The analysis is broadly located within the theoretical frame described in Chapter 5, and follows on from the analysis in Chapter 6. The classification of knowledge in the classrooms, the strategies deployed and the transmission of evaluative criteria draw a focus on *what* was being transmitted in the classrooms. A consideration of the pacing in the classrooms and the nature of the social relations established under the new pedagogic regime describe *how* content was transmitted.

The chapter also considers interview data that was generated in discussions with teachers around their practice and their interpretation of C2005 in relation to what they were doing in their classrooms.

The chapter argues that the collapsing of knowledge boundaries, prized by C2005, was mirrored by a collapse of the instructional regime in these classrooms. Teachers floundered in an unbounded instructional space, lacking the tools to construct an appropriate pedagogic text for themselves and their learners.

The schools and classrooms

The two primary schools in this study were located in Khayelitsha, approximately 30 kilometres from Cape Town. Both schools were formerly administered by the Department of Education and Training (DET). The schools followed a policy of additive bilingualism, whereby children learnt in their mother tongue (isiXhosa in these schools) for the first three years and then switched to English as the medium of instruction in the fourth grade. One of the schools, P1, had, until recently, 'platooned', i.e. it shared premises with a school and provided schooling in the afternoon when the school day of the that school was completed. From April 1998 P1 had a new school building. The area surrounding P1 consisted of shack dwellings. Many residents were recent migrants (mainly from another province, the Eastern Cape) and there was a high rate of unemployment in the area. The school population was drawn mainly from the surrounding community.

P2 was located in a more formalized area, and the surrounding community consisted of largely settled, working-class families. A large number of learners were also bussed in from a nearby shack settlement. A survey of the surrounding communities showed a similarity in relation to parental education levels and occupations. Most parents of learners had not completed high school, and most were engaged in manual labour, in particular domestic labour.

Both schools had sound infrastructure and basic resources; the four classrooms had sufficient desks and chairs for all learners, a teacher's table, bookshelves, a chalkboard and a washbasin. The official student:teacher ratio at the time was 40:1 at the primary level. Only one of the classes had the correct student:teacher ratio (39:1), the other three were 43:1; 52:1 and 73:1. Absenteeism rates were very high, however, with between 15% and 44% of learners in different classes absent across the days of observation.

Many of the learners showed signs of physical neglect such as sores on their bodies and heads, trachoma and obvious undernourishment. About 50% of the learners did not wear school uniform. Learners brought very few of their own resources to the school and many did not have pencils or bookbags. Both schools participated in a school feeding programme and all the learners received bread daily and soup or milkshake on certain days.

The spatial and temporal organization within the schools was loosely bounded. The school day generally began half an hour to an hour after the school bell rang in the morning. There was a free flow of learners between the school and the surrounding area during school hours.

Although there were differences in the location of the schools, there was very little that differentiated their basic functioning. The pedagogy, most notably, was also remarkably similar across the four classrooms. The analysis thus looks at patterns across the four classrooms, rather than comparing schools or teachers. The intention is to gain a picture of dominant pedagogic forms rather than to identify more and less successful practice or compare teachers on other dimensions. Where differences did emerge clearly between teachers, reference is made to these.

Looking in classrooms

Each of the four teachers was observed by three observers for two full school days, between 3 and 18 November 1998, near the completion of the school year. The teachers had been trained to implement C2005 in 1997, and had been "doing OBE" as they put it for about two years. The classes are labeled Class 1, 2, 3 and 4 and the teachers Teacher 1 and 2, (in School P1) and Teachers 3 and 4 (in School P2). A total of 8 days or 44 hours and 25 minutes of observation data was generated across the four classrooms. The time was broken down into *activities* as the unit of analysis, defined here as a segment of time constructed around a single goal, task or theme. These activities comprised both pedagogic activities (time structured for learning purposes) and non-pedagogic activities (time allocated for eating, going to the toilet, break etcetera).

The observation schedule for the collection of the data was designed to gain a comprehensive description of the patterning of the school day, with special focus on recording teacher and learner talk and behaviour. The observations were recorded at a minimum of five-minute intervals in the form of notes, and a synthesis of three sets of notes from three observers produced a data set that provided a detailed and comprehensive account of what happened in the classroom.

The analysis begins with a consideration of the specialization of time and space for learning. The rest of the analysis is concerned with the specialization of the pedagogic text and the structuring of pedagogy. Knowledge is considered in terms of its structure (using classification) and content (drawing on Dowling's notions of specializing and localizing strategies). Framing is used to describe control in the classroom over selection, sequence, pace and evaluative criteria and the social relation between teachers and learners. The focus of the analysis, as in Chapter 6, is on what happens to knowledge, specifically in relation to reading and mathematics, in classrooms where C2005 was being implemented.

Specialization of time and space for learning

Across the four classrooms 58% of the total observation time was allocated to pedagogic activities. Another 32% was allocated to non-pedagogic activities, including breaks, praying, eating, going to the toilet and periods of unstipulated activity. The remaining 10% (over 4 hours) of time was lost to late starting.

Within the time allocated for activities, an estimate of how much time was *actually* spent on both pedagogic and non-pedagogic activities was made (time on task). During the pedagogic activities, it was estimated that learners spent approximately 67% of the pedagogic time (or 39% of the total time) on task. The remainder of the time was lost to periods of unspecified activity. During these times learners either sat silently or spoke to each other. At times several learners were observed to sleep, leave the classroom or play quietly on their own. Learners were learning to wait, waiting to learn.

The reasons for the erosion of instructional time ranged from teacher absence from the class, teacher presence in classroom but occupied with non-school activities or activities going on for far longer than the tasks required (inappropriate time management). The interrupted nature of the school day also accounts for the loss of a large proportion of learning time, the teachers being interrupted up to 11 times in the course of the day.

An examination of the specialization of time and space indicates the extent to which there was the provision of a framework for the pedagogy to proceed. The teachers moved in and out of the classroom during class time, and the boundaries between the classroom for transmission purposes and the rest of the school for attending to other matters were blurred. It was only the non-pedagogic activities that were clearly marked out in terms of when they took place and for what duration. Pedagogic activities were often either allocated too much time, so that learners were not engaged in tasks for the entire period, or the time allocated was cut short and tasks were left incomplete. Classes did not begin on time, and a relatively small proportion of time was first allocated to, and second utilized for, learning. There was a surface, bureaucratic specialization of time and space in that the school day had a beginning and an ending time, and there was a classroom space marked out for the pedagogy to take place. Beyond this, time and space for learning were weakly marked out and hence weakly attended to.

Selection and sequencing – free association pedagogy

Selection and sequencing of the pedagogy is strongly framed: the teacher controls the introduction of content, and the order in which it is presented. This control, however, must be related to the evaluative criteria and the classification of knowledge. If both these are weak, as we will see as follows, although the teacher exerts strong control over selection and sequence, this is not in relation to a particular knowledge object or pedagogic objective. In these cases, what drives the selection and sequence? I present two examples of teaching repertoires (series of activities) below in order to investigate this question.

In an activity that culminated in Teacher 2 instructing the learners to draw a cow and write a sentence about the cow they had drawn, the task was arrived at through what appeared to be a ***free association*** of ideas. A discussion began around the naming of different food, and then moved on to breakfast foods and from cereal to milk. Teacher 2 then proposed: "Let us brainstorm a cow":

Teacher: I want us to talk about milk. What do we do with milk?
Learner: We pour it on cereal. And on tea.

Teacher: Who drank milk this morning?
[No response from learners]
Teacher: Where do we get milk?
Learner: In oats.
Learner: Cornflakes.
Learner: In tea.
Learner: From a cow.
Teacher: Let us brainstorm a cow.

The way in which knowledge was selected in the classrooms frequently appeared to be based on relations of association, both within activities and between activities. This is further exemplified in the following series of activities, structured around the subject of 'pigs' from Class 1:

- The teacher told the story of the 'The Three Little Pigs'.
- The learners were instructed to write the word 'ihagu' (pig) in the sand on the playground.
- The learners were instructed to shape the word 'ihagu' (pig) out of plasticine. The teacher stated: "You'll be pigs now and you are going to make mud [softened plasticine] on top of the paper. You are going to use your mud for writing an 'h' for ihagu".
- The learners participated in a counting exercise focusing on the number of legs a pig has.
- Learners retold the story of the three little pigs in groups and individually to the class.
- Learners commenced a role play of the story of 'The Three Little Pigs'.

The structuring of the tasks was based around relations of closeness in terms of a theme – pigs – rather than the development of particular language or mathematical skills or concepts. Selection therefore, though strongly framed, was derived from theme-based, free association on the part of the teacher.

Learners were not required to produce their own texts in this strong framing over selection. On the few occasions when learners did insert their own texts these were ignored by the teacher. Novel responses were also rejected, ignored or not recognized. In the example below a learner's attempt to relate the oval shape to a rugby ball in Teacher 2's class was dismissed:

Teacher: Listen, we have spoken about peach, pear, pineapple, cabbage. Now give me shapes that you know
Learners: Circle, triangle, square
Learner: Rugby
Teacher: Rugby is the people who play, but that is not their shape.
Learner: The ball has got a shape
Teacher: What kind of fruit can give us a triangular shape?

In telling the story of the Three Little Pigs, an exchange between Teacher 1 and the learners exemplifies how student interventions were not incorporated in the exchanges:

Teacher: The second pig built its own house using wood.
Learner: Our house is built out of tin
Learner: My house is built out of zinc
Teacher: Wolf came again and ate this second pig. The third pig . . .

In other words, there was very little evidence of learner-centred incorporation or evaluation of students' texts for further learning.

Pace

As in selection, it is difficult to exert meaningful control over the pace of learning if the knowledge object is not clear and if student productions or interventions are not used to guide the rate of transmission. Teachers exerted strong control over the pace, and this was evidenced especially in teachers determining the start and end of activities, regardless of whether learners were finished or not. It was also evident in the failure to adjust the pace in relation to learners' errors or interventions. Despite this strong control, the pace was extremely slow. Most activities, pedagogic and non-pedagogic, were allocated more time than they required.

Differentiated pacing (Hoadley, 2003) would entail variation in pace according to the teachers' assessment of the demands of the pedagogical situation, the content of the lesson and the individual rate of learning of learners in the class. In the case of the four classes observed there was no differentiation of pacing – the class was treated as homogenous.

Evaluative criteria

Evaluative criteria lie at the heart of pedagogy, indexing what I have referred to thus far as the 'knowledge object/s' of the lesson. Evaluative criteria can be seen in teachers' mediation of tasks given to learners: in the correction of, or responses to learner productions and in instructions or explanations given to the class, showing what counts or what ideas belong together (Shalem, 2017). Evaluative criteria were also discerned in assessment tasks, and the ways in which these were marked. In order for evaluative criteria to be transmitted, the teacher needs to be aware of what the learners are saying, observe what the learners are doing and intervene where appropriate in order to provide markers towards the realization of the criteria of the task.

There was very little evidence of mediation of tasks across the classrooms. Generally teachers gave the learners instructions and carried on with their own work or were out of class. At no time was a teacher seen to spend a protracted length of time with an individual learner. In addition, very little assessment was seen in

Table 7.1 Nature of the assessment in the 41 pedagogic activities

	No assessment	*Ticks only*	*Ticks and corrects*	*Listens to/watches learners and mediates further learning*
Number of pedagogic activities	28	6	2	5
% of pedagogic activities	68%	15%	5%	12%

the activities. Frequently, the teacher did not see the learners' work as they did it, nor was the work collected for assessment. Table 7.1 gives an indication of how much assessment was apparent across the 41 observed activities.

In the majority of pedagogic activities (82%) there was no assessment or a very restricted form (ticking and signing). There were very few statements with regard to the result or intended outcome of the learning provided, and the criteria for successful learner productions remained implicit. Most activities were based on practice or memory retrieval. For example, learners were told to draw a triangle, a square and a rectangle, without further elaboration.

Classroom discourse patterns

What dominated in the classrooms was an oral discourse that predominantly took one of two forms. The first was chorused responses to low level questions, or the chanting of content (generally rhymes and songs) by the whole class. In these activities there was no feedback on learner productions from the teacher. The second kind of discourse had a catechetic form, involving a series of questions and answers between the teacher and the learners. In these exchanges, learners generally knew the answers to the questions. The questions demanded responses dependent on simple recall of information ("Who was the first person created by God?" (Teacher 2)), or on learners' everyday knowledge, drawn from their own experience ("What does mom do at home?" (Teacher 3)). An exchange in Teacher 4's class went as follows:

Teacher: What does mom do at home?
Learner: She washes the dishes.
Teacher: What else does she do?
Learner: She cooks and cleans.
Teacher: Why do we need to clean?
Learner: When it is dirty.
Teacher: How do you help your parents, Mabhuti?
Learner: I pick up papers.
Teacher: Yonela?
Learner: I wash dishes and sweep the floor.

Again, teachers largely ignored learners' interventions when they strayed from the expected answer to the question, and they did not respond to error. When learners did not know the answers to questions, the course of questioning at times was arrested. In Teacher 2's class:

Teacher:	Today we will read from the Bible. By the way who created us?
Several learners:	God.
Teacher:	Everything on earth was created by God. God worked for 6 days and what did he do on the seventh day? [No response from **learners**]
Teacher:	How many days do you come to school?
Whole class:	5 days.
Teacher:	After working very hard for 6 days, what do you think God did on the seventh day?
Several learners:	He rested.
Teacher:	Who was the first person created by God?
Learner:	Adam.
Teacher:	And who else?
Learner:	Jesus.
Teacher:	No, we said that Jesus is God's son.
Learner:	Eve.
Teacher:	You don't remember things. We are going to the story of the Great Flood.

Principles connecting a series of discrete tasks were not referenced and instructions were generally unelaborated. This resulted in a fragmentation of the learning course with very weak framing over evaluative criteria.

The intended learning or purpose in many of exchanges is often difficult to retrieve. This raises the question of whether these interactions were in fact pedagogic. It is difficult to identify evaluative criteria, either strongly or weakly framed. This was raised in Chapter 2 in relation to a 'zero pedagogy' and I will return to it in Chapter 9. For present purposes, we see in the data several instances of transmission that appears devoid of evaluative criteria. The catechetic form masks a lack of pedagogic substance in the exchange.

The classification of knowledge

The foregoing discussion and data extracts indicate that the knowledge introduced in the classrooms was extremely weakly classified with respect to everyday knowledge. The content of classroom talk was localized, referring to domestic, proximate, everyday meanings, inhering in topics such as food, animals, Bible stories and well-known tales. The emphasis in the classrooms was on an oral form of pedagogy, and a large proportion of the time was spent reciting well-known verses and songs. Very often the content of the verses bore no relation to the preceding or following activities and the reciting/singing was generally unmediated by the teacher.

Table 7.2 Pedagogic activities across two days of observation of the four teachers

	Teacher 1		*Teacher 2*
1	General discussion (child who swallowed fish bone) and prayer	12	Discussion of shapes. Learners draw fruit and label with the proximate shape.
2	Telling of story 3 little pigs and learners act out [pig].	13	Learners draw square and triangle and colour in.
3	Letter recognition – 'h' – writing word pig in sand.	14	Reading single words containing particular phonemes.
4	Letter recognition 'h' – making out of plasticine.	15	Discussion: Food, dairy products, cow.
5	Draw a pig, write name.	16	Learners draw a cow and write sentence about their drawing
6	Recite well-known verse about a pig. Learners count out loud how many legs a pig has and how many legs 2 pigs have.	17	Learners sing well-known songs.
7	Prayer and Bible story – birth of Christ – learners read five words on board.	18	Learners tell fairy tales of their own choice.
8	Draw Jesus' family and write names.	19	Learners sing hymns.
9	Teacher tells and learners retell the story of three little pigs.	20	Bible story – Creation then Noah.
10	Letter recognition – h – locating letter in a pile of letters.	21	Counting up to 10. Counting rhyme. Counting up to 50.
11	Discussion: Food – fruit – vegetables.	20	Discussion: cow – diviner – herbs.
		21	Reading single words from the wall (with particular vowel sounds)
		22	Ordering pictures to construct narrative.

	Teacher 3		*Teacher 4*
22	Days of week – weather Discuss weather.	33	Bible story – loaves and fishes. Questions. Learners retell story.
23	Recite verse about wind. Sing two songs.	34	Draw a fish.
24	Counting with bottletops. Simple subtraction with bottletops.	35	Counting – individuals up to 10. Whole class up to 50 and 100.
25	Learners recount stories from sets of pictures.	36	Addition using number line and story of grandfather who fetches his pension.
26	Sing well-known songs and recite a poem.	37	Recite 7 well-known verses.
27	Learners tell stories of their own choice to the class	38	Sound recognition – 'dy'. Copy 5 words from board.
28	Matching phonemes (consonants) to letter chart.	39	Recite prayer, months of year, days of week.
29	Copying written patterns (non-symbolic).	40	Dictation of 12 single words.
30	Recite poems from wall (led by cleaner who points at words).	41	Consonant recognition in magazines. Cutting and pasting.
31	Draw fresh and stale bread, bananas, apples and oranges (for different groups).		
32	Sing well-known songs.		

A particular interpretation of integration was evident in the classrooms. Tasks were often not finished, and very often the link between one activity and the next could only be discerned in the theme or in the 'free association' pedagogy referenced above. The teachers instructed learners to move from one task to the next, often without assessment or mediation, or closure. Given the weak classification and weak framing of evaluative criteria it was difficult to discern a developmental trajectory that might have produced a shift or change in the learners through the activities.

Table 7.2 indicates, in summary form, the content covered across two days in each of the classrooms. Both the paucity of content covered, as well as the oral and rudimentary nature of tasks, is reflected in the table. The table shows only instructional activity, excluding non-instructional activities such as school feeding, toilet routines and periods where the teacher left the class with no activity set.

Reading

In reading, in all four classes, the emphasis was on reading single words, or on the recognition of consonants and consonant sounds. Very little time was allocated to these activities and participation was extremely variable.

Table 7.3 gives an indication of the nature of the reading activities during the eight-day observation period, the time spent on the activities and the approximate number of learners who participated in the task. An indication of the mediation and assessment employed by the teacher during the activity is also shown.

Not once in the course of the eight days of observation were learners exposed to or required to handle books. They were also not exposed to any extended text. Reading generally consisted of working through lists of single words or sound recognition exercises. No class readers or book corners were seen or used. In the course of the observations, a total of five books were seen in the four classrooms: two bibles, a Grade 5 geography textbook, a book on art ideas for teachers and one large book covering the numbers one to 10 with pictures and text in English. The only books ***used*** were the bibles, from which two of the teachers read.

Similarly, in writing activities, learners wrote only single words and letters. In only one activity were learners required to write a sentence. No scaffolding or evaluation of the task was provided. The learners were instructed: "After you have drawn your cow, write a sentence about your cow". Of the 26 learners present, three were able to write a sentence accurately. Eight learners made no attempt and 17 learners listed a few products derived from a cow.

Of the total 161 learners observed in the four classes, 42 (26%) were unable to write their names accurately. Most learners did not have a grasp of the actual technique of writing and formed letters in unconventional ways and little correction or individual work towards the mastery of name writing was evidenced. Consistent with curriculum stipulations, there were no formal handwriting activities.

Table 7.3 Nature and duration of reading tasks: participation of learners and mediation and assessment by teachers

Class	*Nature of activity*	*Time spent on activity*	*Learner participation in task*	*Mediation*	*Assessment*
Class 1	Letter recognition (letter 'h')	3 minutes	<5 participate	None	None
Class 1	Letter recognition (letter 'h')	2 minutes	<10 participate	None	None
Class 1	Letter recognition (letter 'h')	12 minutes	6 participate	None	None
Class 1	Reading single words	11 minutes	All participate	None	None
Class 2	Reading single words	7 minutes	+/– 50% participate	None	None
Class 2	Reading single words	8 minutes	+/– 70% participate	Assists several learners	None
Class 2	Reading single words	10 minutes	+/– 65 % participate	None	None
Class 3	Letter recognition (consonants)	10 minutes	All participate	None	None
Class 4	Reading single words	16 minutes	+/– 25% participate	Very little	None
Class 4	Letter recognition (consonants)	20 minutes	+/– 75% participate	Demonstrates to several learners	None

Literacy in these classrooms was mostly oral. Table 7.2 gives an indication of the predominance of recitation, choral chanting and singing, and the discussion above points to the fact that learners did not engage with extended written text and did not handle books. Pretorius (2014) argues that, when print-based activities are peripheral, students develop a particular understanding of learning as involving listening (auditory input) and chorusing answers. It is not understood as a text-oriented process (print-based input). And, as Pretorius states pithily: 'only *reading* develops reading' (p. 71).

Mathematics

Very little mathematics was introduced into the classrooms. A total of seven out of the 41 activities involved mathematical content. Three of these were rudimentary counting exercises (in Class 1 up to numerals 4 and 8, in Class 4 up to 10, then 50 and then 100, in Class 2 up to 10 then 50, and in Class 3 up to 10).

All the exercises were at a very low level for children at the end of Grade 1, given that the standard number range for this level is 0 to 100. Two tasks required learners to draw shapes from memory. The only other task requiring learners to write was a lesson on the number line. However, most of this task was oral. It commenced with Teacher 4 giving an account and enactment of a grandfather who walks from his home, rests, and then carries on to a pension office. This was used to demonstrate movement on the number line and a simple addition calculation.

Teacher: I will tell you a story. Others can't count [referring to the counting exercise that preceded this activity]. Okay, there was a grandfather. Who has a grandfather?

Teacher: Grandfather is an elderly man. What does he use for walking?

Learners: A stick.

Teacher: Grandfather walks, and walks and then rests. Why?

Learners: He is tired.

Teacher: He walks and walks and finally arrives at the pension office. Then he goes home. He walks and sits down because he is tired. If you are a grandchild and you help grandfather, count for me how many paces he walked before he rested?

The teacher role-plays the grandfather walking while the children count.

Teacher: You add again when he starts walking. How many paces has he walked?

Learners: Five.

Teacher: After I rested, how many paces did I walk?

Learners: Four.

The introduction of this content through role play was both laborious and distracting. After 55 minutes of oral instruction, learners were told to draw a number line. Most struggled and none were able to use the number line to do a calculation. Rather than facilitating understanding of the number line, the recruitment of an everyday example served to confuse the learners. In the example, what the number line potentially offers is a geometric model for conducting the four basic operations within the number system. Crucially, however, the teacher did not label the start of the number line zero. Learners were therefore unable to grasp the example operation, and failed to connect the steps, rest and destination of the grandfather with a subtraction example introduced by the teacher.

The only other means of representing numbers seen in the classrooms was the use of bottletops as concrete counters to do three simple subtraction sums involving single digits. Apart from this, mathematics was largely an oral activity, with chorused counting the dominant activity observed, suggesting a predominantly rote understanding of number.

Classroom control and the social relations of the classroom

In considering the regulative discourse of the classroom, hierarchical relations were strongly framed. Order was generally kept through direct speech acts based on physical threat. In each of the classrooms, at least four instances of statements involving the threat of corporal punishment were observed. For example, "If I see you talking you will be caned" (Class 1); "If you talk while colouring in I will hit you" (Class 2); "You were laughing but now you don't know the answer. I will hit you" (Class 4); and "Nomthandazo, I will hit you for making a noise" (Class 3).

When the teacher was absent from the classroom, learner behaviour represented a complete break from the order established by the teacher. Learners displayed a significant amount of physical and verbal aggression towards one another. Communication between teachers and learners was minimal and the teachers managed the large numbers of unruly children in aggressive tones. The authoritarian form of social relation probably contributed to the fact that learners rarely asked unsolicited questions or offered comment in the course of the lessons.

The model of the teacher and the learner

Learners were strongly connected by the pedagogy to their local context through the very localized content that was introduced. This exposed learners to content with which they were generally familiar and involved mundane aspects such as animals, food, the Bible and fairy stories. The local, multicultural emphasis of C2005 is the flip side of the culturally distinct and localized community focus of the apartheid curriculum. The effect is the same – that of restricting the learners to their own experiential local environment, here in the name of relevance.

Learners were passive. They were required to restate texts, primarily through the reciting or recall of what they already knew. The implicit subject projected through the pedagogy was the local learner, in need of strict control, incapable of intellectually challenging work and not able to participate in his or her own learning.

The teacher identity resembles that of early socializer, where the activities are localized, close and domestic. The nature of the exchanges approximate what mothers might do with their children in early pedagogic and socialization activities, e.g. helping the child name things, reciting rhymes, playing games, drawing, learning to write their names. They are not empty of pedagogic content or potential but, in relation to learners nearing the end of Grade 1, they represent a form of surface learning inappropriate to this level, and are unlikely to give children access to formal learning and specialized knowledge of early schooling. What we saw was an initial, oral, segmental pedagogy that, crucially, was devoid of written text and opportunities for learners to read and write.

Summary

The analysis of pedagogy is summarized in Table 7.4, in terms of categories presented in Chapter 6.

Table 7.4 Summary of the structuring of pedagogic discourse across classrooms

Instructional	Selection	F^+	Strong – the teacher controls what is taught but with a weak relation to clear pedagogic purpose.
	Sequence	F^+	Strong – the teacher controls the order of teaching but with a weak relation to clear pedagogic purpose.
	Pace	F^+	Strong – the teacher controls the rate of transmission and acquisition, but with a weak relation to clear pedagogic purpose.
	Evaluation	F^-	Weak – knowledge criteria not specified, the teacher does not exert control over defining appropriate and inappropriate productions.
	Classification between subject and other subjects and everyday knowledge	C^-	Weak – everyday knowledge as a resource for mathematics and for literacy, many lessons are theme-driven.
	Classification between areas/topics within subject	C^-	Weak. Reading, number not demarcated as specialized areas, practices. Many of the activities not strictly identifiable in relation to a conventional subject.
Regulative	Framing of social relation (hierarchical rules)	F^+	Strong. Authoritarian relation in the classroom.
	Model of the teacher		Caretaker, early socializer. But repressive.
	Model of the learner		Locally-defined, culturally-affirmed. Passive. Communalized.

To summarize, teaching comprised mainly unelaborated instructions by the teacher, without a sense of the learning rationale or trajectory behind the selection of tasks and content. At times activity in the classrooms appeared to be driven by a theme, but this was not consistent across the days or classrooms. The knowledge content introduced in the classroom was localized and fragmented, with very weak classification between school knowledge and everyday knowledge. The cognitive demand of tasks demanded was very low, and framing over the evaluative criteria was exceptionally weak. Teachers seldom responded to learners' interjections and generally did not mediate the work that learners produced in the classroom. As well as activities in the classroom being brought together on the basis of assertion, control in the classroom was based on censure and threat. The learners in the classrooms were passive, and the relationship between the teacher and students was strongly framed.

The extent to which the practice in the classroom represents the stipulations of C2005 is uneven across the dimensions identified. Along the lines of learner-centredness, C2005 stipulates that all of the instructional discourse be weakly framed and weakly classified. In the practice of the teachers here, selection, sequence and pace were strongly framed, while evaluative criteria were weakly framed. There was weak classification of subject knowledge. The question as to whether these evaluative criteria were weak, or indeed absent, was raised above and will be returned to in the chapters to come. The social relations of the classroom remained determinedly authoritarian despite the child-centred relation advocated by C2005. The model of the learner, as opposed to the individualized, critical, engaged and enquiring learner of C2005, was passive and treated as part of a homogenous group. Students were not seen to ask questions and seldom made their own interventions in the pedagogy.

While the influence of C2005 could be read off some elements of the teachers' observed pedagogy and in their accounts of their practice (as follows), it would seem that much of what they did in the classrooms was derived from pre-existing practices, those that are consistent with the types of practices described under apartheid. Collective chanting, chorus and drill were in evidence, reproducing the rite of rote and surface learning. Social relations appeared to have changed little from the authoritarian forms of the past. After the first major post-apartheid progressive reform, and despite the strong ideological project of C2005 and teachers' espousal of it having shaped their practice, pedagogy looked much like broader descriptions of pedagogy in the past and fit, to a large extent, the descriptions in developing countries more widely.

The most significant shift from apartheid pedagogy to C2005 would appear to be the position of knowledge in the pedagogy. Whilst pedagogy under apartheid entailed repetitions of low level content, under C2005 the circulation of everyday meanings and local, experiential knowledge predominated.

The demise of knowledge-to-be-taught

The four teachers were interviewed in order to retrieve their own rationale for the observed pedagogy. The teachers were asked specifically for their response to C2005, requesting them to rate the extent to which it affected the way they taught, and in what ways. In the accounts given, the teachers articulated a specific understanding of some of the main tenets of the progressivist discourse underlying C2005/OBE, such as learner-centredness, the teacher as facilitator and exploratory learning. In a number of these comments the position of knowledge in the classroom was the focus. In some accounts the teachers understood their role as *not* providing students with knowledge:

> I don't have to tell them everything, they find out for themselves, in fact my teaching is being guided by the learners.
>
> (Teacher 3)

> In maths, for instance, the teacher does not have to tell the kids that today we are going to learn fractions, it automatically enters into the lesson.
>
> (Teacher 2)

> The children no longer need to be spoon-fed with information, instead I give them problems, they find solutions.
>
> (Teacher 4)

The notion of facilitation is also emphasized, but it is understood as requiring less of the teacher:

> The teacher is to facilitate. Most of the work must be done by the learners, even talking. Learners are forced to do research in their learning areas.
>
> (Teacher 4)

> There's less talking and chalkboard writing from me, most of the talking and writing is done by the learners. There's no pressure of completing the syllabus, I have the autonomy power of choosing what to teach, when and how.
>
> (Teacher 2)

> In a way that I have to be less active, and allow my learners to do most of the work.
>
> (Teacher 1)

> I'm just a facilitator most of the time. About 90% of work is done by learners.
>
> (Teacher 3)

There are references to learners "doing research", "learning things on their own" and "being more active". Negative comments focused on teachers' confusion or uncertainty about aspects of C2005, but there was only one direct criticism: "In teaching reading and writing, where I need to do vowels and phonics, it doesn't give me much allowance to do so. It's designed less with African languages in mind" (Teacher 1).

The comments could account for the extent to which the learners are left to work on their own, with little mediation and assessment. It could also account for the predominating mode of unelaborated instructions and the absence of elaboration within tasks of evaluative criteria. It also accounts for the absence of the systematic and explicit introduction of knowledge in the classroom. Nykiel-Herbert (2004) confirms the teachers' (mis)readings of the policy intention of C2005 across a number of research studies, arguing that the interpretations are particularly damaging because they undermine core educational beliefs including the teacher's role and responsibility to convey new information to students (p. 260).

What C2005 did was undermine the idea that a pedagogic relation necessarily entails both teachers and learners having, at least, an implicit understanding that criteria are to be transmitted and acquired, and further that these criteria *rest with the teacher*. A combination of very weak boundaries between school knowledge and everyday knowledge, and weak evaluative criteria, provides the learners with very limited opportunity to acquire the formal discourses of schooling.

At the most simple and devastating level, MacDonald (2002) confirms the findings of this small study – that teachers stopped explicitly and systematically teaching their students to read and write. The teaching of phonics ceased, possibly in reaction to previous behaviourist approaches that focused on oral drill sequences and a strong reliance on technical, decontextualized decoding skills, with little understanding of the meaning of text (MacDonald, 1990; Flanagan, 1992). However, it was replaced with "an unorganized confusion of contrived realism" (Taylor and Vinjevold, 1999, p. 121), where superficial appeals to learners' personal experience replaced conceptual development.

Teacher knowledge and the new scripture

From a wide range of research, the argument is made that under C2005, in former (mostly white) historically-advantaged, schools, teachers continued to teach basic reading, writing and number concepts. Integration was relegated to the Life Skills component of the curriculum, while Language and Mathematics remained strongly classified. Utilizing existing and new resources, these well-trained teachers were able to put together their own, well-established programmes of learning in the absence of content specification in the curriculum. Having been exposed to progressive elements of practice, they were probably best placed to evaluate and select what was useful from C2005 without deploying it wholesale (Harley & Wedekind, 2004).

However, for teachers in former DET (and persistently black) schools, the progressivism of People's Education of the 1980s had, in C2005, hardened into dogma (DOE, 2000:31), and C2005 was widely and uncritically taken up with much praise from teachers for the reform (Jansen & Christie, 1999). To criticize it was, in some quarters, to be disloyal to the political project, and it took on a 'scriptural' nature, such that it required a kind of belief: 'If we are opposed to apartheid education then we must be in favour of OBE' (Morrow, 2001). But, in reaction to the content-laden syllabi of apartheid, in C2005 the content was removed and replaced with themes, generic outcomes and broad competences and strategies to be undertaken. Muller sums up the class implications of this kind of curriculum:

> A success can be made of such an under-stipulated curriculum, but only if the teacher has a well-articulated mental script of what should be covered, and if the pupils come from homes where they have been well prepared to respond to such putative freedom, in other words, only in schools by and for the middle class.
>
> (Muller, 2000, p. 14)

The fundamental issue was that most teachers did not possess this mental script. Taylor and Vinjevold (1999), reporting on a large set of classroom-based studies conducted during the time of C2005 showed a convergence in the findings of the research around teachers' extremely poor conceptual knowledge. They also found that teachers lacked the knowledge base to interpret Curriculum 2005, and were unable to deal with integration and 'ensure that the everyday approach prescribed by the new curriculum will result in learners developing sound conceptual frameworks' (Taylor and Vinjevold, 1999, p. 230).

The first post-apartheid curriculum reform, along with the legacy of apartheid educational forms, produced a pedagogy that effectively locked out those children most in need of access to school knowledge. While its intentions were laudable, its outcomes would set the process of transforming the education system back considerably. The case suggests how the radical learner-centred reform of C2005 was subsumed into existing practice, especially in the face of poor teacher knowledge that could not compensate for the lack of knowledge signaling in the curriculum.

Note

1 The study, the Learner Progress and Achievement Study, was located at the University of Cape Town and led by Dr Heather Jacklin. The study formed part of the President's Educational Initiative, which, under the Mandela administration, was funded to conduct studies of classrooms. Over 30 studies produced some of the first systematic studies of classrooms in South Africa.

References

Department of Education. (2000). A South African curriculum for the twenty-first century: Report of the review committee on Curriculum 2005. Pretoria: South African Department of Education.

Flanagan, W. (1992). Pedagogical discourse, teacher education programmes and social transformation in South Africa. *International Journal of Educational Development*, *12*(1), 27–35.

Harley, K., & Wedekind, V. (2004). Political change, curriculum change and social formation, 1990 to 2002. In *Changing class: Education and social change in post-apartheid South Africa* (pp. 195–220). Pretoria: HSRC Press.

Hoadley, U. (2003). Time to learn: Pacing and the external framing of teachers' work 1. *Journal of Education for Teaching: International Research and Pedagogy*, *29*(3), 265–277.

Jansen, J., & Christie, P. (Eds.) (1999). *Changing curriculum: Studies on outcomes-based education in South Africa*. Cape Town: Juta and Company Ltd.

MacDonald, C. (2002). Are the children still swimming up the waterfall? A look at literacy development in the new curriculum. *Language Matters*, *33*(1), 111–141.

MacDonald, C. A. (1990). Swimming up the waterfall: A study of school-based learning experiences. Pretoria: Human Sciences Research Council.

Morrow, W. (2001). Scriptures and practices. *Perspectives in Education*, *19*(1), 87–106.

Muller, J. (2000). *Reclaiming knowledge*. London: RoutledgeFalmer.

Nykiel-Herbert, B. (2004). Mis-constructing knowledge: The case of learner-centred pedagogy in South Africa. *Prospects*, *34*(3), 249–265.

Pretorius, E. (2014). Supporting transition or playing catch-up in Grade 4? Implications for standards in education and training. ***Perspectives in Education***, *32*, 51–76.

Shalem, Y. (2017). Scripted lesson plans: What is visible and invisible in visible pedagogy? In B. Barrett, U. Hoadley & J. Morgan (Eds.), ***Knowledge, curriculum and equity: Social realist perspectives.*** London: Routledge.

Taylor, N., & Vinjevold, P. (1999). Getting learning right: Report of the president's educational initiative research project. Johannesburg: The Joint Education Trust.

8 One step forward

The compromise National Curriculum Statement

Introduction

In 1999, barely two years after its implementation, the Minister of Education called for a formal review of Curriculum 2005 (C2005), the first curriculum of the newly democratized South Africa. Despite its laudable political goals, the educational shortcomings of the C2005 project had quickly become apparent and criticism was swift and vociferous. Prominent critiques focused on training and implementation, system failures and curriculum design. For Jansen (1999) the curriculum had failed because it was driven by policy imperatives with no conception of the realities of classroom life. Jansen (2001) argued that C2005 had served the purpose of 'political symbolism', helping to mark the shift from apartheid to post-apartheid education and establish the ideological and political credentials of the new regime. But as a pedagogical project it had failed.

Reviewing the first post-apartheid curriculum so soon after its implementation was, however, politically difficult for the state. The review was thus cast as a process of 'strengthening and streamlining of C2005'. As a result of this framing, and the fact that particular design features of C2005 were retained (most notably outcomes), there was a significant amount of continuity between C2005 and the NCS. The NCS did however, in contrast to C2005, recognize the distinctiveness of the schooling sector and its particular purposes, and set out to describe a curriculum to be mastered by school children in conventional graded classrooms as opposed to the generalized learner of C2005, where every site was potentially pedagogic. There was also an attempt to reintroduce subject knowledge as the basis for curriculum organization.

The review of C2005 was marked by significant contestation, however. There were strong interest groups at play in the process, attempting to pull the curriculum in different directions. The resulting NCS was a hybrid and at times contradictory curriculum which could be read in a number of different ways. As in Chapter 5, in this chapter I discuss the reform through an analysis of the NCS curriculum for reading and number in Foundation Phase. The analysis shows how the possibilities of the resulting curriculum influencing practice would depend on which parts of the curriculum were read and how they were read.

Official pedagogic discourse

> The discontent churned up by an unemployment rate of 37,6 per cent, of poverty levels that match those under the final years of apartheid and of widening inequality is still radically muffled and disorientated by a party that monopolises the discourse of transformation.
>
> (Marais, 2001, p. 186)

This was Hein Marais's distillation of the broad political and economic environment in 2000. The government persisted doggedly with its internal structural adjustment programme, GEAR, despite a stagnating economy and massive job losses in the preceding years. Official pedagogic discourse also persisted in hinging around human capital theory and the idea that improving the output of more educated and skilled individuals would lead to economic growth. How this discourse translated into actual schooling processes and outcomes was, however, far from clear. Little had changed for the most disadvantaged and their experience of the schooling system.

Baatjes and Mathe (2004) suggested at the time that there were few effective programmes addressing even minimal skills training of workers. At the school level, little was done to address the challenge as well, perhaps the most notable programmes being the QIDS-UP programme aimed at achieving high levels of literacy and numeracy skills in the lower grades, and the mathematics and science 'Dinaledi' programme in 529 high schools aimed at doubling mathematics and science high school graduates. Neither of these programmes showed significant effects for their target communities.

In 1999 the then Minister of Education, Kader Asmal declared the system to be in crisis. The only measure of learning outcomes at the time was the school-leaving (Grade 12) National Senior Certificate examination results, and these had declined. Overcrowded classrooms, the ongoing decline in the ethos of teaching and learning and lack of textbooks and other materials had become pressing issues not yet addressed by the democratic state. Strong criticism of the curriculum made this an obvious area for intervention.

Contestation and interests in the review of C2005

The 2000 review of the first post-apartheid curriculum was a significant chapter in South Africa's post-apartheid education history. The process was a complex one, which was riven with strong interests which pulled the idea of a revised curriculum in different directions. Critically, the government of the day dug its heels in on its economic policies, and was reluctant to go back on education decisions, like outcomes-based education, that were linked to these. But an outcomes-based, economistic focus was only one interest at play. There were a number of others that I attempt to tease out below.

On one level the recommendations of the review were straightforward and sensible given criticisms of C2005, and included that:

- The design of the curriculum be simplified;
- Curriculum overload be addressed, including the reduction in the number of Learning Areas in the Intermediate Phase;
- The terminology and language of the curriculum be simplified;
- Assessment requirements should be clarified;
- Content be brought into the curriculum, and specified;
- A plan be developed to train teachers effectively for a new curriculum;
- Textbooks and reading be reintroduced.

How these would play out in the actual revision, however, was more complex given different positions at play in the review.

Chisholm (2005) argued that it was not possible to find a neat fit between interests in the process and the outcome of the review. She argued, however, that SADTU, the dominant teacher union, played a critical role in keeping the fundamentals of outcomes-based education on the agenda. SADTU's main concerns centred on alignment of the revised curriculum with the National Qualifications Framework and the original conceptualization of outcomes-based education. SADTU saw any shift away from outcomes as moving towards 'the old style syllabus' reminiscent of the apartheid era (Chisholm, 2005, pp. 90–91) and insisted on what they saw as the democratic ideals contained in C2005.

On the other hand, Chisholm argued that apart from the retention of outcomes, in the NCS there was now almost no reference to the strong emphasis around C2005 on the integration of education and training. In seeking a curriculum solution *for schools* separate from the world of training, the review "broke the umbilical cord that had hitherto existed in all references to the apparently integrated worlds of 'education and training'" (Chisholm, 2005, p. 95). Chisholm argued that underpinning the report was the argument that education and curriculum could not be reduced to concerns around the economy and industrial training. "The dominant discourse in the curriculum was accordingly not an economic rationalist one but, despite the limitations even here, one of rights, social justice and equity" (ibid.). Her argument was that the review leant towards a human rights logic (which would be seen in cross cutting bodies in the revision process ensuring that human rights, inclusion and indigenous knowledge were attended to).

Finally, Fataar (2006) provided a fascinating 'networks' account of the process, arguing that while a 'labour policy network' was dominant in the construction of C2005, an 'academic policy network' held sway in the NCS review process. On closer inspection, however, there was only one academic on the review committee fitting Fataar's description. Interests and positions in the review then, seemed not to fall along occupational (or field) lines, but rather on intellectual and political positions taken in relation to the question of outcomes and the question of subject knowledge (review committee member, personal comment). So a third interest and position – an academically-oriented concern around the centrality of subject knowledge in curriculum making – underpinned the review process.

In sum, the tensions in the review of the NCS (and evident in the report) can be seen as pulling in three directions: towards social objectives, towards economic imperatives (outcomes) and towards knowledge. I elaborate on the knowledge argument that was made in the review below.

The argument for subject knowledge

Through the Curriculum 2005 Review Report academic arguments around knowledge and its organization in the curriculum entered official discourse. Based on a critique of curriculum integration developed by Muller (2000), the report argued that while the socio-political rationale for integration in C2005 was clear, the pedagogical purposes were not. Removing most of the content for subjects and replacing it with outcomes expressed as generic skills, meant that teachers were expected to select the appropriate content and design 'learning programmes' themselves. In a country where teachers had vastly different capacities to do this given recent history, this served to greatly disadvantage those whom the curriculum was most urgently needed to serve.

Preceding and around the time of the review of C2005, there was a strong critique of the radical constructivism which underpinned C2005. The critique argued that "by ignoring the boundary between school and everyday knowledges, radical modes increase the difficulties that working-class children will have in trying to acquire formal discourses" (Taylor & Vinjevold, 1999, p. 129). These arguments derived from a number of papers on the distinction between everyday knowledge and school knowledge from the mid-1990s (Dowling, 1995; Ensor, 1997; Davis, 1996; Muller & Taylor, 1995). Grounded in Bernstein's (1990) conceptualizing of boundaries, the arguments focused centrally on the unequal distribution of types of knowledge to different students, often on the basis of social class. Dowling's (1998) research in particular showed how the working-class and lower ability student "paradoxically, is left free to be a local individual but a failed mathematics learner" as Muller (2000, p. 68) put it.

Through the Review Report, these arguments around the distinction between everyday knowledge and school knowledge, and the implications of integration entered the formal domain in a way that was accessible to a broader readership, including those in government. Drawing implicitly on Bernstein's theory of knowledge, the Review Report presented a realist view of knowledge and of school knowledge as having an objective conceptual structure (especially in terms of the selection and sequence of knowledge). The major design flaw of C2005 was identified as curriculum subjects having no conceptual sequence and hence no learning progression path. "It is true that different learners approach learning in different ways, and might even learn concepts in a non-prescribed sequence. But this non-prescribed sequence must be an alternative route up the same conceptual ladder. There is no such thing as an alternative ladder, of optional and replaceable concepts" (South African Department of Education, 2000, p. 44).

The problem of outcomes

Despite the strength of the knowledge arguments made in the review report under pressure from the unions and with the support of the Minister (Chisholm, 2005), outcomes-based education (OBE) as the curriculum organizing principle was retained. This meant that certain pedagogical and curriculum features associated with outcomes would also be retained. These were identified by the Review Report itself, arguing approvingly that OBE had come to be associated with certain curriculum features that were current the world over:

- the active learner and ideas of uniqueness and difference
- the active teacher who, rather than following a prescriptive syllabus, makes decisions about what to teach and how to teach it
- the relative importance of activity and skills as a basis for knowing and knowledge
- the relative importance of induction over deduction (Department of Education, 2000, p. 47)

The Review Report had provided a clear and coherent critique around knowledge and the need for greater conceptual coherence and progression, knowledge stipulation and attention to disciplinary structure. However, in arguing for the continued emphasis on the four pedagogical aspects bulleted above, the pedagogical project of C2005 was retained along with the retention of outcomes. Thus, specific progressivist and constructivist elements were reasserted by association: local choice of content, a skills-based approach and an emphasis on experiential knowledge (by asserting inductive approaches). A fourth interest group then emerges: the progressives who wanted to retain the gains of the learner-centred philosophy established in C2005. The resulting review report then could be read in different ways and, unsurprisingly, the curriculum that resulted from this review process was a hybrid curriculum.

The recontextualizing rules: revising the NCS

Several papers have reflected in detail on the policy processes involved in the revision of C2005 that followed its review, to produce the National Curriculum Statement (Chisholm, 2003, 2005; Fataar, 2006), again analyzing the play of power among different interest groups in this revision process. Revision of the curriculum began in January 2001. According to Chisholm, the role of academics and university-based teacher educators in this process was fought for (following their marginalizing in the writing of C2005), and in the end they mostly played an equal role in writing the curriculum to the unions and department officials.

Outcomes in the process of revision proved problematic. The lack of knowledge stipulation in C2005 had to be addressed, whilst the retained outcomes focused on attitudes, dispositions and competencies, failing to direct adequate specification of subject content. The revision attempted to deal with this tension by introducing 'assessment standards' and various forms of content frameworks that would provide the subject knowledge teachers were required to teach, while still retaining outcomes. The result, however, was an uneven specification across learning areas, subjects and grades. Over time additional documentation would have to be produced to address these gaps.

The NCS revision process aimed to simplify the curriculum and many of the design features of C2005 were done away with, including phase organizers, programme organizers, performance indicators and range statements. The critical and developmental outcomes of C2005 were retained in exactly the same form. What changed was that new learning area outcomes (which were the same across the grades) were linked to grade-specific assessment standards. These became one of the central organizing devices for the new curriculum. Assessment standards, in the fashion of OBE, were 'designed down' from learning outcomes to produce statements of what a learner should be able to do. The learning outcomes were broad orienting topics, and generally precluded the statement of content. The idea was that content, as well as progression be written into the assessment standards. In certain subjects, knowledge frameworks were also provided, which listed topics to be covered.

In the NCS revision process the assessment policy that came with C2005 was retained. This was because the review could not resolve the issue of whether the school assessment system should reintroduce test and exam-based assessment, or whether there should continue to be more emphasis on other school-based, formative forms of assessment. In the absence of agreement, the C2005 policy prevailed. There was already substantial confusion around what continuous and summative assessment, and formal and informal assessment entailed and there were numerous attempts to clarify an assessment policy over time. What resulted in the NCS was largely a poorly understood assessment policy, with a de-emphasis on tests and examinations but an extremely onerous process for teachers in terms of its administrative (recording and reporting) requirements of projects, portfolios and other forms of continuous assessment.

The eight learning areas from C2005 were retained with slight changes to what they were called: Languages; Mathematics; Natural Sciences; Social Sciences; Arts and Culture; Life Orientation; Economic and Management Sciences; Technology.

The NCS curriculum was comprised of three documents for each learning area: The National Curriculum Statement document ('Statement' below), Assessment Guidelines and Learning Programme Guidelines (LPG). There were significant contradictions across the three documents, and some of the tensions discussed above are reflected in these documents with different information based on different curriculum principles and with different philosophical positions across the documents.

Over time districts and provinces also developed curriculum documentation in order to provide teachers with greater specificity around teaching. These included work schedules, lesson plans and assessment exemplars. As in C2005, the curriculum required that teachers structure and design their own 'programme of learning', taking into account a vast array of documentation, outcomes and principles. Thus, the model of the teacher again assumed an autonomous professional capable of constructing appropriate courses of leaning. How the documentation was constructed and what this meant in terms of the model of the teacher and learner is elaborated below in relation to mathematics and reading.

Having it both ways: the constitution of reading in the NCS

In considering the classification and framing of reading in the NCS, I analyzed four relevant documents: the NCS Statement for Languages (DOE, 2002a), the Learning Programme Guidelines (LPG) for Languages (DOE, 2003c), the Assessment Guidelines for Foundation Phase (2003b) and a document entitled *Teaching Reading in the Early Grades* DOE (2008). Significant differences were found between the documents in how the teaching of reading in the NCS was understood and stipulated. The differences and specifics of the documents are discussed below.

The NCS Statement – a 'balanced approach'

Literacy in the NCS Statement is organized into six learning outcomes with associated assessment standards. The learning outcomes are listening, speaking, reading and viewing, writing, thinking and reasoning, language structure and use. These outcomes are very different to the seven specific outcomes of C2005, replacing the emphasis on meaning, multiple texts and socio-affective competences with reference to specific and more conventional content/skill areas for literacy.

The NCS Statement claims a 'balanced approach' to reading instruction, which is broadly defined as incorporating phonemic awareness and phonics (understanding the relationships between sounds and their written representations), fluency, guided oral reading, vocabulary development and comprehension (elements associated with a whole language approach) (National Reading Panel, 2000). The learning outcome for reading emphasizes reading for meaning, "Reading and viewing: The learner will be able to read and view for information and enjoyment, and respond critically to the aesthetic, cultural and emotional values in texts" (DOE, 2002a, p. 6). However, both reading for meaning and phonics form part of the assessment standards for reading and viewing, seen in Table 8.1.

The sixteen Assessment Standards across Grades 1, 2 and 3 that are attached to the Reading and Viewing learning outcome are shown in Table 8.1, and focus on phonics and letter and word recognition as well as reading for meaning, information, enjoyment and personal response. For each Assessment Standard there is a set of bullet points that, with varying levels of detail, elaborate the assessment standard. So, further specific components of reading such as fluency, word recognition, print genres, vocabulary, development of comprehension and phonemic awareness are found in text accompanying these outcomes, although these are

Table 8.1 Assessment Standards for Reading and Viewing in the NCS

Grade 1	*Grade 2*	*Grade 3*
Uses visual clues to make meaning	Uses visual clues to make meaning	Uses visual clues to make meaning
Role-plays reading		
Makes meaning of written text	Makes meaning of written text	Makes meaning of written text
Recognizes letters and words and makes meaning of written text	Recognizes and makes meaning of letters and words in longer texts	Reads texts alone and uses a variety of strategies to make meaning
Develops phonic awareness	Develops phonic awareness	Consolidates phonic awareness
Reads for information and enjoyment	Reads for information and enjoyment	Reads for information and enjoyment

- Makes meaning of written text:
  - comments on a story or poem the learner has read and demonstrates understanding by answering questions on:
    - main idea,
    - key details such as main characters, sequence of events, setting, cultural values,
    - cause-effect relations,
    - conclusions (e.g. 'What does this story/fable teach us?').
    - whether or not the story was liked and why;
  - reads instructions related to real life interests and needs;
  - reads a wide variety of fairly complex texts such as fiction and non-fiction books, tables of contents and indexes

Figure 8.1 Example of assessment standard

often incomplete or fragmentary. For example, 'Makes meaning of written text' is extended as shown in Figure 8.1 (for Grade 3). Here some attention is drawn to narrative structure as well as reference to genre. However, these aspects are incomplete and not clearly signaled for teachers. No particular texts are named or prescribed, and no examples provided regarding text length and complexity are given, so that what a "fairly complex text" might be at this level is not made explicit. In other cases, information is fragmented. For example, only one reference is made to 'sight words' (Dolch words), in Grade 1: "recognises some high-frequency sight words such as 'the', 'a', 'to', 'my', 'your', 'like' and including own name and print in the environment" (DOE, 2002a, p. 36), and then are not referred to again. The list of phonics to be learnt is also incomplete.

Although the NCS Statement document refers to the importance of integration and themes as organizers for learning, this is not a focus. The NCS Statement defines reading as a specific area to be taught, it specifies the approach (balanced) and although sometimes incomplete and fragmented, provides detail on what this would entail. Evaluative criteria, in comparison to C2005 especially, can be characterized as quite strongly framed (F^{+}) and reading as a content area quite strongly classified (C^{+}). The further stipulations of the assessment standards do indicate progression across the grades and differences in the requirements across the grades stated. All specifications are limited, however, given the outcomes framework. Both learning outcomes and assessment standards and their elaboration remain statements of what learners can *do*, as opposed to *what* should be taught.

Learning programme guidelines (LPG): focus on 'whole language'

In contrast, in the LPGs (DOE, 2003c) the approach to reading is based on a whole language approach. Here phonics is not referenced, and the statements of purposes and approaches closely resemble that of C2005. The approaches privileged are new literacies and multiliteracies (citing the C2005 document) as well as a communicative approach to learning language, which according to the document meant that "Language is *acquired* through a gradual and mainly subconscious process; it cannot be quickly and consciously 'learned', i.e. through teaching grammar structures (however, this should not be understood to imply that grammar structures may [sic] or cannot be taught)" (DOE, 2003c, p. 49).

The emphasis on acquisition is reminiscent of the constructivist approach found in C2005, along with references to *all* learners entering school with high levels of language knowledge. There is a strong emphasis on language for social purposes and for empowerment and the strong ideological thrust of C2005 in the discussion of the selection of texts: "Reading will then become a means of developing language and a vehicle for experience of a wider world than that in which the learner finds himself or herself. Important social issues can be encountered and explored from early on in the language learning process" (DOE, 2003c, p. 49). A whole language approach is adopted in the description of how children learn to read without reference to specific skills entailed in its teaching.

There is also a strong emphasis on integration in the LPG – both between subject areas, and between school knowledge and everyday knowledge. This is reflected in the somewhat cryptic definition of a text:

> The word "texts' is used very broadly to cover a range of print and non-print media. This is meant to include experiences in the world at large that may

result in some kind of print or non-print text, for example the landscape or environment in which the learner finds him- or herself.

(DOE, 2003c, p. 42)

Reading in the LPG is more weakly classified, both with respect to what constitutes reading, as well as the relation between reading and everyday activities, and reading and other areas in the language curriculum. It is weakly framed in that evaluative criteria, sequence, selection and pace requirements for its teaching are not explicit

In summary, the LPG provides multiple definitions of approaches that don't articulate with the assessment standards of the NCS Statement. The latter provides a more balanced approach in relation to whole language and phonics. Given that the NCS documents contradict one another, the NCS is difficult to code in the way that C2005 was. On a number of the analytic dimensions it is a hybrid.

Assessment guidelines

The third document that forms part of the NCS is the Assessment Guidelines (DOE, 2003b), and these are developed per phase. The document provides a largely generic explanation of assessment planning, recording and reporting. It also explains in detail forms and purposes of assessment, what is meant by Outcomes-Based Assessment (OBA), principles of assessment and how to conduct integrated assessment. The implications of retaining outcomes are perhaps most starkly seen in this document in its production of generic statements of assessment. For example, the 'principles of OBA' are given as: design down; clarity of focus; high expectations; and expanded opportunities. And the characteristics of OBA are then described as

> OBA is integrated throughout the teaching and learning process; OBA is participative, democratic and transparent; OBA is continuous – it is ongoing, takes place over a period of time, and supports growth and development; OBA encourages reflection and regular feedback, with timely interventions.
>
> (DOE, 2003d, p. 11)

Nowhere in the document is the teacher given guidance on how to assess reading or writing, information on reading benchmarks and reading remediation.

The assessment guidelines present a complex approach to integration, with multiple tables and exemplars showing possible relationships between learning outcomes and assessment standards *across* different learning areas. The diagram seen in Figure 8.2 is an example from the document of how to plan integrated assessment, LO referring to learning outcomes and AS to assessment standards. In this example, four assessment standards in two learning outcomes in mathematics are matched to assessment standards and learning outcomes in Languages, Arts and Culture and Technology.

Content, levels of complexity and cognitive demand are unspecified. Integration becomes a process of matching discrete bits of learning (assessment

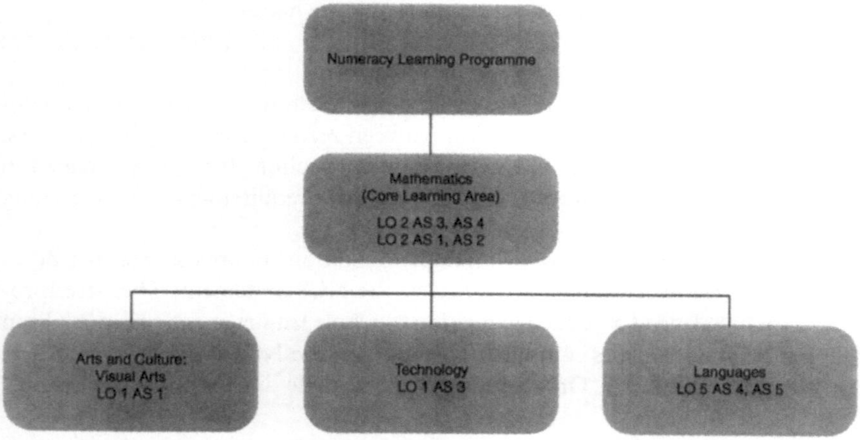

Figure 8.2 Extract on planning integrated assessment from the Assessment Guidelines (DOE, 2003b)

standards) or sometimes keywords from assessments standards from a range of learning areas, without an indication of the conceptual logic of how this knowledge fits together within the subject and what conceptually drives the integration.

Only at one point is a checklist provided of criteria for consideration in assessing reading, shown in Figure 8.3.

The 'checklist' is broadly defined. What the specific grade level expectations are regarding these different components of reading is not specified. Definitions of criteria are not given – for example, what constitutes a 'low rate of speed'? How many words per minute at what grade level? Also, because the checklist only focuses on omissions or incorrect practice, a host of criteria that may be used to judge competence are omitted, for example a learner's ability to use cueing systems.

In the Assessment document the generic specification of assessment practices constructs reading (and mathematics) as weakly classified and evaluative criteria weakly framed. The specificities of assessment in reading are not made explicit.

Teaching reading in the early grades

An additional document, *Teaching Reading in the Early Grades* (2008) was developed six years on from the implementation of the NCS to supplement the weaknesses of the NCS Statement in providing a guide to teachers teaching reading. The document contains explicit instruction, as well as rationales for teaching reading. It is written in plain, simple language and identifies and explains the widely accepted five components of learning to read: phonemic awareness; word recognition (sight words and phonics); comprehension; vocabulary; and fluency.

This checklist is for reading diagnostics, which can he adapted for Grades 1-3.

Learner Ziyaad, Grade 2

Key: 1 = Difficulty recognised   2 = Learner progressing   3 = No longer has difficulty

		1st check	2nd check	3rd check	Comments
1	Word by word reading	1	2	2	
2	Omissions	1	2	3	
3	Repetitions	1	1	2	
4	Reversals	1	2	3	
5	Substitutions	1	1	2	
6	Basic sight words does not recognise.	1	2	2	
7	Guesses at words	1	2	2	
8	Consonant sounds not known	1	2	2	
9	Vowel sounds not known	1	2	2	
10	Blends, digraphs or diphthongs not known	1	1	1	
11	Sight vocabulary is not up to grade level.	1	1	1	
12	Unable to use contextual clues.	1	1	2	
13	Low rate of speed	1	1	2	
14	Contractions not known.	1	2	2	

Figure 8.3 Example of an assessment checklist for reading (DOE, 2003d, p. 86)

Specific teaching strategies such as shared reading, 'word attack' (i.e. decoding) skills and independent reading are explained in detail, and detailed suggestions of how the strategies might be undertaken are made explicit.

The document also provides detail on the assessment of reading and how to determine reading levels, providing checklists for these levels. For example, Stage 3: The Early Reader includes the following aspects:

- Knows most letter sounds and names;
- Recognizes some common words
- Uses pictures to make meaning;
- Reads aloud when reading to self;
- Still reads word by word – not yet fluent (DOE, 2008, p. 9)

Five reading levels are clearly differentiated: emergent readers, early readers, developing readers, transitional readers, and independent readers. The kinds of reading competences and characteristics associated with each level are precisely specified.

For each level an assessment checklist is given, as in the example in Figure 8.4.

The document is characterized by stronger classification of reading and stronger framing of the evaluative criteria in relation to a balanced approach to reading, identifying particular components of teaching reading. However, the decoding elements again lack precision. In 'knows some letter sounds' would five sounds suffice? The stages are not pegged to particular grades: would Stage 3 be

Emergent level					
Learner's name:		Tests			
Pre-Reading Skills		Date	Date	Date	Date
Give the learner a text at the correct level. Observe him/her read a few pages. Ask: What is in this picture?	Holds the book the right way.				
	Knows where to start reading.				
	Reads from left to right.				
	Can say what is in the picture.				
Word recognition					
Point to some letters in the text. Ask: What is the name of this letter? What sound does it make? Is it a capital or a small letter?	Can say the *names* of some letters in the text, if the language allows this.				
	Can say the *sounds* of single letters in the text.				

Figure 8.4 Extract from reading assessment checklist from *Teaching Reading in the Early Grades* (2008)

appropriate for Grade R or Grade 1? Thus, although representing a significant shift from C2005, specification remains an issue in the NCS.

Summary

Clear contradictions across different documents are evident from the discussion above. Taken as a whole, the NCS still represents a significant shift from C2005. Reading is more strongly classified and framing of evaluative criteria in some instances more explicit. However, the focus on outcomes constrains specification and leads to generic statements of learning (especially in assessment). In addition, adherence to C2005 principles of integration and constructivist approaches mitigates a clearly bounded understanding of reading as a specific content/skill area that requires the transmission and acquisition of specific skills, techniques and sensibilities.

Content and outcomes in tension: number

The NCS documents relevant to the teaching and learning of number in the Foundation Phase suffer from the same contradictory messages across different documents as those for reading. The NCS Statement document (DOE, 2002b) is a notable departure from C2005. Starting with the definition, the notion from C2005 that mathematics is "the construction of knowledge that deals with qualitative relationships of space and time" is replaced with the assertion that mathematics consists of specialized knowledge and practices: "Mathematics uses its own specialised language that involves symbols and notations for describing numerical, geometric and graphical relationships. Mathematical ideas and concepts build on one another to create a coherent structure" (DOE, 2002b, p. 4). The definition also draws attention to the 'vertical integration' or progression emphasized in the review report.

Unlike in C2005, where number concept development, counting and calculating were dispersed across the specific outcomes, in the NCS statement they are clustered into two learning outcomes, specified as follows:

> Learning Outcome 1: Number, operations and relationships: The learner will be able to recognize, describe and represent numbers and their relationships and to count, estimate, calculate and check with competence and confidence in solving problems.
>
> Learning Outcome 2: Patterns Functions and algebra: The learner will be able to recognize, describe and represent patterns and relationships, as well as to solve problems using algebraic language and skills (DOE, 2002b, p. 6)

The curriculum specifies a number range for the Foundation Phase, that "by the end of Grade 3 includes whole numbers to at least 1 000, and unitary and non-unitary common fractions" (DOE, 2003d, p. 8). The assessment standards stipulate goals to be achieved by the end of each grade, and in this way grade-level pacing is made explicit, though not within-grade pacing. Conceptual progression is made visible, with increases in number ranges and increasingly complex calculation strategies demanded. Everyday knowledge is significantly backgrounded by comparison with C2005, and in the learning outcomes and assessment standards almost all reference to everyday knowledge has been excised thus strengthening classification of knowledge in the curriculum.

Despite the significant shift in the NCS Statement document, as in reading, the LPG takes the NCS right back to C2005. Directly referencing the C2005 numeracy document of 1997, it states that the purpose of numeracy, amongst other things, is to:

- use the learner's own innate, intuitive and experientially acquired knowledge and ability in number and space as a springboard into continued learning,
- ensure the enjoyment of the experiences provided,
- engender confidence in the young learner's own mathematical abilities,
- encourage learners to develop their own approaches to working with number,
- build on the learner's experience of space, time and motion in their everyday lives in order to assist in structuring and interpreting it through concrete and diagrammatic representation, estimation and measurement (DOE, 2003d, p. 53)

In this way the constructivist underpinnings of C2005 are reasserted, and the emphasis on the relation between school and everyday knowledge resurrected.

Integration with other subjects and with learners' everyday cultural worlds is also emphasized in statements like:

> People can use mathematical tools to describe and analyse natural occurrences such as patterns and shapes in plants, rock formations, the weather and the movements of the planets. They can also use these tools to create and construct useful and beautiful cultural artefacts from homemade beadwork to that produced in factories, and to describe and predict social occurrences such as population growth, the spread of infections and the allocation of resources to needy areas.
>
> (ibid., p. 57)

The LPG also places a strong emphasis on the critical and developmental outcomes. The planning process set out in this document resembles that of C2005 – an extremely complex process that leaves much of the decision-making to teachers, and where integration of other learning areas and choice of context are left to teachers. The complexity of planning is shown in Figure 8.5.

In this diagram content and context are left for the teacher to decide: "choose knowledge focuses that are age and grade appropriate" (DOE, 2003d, p. 37). In

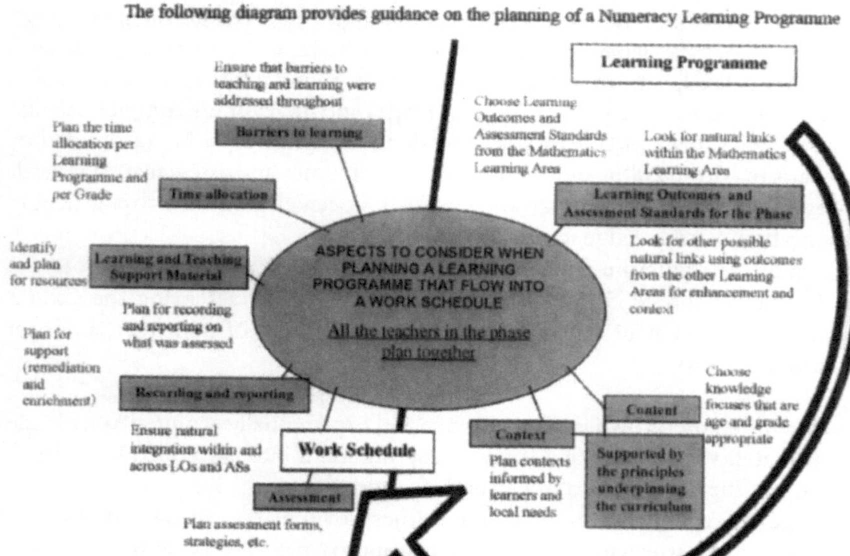

Figure 8.5 Planning process for numeracy, Learning Programme Guidelines (DOE, 2003d, p. 53)

other words, content is separate from learning outcomes and assessment standards, not contained within these. In all likelihood this approach to planning is a hangover from the 'design down' approach of the NQF. In this logic content, context (i.e. student's interests/experience), methods and assessment must be selected in order to achieve the outcome. Allais (2012) explains the curriculum implication: "The outcome, not the content, would need to be stipulated. Learning programmes should not be designed based on the internal requirements or logic of a knowledge area; instead, knowledge areas should be selected on the basis that they can lead to the competence in question" (p. 25).

The Assessment Guidelines suffer from the genericism indicated in the discussion of reading above. The Guidelines emphasise integration once again, and provide little specificity regarding the evaluative criteria relevant to particular topic areas of mathematics. For example, in discussing assessment of "classifying and sorting 2D shapes from 3D objects", the text indicates simply that teachers should "observe whether learners can sort 2D shapes from 3D objects" (DOE, 2003a, p. 29). The underlying conceptual competences and content detail are not spelt out, neither are common errors or misconceptions. In other words, evaluative criteria that would inform assessment in this document are weakly framed, focusing on procedural mechanisms for ensuring integration in assessment tasks and recording marks.

The model of the learner

The NCS places emphasis on both what the learner needs to learn (strongly stated in terms of skills) and an emphasis on the full potential of each learner as a citizen of a democratic South Africa, "a lifelong learner who is confident and independent, literate, numerate and multi-skilled, compassionate, with a respect for the environment and the ability to participate in society as a critical and active citizen" (DOE, 2003e, p. 8). The 'developmental outcomes' that frame the curriculum, however, are more vocationally-oriented, listed below:

- Reflect on and explore a variety of strategies to learn more effectively.
- Participate as responsible citizens in the life of local, national and global communities.
- Be culturally and aesthetically sensitive across a range of social contexts.
- Explore education and career opportunities.
- Develop entrepreneurial opportunities (DOE, 2003d, p. 11)

The time of the construction of the NCS was defined by a realization of the contradictions between the hopes of the new democracy and the realities of persistent inequality, a lack of social transformation and poor economic development. These two sides are reflected in the model of the learner projected in the curriculum – the critical, democratic citizen as well as the subject that needs to take responsibility for their own economic well-being as articulated in the developmental outcomes above.

The model of the teacher

The 'envisaged teacher' of the curriculum is also explicitly stated in the curriculum document, as one who has a broad range of roles:

> mediators of learning, interpreters and designers of Learning Programmes and materials, leaders, administrators and managers, scholars, researchers and lifelong learners, community members, citizens and pastors, assessors and learning area/phase specialists.
>
> (2003e, p. 9)

These are drawn from the teacher education policy that was developed for C2005 and show the broad function that was envisaged for schooling at that time. The teacher's role in social transformation is once again emphasized in the NCS, and the curriculum "envisions teachers who are qualified, competent, dedicated and caring" (ibid.). The retention of planning procedures from C2005, and the demand for integration between subjects as well as a curriculum that was still unspecified, envisages a teacher who is well-versed in their subject, able to make conceptual connections between subjects and appropriately select and design learning and assessment opportunities for learners.

Framing of the social relation

Less is explicitly made of the social relation between learners and teachers in the NCS than in C2005; however, a learner-centred approach is maintained and reasserted: "The outcomes and assessment standards emphasise participatory, learner-centred and activity-based education. They leave considerable room for creativity and innovation on the part of teachers in interpreting what and how to teach" (DOE, 2003e, p. 12). Also, in some of the documentation, especially the learning programme guidelines, a constructivist approach, which affirms and acknowledges the existing knowledge and experience of the learner, is emphasized. Finally, integration as a curriculum principle features prominently across the documents, asserting that the NCS will "emphasise the principle of integrated learning and the achievement of an optimal relationship between integration across learning areas and conceptual progression from grade to grade" (ibid.).

The coding of the NCS is shown in Table 8.2, reflecting the hybrid nature of the curriculum policy.

Conclusion: a contradictory curriculum

Although gains were made in the NCS from C2005 in relation to greater knowledge specification, one of the restrictions in the reform was the retention of outcomes. The curriculum organizing feature of designing down placed limits on the specification of content as well as the articulation of progression. Multiple, contradictory documents produced conflicting statements around the nature of

Table 8.2 Summary of the structuring of pedagogic discourse in the curriculum

Instructional	External framing curricular knowledge	$F^{c+/-}$	Contradictory across documents, stronger in the Statements, but generally weak framing of selection, sequence, pace and evaluative criteria in the LPGs.
	Classification between subject and other subjects and everyday knowledge	$C^{+/-}$	Less integration in the Statements – there is a focus on meaning ***and*** phonics in reading and clear mathematical statements around counting and calculation. But strong emphasis on integration in Learning Programme guidelines and Assessment docs and strong commitment to integration in overview document.
	Classification between areas/ topics within subject	$C^{+/-}$	Stronger. Reading and number are clearly specified areas of learning. But integration still key principle.
Regulative	External framing of social relation (hierarchical rules)	F^{c+}	Retains commitment to specification of child-centred, constructivist pedagogy in some of the documentation. Not as strongly specified as C2005.
	Model of the teacher		Competent in a balanced approach to reading instruction and competent in mathematics instruction and activity-based learning and learner-centred methods across both. Teacher as critical agent of social transformation
	Model of the learner		In Statement not yet competent reader and yet to master the rudiments of mathematics. In LPG existent knowledge is emphasized.

knowledge and learning in the curriculum. This partly stemmed from the fact that government wished to underplay the revision of the first post-apartheid curriculum so soon after its implementation. Calling it a 'streamlining' of C2005, and emphasizing that it was ***not*** a new curriculum opened up the space for provincial and national Department of Education officials to blend C2005 into the NCS (DBE, 2009, p. 14).

While the NCS Statements represented a break with C2005, the LPGs asserted continuity with C2005 and its emphasis on pedagogical constructivism and integration. The assessment guidelines suffered from the genericism arising out of an outcomes-based framework, providing little subject-content based guidance to teachers on what and how to assess. In the NCS there were three obstacles to establishing a subject knowledge-based curriculum: 1. the insistent genericism of the outcomes-based framework, especially its assessment procedures, 2. the backgrounding of formal knowledge in privileging pedagogical constructivism, and 3. curriculum integration as a curriculum principle underpinning both 1. and 2.

The compromise that was the NCS may also be explained by the complexity of the recontextualizing field at the time alluded to above. On the one hand, within the ORF, there was a reforming impetus from Minister Asmal and other pro-change bureaucrats. However, there were also bureaucrats (including the Minister) who wanted to retain outcomes, some for political reasons and some because they were heavily invested in C2005 either ideologically or materially. Within the PRF, there was a contest between three groupings: the knowledge realists who wanted priority given to the notion of curriculum as an organization of subject knowledge; the pedagogic constructivists or progressives, who privileged the social and political purposes of curriculum and knowledge construction; and the unions who were committed to OBE. Knowledge realists made some gains in the Statements, but the C2005-aligned bureaucrats produced the LPGs that reasserted C2005 principles, of integration, constructivism and learner-centred pedagogies.

The complex and hybrid nature of the NCS was partly about the difficulty of reviewing C2005 so soon after its heralding as the first curriculum of the democratic nation. But it also reflected the tensions of the review process, where different interests inscribed in the report allowed for different readings in the actual revision of the curriculum. The possibilities of the resulting curriculum influencing practice would depend on which documents were read and how they were read. But they were more likely to sow further confusion for teachers in how to proceed in planning, teaching and assessing than provide robust guidance for teaching subjects.

References

Allais, S. (2012). Claims vs. practicalities: Lessons about using learning outcomes. *Journal of Education and Work, 25*(3), 331–354.

Baatjes, I., & Mathe, K. (2004). Adult basic education and social change in South Africa (1994–2003). In L. Chisholm (Ed.), *Changing Class* (pp. 393–420). Pretoria: HSRC.

Bernstein, B. (1990). *Class, codes and control: The structuring of pedagogic discourse*, vol. 4: The structuring of pedagogic discourse. London: Routledge.

Chisholm, L. (2003). The state of curriculum reform in South Africa: The issue of Curriculum 2005. In J. Daniel, A. Habib & R. Southall (Eds.), *State of the Nation: South Africa 2003-2004* (268–289. Cape Town: HSRC Press.

Chisholm, L. (2005). The politics of curriculum review and revision in South Africa in regional context. *Compare: A Journal of Comparative and International Education, 35*(1), 79–100.

Davis, Z. (1996). The problem-centred approach and the production of the vanishing pedagogue. Paper presented at *Kenton-at-Wilgespruit Conference*, Johannesburg.

Department of Basic Education. (2009). Report of the task team for the review of the implementation of the national curriculum statement. Pretoria: South African Department of Basic Education.

Department of Education. (2000). A South African curriculum for the twenty-first century: Report of the review committee on Curriculum 2005. Pretoria: South African Department of Education.

Department of Education. (2002a). Revised national curriculum statement grades R-9 (schools): Languages. English – home language. Pretoria: Department of Education.

Department of Education. (2002b). Revised national curriculum statement grades R-9 (schools): Mathematics. Pretoria: Department of Education.

Department of Education. (2003a). National curriculum statement general education and training: Assessment guidelines for foundation phase grades R-3. Pretoria: Department of Education.

Department of Education. (2003b). National curriculum statement general education and training: Assessment guidelines for foundation phase grades R-3. Pretoria: Department of Education.

Department of Education. (2003c). Revised national curriculum statement grades R-9 (schools): Teacher's guide for the development of learning programmes: Languages. Pretoria: Department of Education.

Department of Education. (2003d). Revised national curriculum statement grades R-9 (schools): Teacher's guide for the development of learning programmes: Mathematics. Pretoria: Department of Education.

Department of Education. (2003e). *Revised national curriculum statement grades R-9 (schools): Overview*. Pretoria: Department of Education.

Department of Education. (2008). *Teaching reading in the early grades*. Pretoria: Department of Education.

Dowling, P. (1995). Discipline and mathematise: The myth of relevance in education. *Perspectives in Education*, *16*(2), 209–226.

Dowling, P. (1998). The sociology of mathematics education: Mathematical myths/pedagogic texts. London: Falmer.

Ensor, P. (1997). School mathematics, everyday life and the NQF: A case of non-equivalence? *Pythagorus*, *41*, 36–44.

Fataar, A. (2006). Policy networks in recalibrated political terrain: The case of school curriculum policy and politics in South Africa. *Journal of Education Policy*, *21*(6), 641–659.

Jansen, J. (1999). The school curriculum since apartheid: Intersections of politics and policy in the South African transition. *Journal of Curriculum Studies*, *31*(1), 57–67.

Jansen, J. (2001). Explaining non-change in education reform after apartheid: Political symbolism and the problem of policy implementation. In Y. Sayed & J. Jansen (Eds.), *Implementing Education Policies: The South African Experience* (pp. 271–292). University of Cape Town Press: Cape Town.

Marais, H. (2001). South Africa: Limits to change: The political economy of transition. New York: Palgrave Macmillan.

Muller, J. (2000). *Reclaiming knowledge*. London: RoutledgeFalmer.

Muller, J., & Taylor, N. (1995). Schooling and everyday life: Knowledges sacred and profane. *Social Epistemology*, *9*(3), 257–275.

National Reading Panel, (National Institute of Child Health & Human Development, (2000). Report of the national reading panel: Teaching children to read: An evidence-based assessment of the scientific research literature on reading and its implications for reading instruction: Reports of the subgroups. Washington DC: National Institute of Child Health and Human Development, National Institutes of Health.

Taylor, N., & Vinjevold, P. (1999). Getting learning right: Report of the president's educational initiative research project. Johannesburg: The Joint Education Trust.

9 The communalized classroom

Pedagogy under the National Curriculum Statement

Introduction

The analysis in Chapter 8 suggested that the National Curriculum Statement (NCS) reform could potentially have steered classroom practice in the direction of stronger classification and framing of knowledge on the one hand, or the reproduction of the classifications and frames of C2005 on the other. The discussion there showed how through contradictory documents and the billing of the NCS as a 'streamlining' of C2005 significant and clear differences between the NCS and C2005 were not uniformly achieved or broadly understood. Thus, the enduring 'scriptural' nature of OBE (Morrow, 2001), entwining groupwork, learner-centredness and integration, persisted in framing the practices in classrooms analyzed in this chapter.

Although investigating the same dimensions of pedagogy as Chapter 7, the present chapter offers a more theoretically refined analysis of pedagogy. In Chapter 7, classification and framing were used heuristically to explore and characterize pedagogy. Here the concepts are elaborated in relation to an external language of description, providing a more precise 'anatomising of pedagogy' (Fitz et al., 2006). A full description of the analytical methodology is provided in Appendix B. I focus in this chapter on the findings.

The study on which this chapter is based compared classrooms located in the same township described in Chapter 7 with a set of middle class, affluent suburban schools. While pedagogy and the classroom in accounts of social class reproduction are often treated as a black box, these two contrasting contexts were used to focus on the specific question of how social class difference is reproduced *through pedagogy* (Hoadley, 2005, 2007, 2008). In the broader study I argued that the kinds of pedagogy found in working-class contexts failed to provide opportunities for learners to access the specialized skills and knowledge of mathematics and language.

In this chapter I provide an account only of the data drawn from the working-class context. The focus here is on continuities and shifts from C2005, exploring the instructional and regulative features of four classrooms. The interest, following the review of C2005 and implementation of the NCS, is whether and how students gain access to formal school knowledge. Everyday knowledge, emphasized in the progressive and learner-centred agenda, had persistently framed the way to empower learners and facilitate their access to school knowledge. The analysis finds that a 'communalizing pedagogy' persisted in classrooms under the NCS curriculum regime, and students were exposed to everyday knowledge at the expense of the specialized knowledge of subjects.

Looking in classrooms five years on

The study reported on in this chapter was conducted five years on from the classroom study of Chapter 7. Classroom data was collected from two schools in Khayelitsha. I observed and collected video data from four Grade 3 classrooms. I refer to the teachers of these classrooms in this chapter as Teachers E, F, G and H. These teachers had been trained in the NCS and had been implementing it in their classrooms for about two years. The children in their classes came from very poor homes, where parents were either in unskilled jobs or were unemployed. The surrounding areas of the schools consisted of a combination of shacks and formal housing. The schools were adequately resourced, although the grounds like the surrounding area were dusty, exposed and littered. The teachers lived close to the schools and had themselves attended similar schools to those in which they now taught. The teachers had all completed their schooling before 1985 under bantu education and they had all subsequently trained at Good Hope College, a teacher training institute in Khayelitsha in Cape Town, originally established for the training of black teachers.

From the data, mathematics and language lessons were extracted, and each of these lessons was broken down into tasks – the unit of analysis for considering the pedagogy in the classrooms. A task is defined as an activity with a single goal or theme that the learner is required to do. In structuring the data for analysis, 20 tasks from 11 lessons in mathematics, and 25 tasks from 20 lessons in language were identified across the four teachers. The data was analyzed using the concepts of classification and framing (Bernstein, 1996), strategies and domains (Dowling, 1998) and organizational form (Pedro, 1981), elaborated in Chapter 5 and Appendix B.

How a tree lives and grows: pedagogic forms in the classrooms

I present a number of extracts from the data in discussing the findings of the analysis. The first extract was taken from Teacher G's class, where she gave a mathematics lesson on 'rounding off'. In other literacy and life skills lessons during the course of that day, the theme of trees had predominated. In the extract below we see the theme directing the lesson in mathematics as well. Two tasks were identified in this extract. The first was the introduction of a word-problem and discussion of trees. The second was an explication of the concept of rounding off.

Extract 1: hey! That's a lot of trees

Teacher G has selected a word-problem for a numeracy lesson on the basis of a predetermined theme – trees. The first part of the lesson consists of the chanting of the wording of the word-problem, exemplified in the following:

Teacher: Listen, on page 63, how a tree lives and grows. It says that . . . what does it say people? How a tree lives and grows. What does it say?

Learners: How a tree lives and grows.

Teacher: What does it say?

Learners: How a tree lives and grows.

Teacher: What does it say?

Learners: How a tree lives and grows.

Teacher: Umthi uphula njani ukhube nyani. Say it in Xhosa.

Learners: Umthi uphula njani ukhube nyani.

Teacher: Say it again in English, how a tree lives and grows.

Learners: How a tree lives and grows.

Teacher: There are those who are not talking. I don't hear you. How a tree lives and grows.

Learners: How a tree lives and grows.

Teacher: I don't hear some [of you], how a tree lives and grows

Learners: How a tree lives and grows.

Teacher: I don't hear you Thondo. How a tree lives and grows.

And so on. In a similar way the teacher and learners work their way through the word-problem:

'Pulani has about 289 trees on her farm. Write the number of trees to the nearest hundred'. Later in the lesson the teacher introduces the question. It would appear she 'stumbles' on the question, not having anticipated it:

Teacher: That's right. You must listen to others before you say it. Hey! That's a lot of trees. Two eighty-nine is a lot of trees. It's like a whole day! [The teacher draws two trees on the board.] Do they all look the same?

Learners: No.

Teacher: Yes it's different kinds of trees. There are trees shaped like an umbrella, like a circle. And what else did we say trees are shaped like?

Learner: Like a circle.

Teacher: The writer says that Pulani has all those kinds of trees. They fill her farm. Now he says, 'Write the numbers of trees to the nearest hundred'. That's the question.

The teacher writes a number – 79 – on the board for learners to calculate 'the nearest hundred'. When learners are unable to solve the example, the teacher presents them with a rule, which the learners take up in a chant:

Teacher: I say to you if the number is over 50 then it's a 100, if it's over 100 then it's 200, if it's over 300

. . .

Learners: [chant] Then it's 400, if it's over 400 then it's 500.

The teacher writes 6 numbers on the board that the learners call out from the textbook and she asks them to write the numbers 'to the nearest hundred'. It becomes clear that the learners are unclear how to proceed.

Teacher: You haven't started writing. I want the nearest hundred. Write. I said to you if it is over 50 the nearest hundred, it goes to hundred. If it is below 50 it doesn't go to a 100. If it is above 150 something it goes to 200. If it is below 150 something then it doesn't go. Do you understand? Same as if it's above 200 and something. If it is 250 something and above it goes to 300, if it doesn't go above 250 something, then it doesn't go to 300. It remains 200, ne? Do you understand? We are going to explain it again tomorrow.

Finally, the bell rings and the lesson is terminated. Learners do not return to this exercise later, or on the following day. The learners have not successfully completed the problems, but have copied out the word-problem and the numbers from the board.

In this lesson the decision around what to teach was determined by the theme – trees. The teacher, by her own account, paged through the textbook and recognized the theme in the textbook iconically, and proceeded to work through the text with the learners. Twenty-four minutes of the 35-minute lesson were spent working through the wording of the problem, chanting phrases from the problem, and discussing trees. The focus of the lesson became trees, and the theme was foregrounded in the extensive repetition and chanting of the word-problem and in a short discussion of trees. The semantic resources for the lesson thus lay in everyday knowledge, or the theme, rather than mathematical knowledge. The focus was particularly clear as the teacher began to talk about trees, and then moved beyond the given text, saying, 'The writer says that Pulani has all those kinds of trees. They fill her farm'. Also beyond the text, and the mathematical purpose, were the teacher's further descriptions of the shapes of trees (which were not represented in the textbook). In this way, conceptual understanding was firmly subordinated to the theme. The boundary between school knowledge and everyday knowledge was weak, and the lesson was coded as C^{--} for the classification of discourses. The pedagogic form was akin to the 'free association' pedagogy described in Chapter 7.

Teacher G did not use the terminology 'rounding off' at all in the lesson, but used the expression of the word-problem, 'to the nearest hundred'. When she did broach the concept of rounding off it was obvious that she did not have a grasp of the necessary mathematical knowledge to explain it. When she did attempt to present the learners with a rule, it was erroneous: 'I say to you if the number is over 50 then it's 100, if it's over 100 then it's 200, if it's over 300 . . .'. She transmitted no concept of rounding up and rounding down.

Framing relations with respect to the teacher-student relation were strong (F^{++}); the teacher gave direct orders to the learners in controlling the classroom activity: 'You haven't started writing. I want the nearest hundred. Write'. The teacher also controlled what knowledge was selected, its sequence, and the pace of the lesson (F^{++}). With respect to the evaluative rules, however, the framing was characterized as F^0 in the first task relating to the discussion of trees (where no mathematical knowledge is transmitted) and extremely weak in the second task (F^{--}) where the criteria and requirements for the task were unclear.

The first task, the chanting of the word-problem and a discussion of trees, was coded as localizing non-mathematical. There was no reference to mathematical knowledge, and the task required no specialized activity on the part of the learners (see Appendix B for details of this coding scheme). The second task, the explication of a rule for rounding off, was coded as specializing-procedural, despite the fact that the procedure was erroneous. The learners were given a 'mathematical' procedure for the completion of the task, even though they were unlikely to realize the appropriate production as a result.

Considering evaluative criteria and F^0

Below I give another example of a mathematics lesson and the weak framing of evaluative criteria in the context of localizing strategies. In this case the question of the presence of pedagogy, raised in Chapters 2 and 7 in relation to 'zero pedagogy' is discussed. Bernstein's suggestion that instructional discourse can be suspended such that the discourse is wholly regulative (Bernstein, 1990, p. 92) as addressed in Chapter 5 is also considered.

Extract 2: write! Even though you don't know

Teacher numbers a set of leaves she has drawn on the board and the learners shout out the numbers as she writes them. The teacher then moves directly onto the next section in the book on trees.

Teacher: He says here there are parts of the tree, that's what I like, but then he says we don't tell colours as they are. So here are the parts of the tree. He says write them in their order from the biggest to the smallest. Read these as I write them on the board.

The teacher writes on the board: tree, leaf, branch, bush, and addresses the learners.

Teacher: Which are found at the bottom of a tree?

Learner: Roots are found at the bottom of the tree.

Teacher: No no. Don't tell me things you haven't seen. I'm not asking for what you've thought about,

I'm asking for what you've seen. Okay, from the tree, bush, leaf and branch, which one do you get from the bottom of the tree? Things that you get at the bottom. Bottom, bottom.'

The teacher underlines 'bottom' on the board. Another learner says roots. After a while the teacher looks back at the textbook and realises that she has made a mistake, reading 'tree, bush, branches, leaf', instead of 'stem, roots, branches, leaves'. She moves directly on to the next question, which requires writing from biggest to smallest, tree, branch, leaf, bush. Learners respond and the teacher writes each word on the board. She then returns to the question of what is found at the bottom of the tree. As she writes, learners repeat the words over and over again. The following exchange occurs as she moves onto the next section in the book:

Learners: leaves, leaves, leaves, leaves, leaves, leaves leaves, leaves, leaves leaves, leaves, leaves leaves, leaves, leaves

Teacher: Hey stop. The reason why we are repeating this is because you do your own thing when I turn my back on you. Now the writer says the same words rhyme at the end. Now we've done a tree. Haven't we done a tree?

Learners: Yes Miss. Yes we've done it.

Teacher: Now we know how a tree is formed. Now the writer says there are certain words that rhyme at the end. This is what I like. And he also says write those that rhyme in the box. [Teacher looks at the book for a while] Ja, here's work. Close your books. I'll give you work on the board. Don't talk Grade 3. Don't talk, don't talk. Sleep on your desks. Lower your heads. The teacher writes 6 words on the board: tree, fruits, home, flowers, smoke, bushes, roots.

Teacher: Listen, listen. I did not say shout on the top of the roof. Now write the rhyming words.

He [the author of the textbook] says some words are rhyming at the end so he wants you to write those that rhyme at the end. Here's the correct date, the thirty-first. Let's write. Let's work. No talking. I want rhyming words. I want rhyming words. I want rhyming words.

Later the teacher bangs on her table with a ruler and shouts at the learners to be quiet.

Teacher: Write! Write! Even though you don't know.

The teacher sits at her desk for the remaining 23 minutes of the lesson. At no point does she see what learners are writing. The bell rings for break and learners close their books and go out.

In terms of regulative discourse, the hierarchical rules in this lesson were coded F^{++}. The control relation was generally about constraint and is based on formal teacher/pupil hierarchy, rather than an explication of rules or principles for the commands. In this imperative form (F^{++}) the acquirer is given no options in responding to the control of the teacher, apart from an explicit challenge to authority. Selection and sequence in this instance were both be coded F^{++}. Learners were not given opportunities to alter the selection and the sequence of the knowledge, even where, at one point ("roots are found at the bottom of the tree") their interjections potentially were a corrective to the teacher's misreading of the text.[1] Although it was clear that the pace of the lesson is extremely slow, it was the teacher who controlled the pacing. Learners did not intervene when they had completed work well ahead of time. Pacing was therefore also coded F^{++}.

A problem arose, however, in the coding of the evaluative criteria. The required performance of learners ultimately was to copy down words that rhymed, but no concept of rhyming was transmitted, and its recognition was potentially opaque to the learners. Because the evaluative criteria had not been transmitted, the teacher could only elicit the legitimate text from the learners on the basis of assertion: 'Write, write, even though you don't know.' And that legitimate text appeared devoid of instructional content. The learners were required to write; what they wrote appeared arbitrary.

Similarly, an earlier exchange in the same lesson unfolds as:

Teacher: Now we've done a tree. Haven't we done a tree?
Learners: Yes Miss. Yes we've done it.
Teacher: Now we know how a tree is formed.

Again, the legitimate text is extracted on the basis of assertion. The learners had merely named parts of a tree up to this point; they had not addressed 'how a tree is formed'. The framing of the evaluative criteria was difficult to categorize as either weak or strong. Thus, the category F^0 in the coding scheme was developed in order to capture such instances of transmission, which appear devoid of evaluative criteria relating to the instructional discourse, or where these are obscured by regulative criteria. There was not an absence of control. The teacher asserted control here, but there was no evidence of the teachers' specialized voice. Without the evaluative criteria – that which specifies the legitimate text – students were unable to recognize what was required, and the teacher did not evaluate their productions according to instructional criteria. Consequently, framing of the evaluative criteria was coded F^0. All was about comportment, form or behaviour.[2]

The evaluative criteria could also not be coded as extremely weak (F^-), as this would imply that it was the learners who had 'apparent' control over defining the legitimate text. The strong framing over the hierarchical rules and rules of selection mitigated this. It must be emphasized that F^0 does not lie on the continuum (i.e. it is not extremely weak framing), but rather is a rupture. F^0 represents an inability to observe the code. It may also point to a breakdown in pedagogic discourse, or the absence of (a particular dimension of) pedagogy.

This suggests that a learner can be positioned within the school (that is, get sorted into the social relation) but have no access to the means to participate in knowledge exchange (evaluative criteria). The learner is merely sorted. Stuck.

F^0 (elaborated in Hoadley, 2006) was what sparked the debate I referred to in Chapter 2 around zero pedagogy. There I explain how Hugo and Wedekind (2013) argue that absence of one dimension of the pedagogy (knowledge transaction or instructional discourse) translates to the absence of pedagogy or 'zero pedagogy'. I would argue, however, that a form of pedagogy subsists, and that regulative criteria are still being transmitted. Learners are acquiring certain comportments, behaviours and routines and they are also acquiring a particular pedagogic identity (an understanding of what it means to be a student). Hugo and Wedekind's (2013) argument is important in drawing attention to the 'ordering principle' of pedagogy (which they argue should be specialized knowledge). However, as I argued in Chapter 2, and return to later, it is important to keep instructional and regulative features visible and in tension to describe the pedagogic form and to consider how it may be shifted. There is not nothing going on here, even though specialized knowledge is not evidently ordering the pedagogy.

Classification and framing

All lessons were coded and assigned values for classification and framing. What emerged were consistencies across the classrooms with respect to classification and framing of pedagogic practice. The results from the analysis of classification and framing in the 20 lessons for mathematics and 25 lessons for language are shown in Table 9.1. The results are aggregated across teachers, where differences were minor.

Table 9.1 Summary of the structuring of pedagogic discourse across classrooms

Instructional	Selection	F^{++}	Strong the teacher controls what is taught
	Sequence	F^{++}	Strong the teacher controls the order of teaching
	Pace	F^{+-}	Strong the teacher controls the rate of transmission and acquisition
	Evaluation	F^{-}	Weak. Knowledge criteria not specified, the teacher does not exert control over defining appropriate and inappropriate productions.
	Classification between subject and other subjects and everyday knowledge	C^{-}	Weak. Everyday as a resource for mathematics and for literacy. Theme/experiential knowledge dominates.
	Classification between areas/topics within subject	C^{-}	Weak. Reading, number not demarcated as specialized areas, practices. Many of the activities not strictly identifiable in relation to a conventional subject.
Regulative	Framing of social relation (hierarchical rules)	F^{+}	Strong framing, hierarchical relation between teacher and students

Across the classrooms there was strong control over sequence and selection. The framing over pacing in the classrooms was very strong, where learners were not given control over the rate of acquisition but worked (or waited) according to times stipulated by the teacher. The evaluative rules were generally unclear and implicit. This very weak framing over the evaluative rules (F^{--}) meant that students often did not know how to proceed with a task, and the conceptual content of exposition was implicit or absent. The hierarchical rules, that describe the social relations of the students and teachers, were strongly framed, the authority and control of the teacher was overt; non-negotiable rules and assertions dominated (F^{+}), although threats and acts of physical punishment were not in evidence as before.

There was weak classification of literacy and mathematical knowledge from everyday knowledge. Theme-driven pedagogy often obscured the knowledge object of lessons. Distinctions between content areas – such as phonics, reading and writing in literacy – were not observable. The pedagogy was predominantly oral with very little written text. Reading activities across the classrooms consisted mainly of the teacher reading to the class, or the class reading out a passage together. Graded or other readers were not seen or used in any of the classes, and only on one occasion did learners read individually, aloud or to themselves. There were also very few writing activities and no extended writing.

Strategies – localizing and specializing

Two further extracts are given below to show the operation of specializing-principling and localizing-mathematical strategies (following Dowling, 1998), and to draw out the difference in these strategies.

An example of a localizing-mathematical strategy is shown below, taken from Teacher H's class; learners were required to make equal groups of trees on a worksheet from the numbers 16, 25, and 20. The explanation given to learners is shown in extract 4 below.

Extract 4: let's count the trees

The teacher draws three rows of four trees on the board. The following exchange takes place:

Teacher: Here are rows 1, 2, 3. Let's count the trees.
Teacher points as learners count.
Learners: 1, 2, 3, 4.
Teacher: Now count the rows and say 'three', and count the trees and say 'four'. It becomes 3 times 4. What is the answer?
Learner: 7.
Learner: 9.
Teacher: 3 times 4?
Learners: 12.
Teacher: Now who doesn't understand so that I can give you another example? Who does not understand?

Learner: I don't.

. . .

Learner: 3.
Teacher: 3. And what's double 10?
Learner: 20.
Teacher: And what's double 3?
The teacher circles the three rows of trees
Teacher: These are the 3 rows. Now 3 stands for?
Learners: For rows.
Teacher: And 4?
Learners: Four stands for the number of trees in a row.
Teacher: Now what does 12 stand for?
Learners: For trees altogether.
Teacher: Now is there anyone who hasn't understood?
Learners: No Miss.
Teacher: Can I give you your own trees to count?
Learners: Yes Miss.

In relation to the task, it would have been more helpful to the learners had the teacher showed them grouping rather than multiplication in the first instance. The teacher did not extract a rule for the learners to apply in the task, apart from possibly trial-and-error but this was not made explicit. In her second attempt at an explanation, rather than give an account of how the two dimensions might have been derived, she restated her first account: the 3 'stands for rows', and the '4 stands for the number of trees in the row'. Instructions for the task became emptied of mathematical content, and the connections between the task and the mathematical concept became attenuated. The task was classified as localizing-mathematical. The localizing strategy illustrated above contains mathematical content, and is different to that of tasks such as colouring-in or chanting, where there is no mathematical content visible. However, the mathematics concepts for use in approaching the calculation remain implicit. In this way the distinction is made between localizing-mathematical and localizing-non-mathematical. Localizing-mathematical displays mathematical content, but the principles and procedures for completing the task are absent (for more detail on these categories see Appendix B).

Finally, two localizing strategies – ritual and nominal – are discussed briefly below, especially given their identified dominance in South African and developing country classrooms more broadly.

Localizing-ritual strategies entail the call and response or catechetic exchanges identified earlier and were a common pedagogic form deployed by the teachers in the classrooms. An example is given for Teacher G:

Extract 5: in your mind

Teacher: Do you agree with him? He says the same thing as Simvuyile. I am expecting those who are not talking to talk. Let's talk people. In summer it is very hot. It is what?

Learners:	It is very hot.
Teacher:	How is summer?
Learners:	It is very hot.
Teacher:	How is summer?
Learners:	It is very hot.
Teacher:	How is summer?
Learners:	It is very hot.
Teacher:	I am waking up all those who are sleeping and not talking. You must talk so that you can keep things where?
Learners:	In your mind.

The extent to which this pattern of exchange of meanings was entrenched is evident in particular in the last two sentences of the exchange. The learners were familiar with the first part of the exchange – 'so that you can keep things where' – and automatically responded, 'In your mind'.

This localizing-ritual was also a feature of reading. It was seen particularly in instances where learners repeated words and phrases from a text after the teacher, and were not required to read themselves. This kind of reading activity did not provide skills or strategies for engaging with text but rather oral repetition after the teacher.

Finally, localizing-nominal was the most common strategy found in the analysis of the tasks in the working-class context. This strategy consisted of the teacher and learners naming things – usually in relation to a theme. The following extract comes from Teacher D's class, where learners are going through different shapes of leaves shown in the textbook.

Extract Teacher D: long leaves, palm leaves . . .

Learners:	Big and pricking leaves.
Teacher:	These are oak tree leaves. You can never touch them because they are pricking. Continue.
Learners:	Featherlike leaves.
Teacher:	There are pricking leaves from the oak tree, but there is no oak tree here so I can't show you. Next one.
Learners:	Long leaves.
Teacher:	Long leaves.
Learner:	Long and thin leaves.
Learners:	Those shaped like heart.
Teacher:	It says there are heart-shaped leaves. Now we saw the top leaves, now let's look at the bottom ones.
Learners:	Ipayina [pineapple tree].
Teacher:	Ipayina.
Learners:	Ipayina.
Teacher:	It's a pine tree.
Learners:	Peach tree leaves.
Teacher:	Peach tree leaves.

Learners: Isundu [Palm].
Teacher: We don't have a lot of these trees around in Harare [surrounding area]. When you get to go to a forest you will see all the kinds of trees and leaves. You will see them. There are many kinds of trees. We could talk about them the whole day. Palm, and it's got palm leaves.

There were no discernible literacy strategies evident in this exchange and others like it. It is evident in Teacher D's statement: 'There are many kinds of trees. We could talk about them the whole day'. A clear pedagogic trajectory from these kinds of exchanges was not retrievable; rather the pedagogic process consisted of building up a series of words and images in relation to a theme.

Summary – strategies

In mathematics across classrooms there was an equal number of localizing strategies and specializing-proceduralizing strategies (Table 9.2). Within the localizing category, the dominant strategy was localizing-mathematical. Although the tasks 'looked like' mathematics, the explanation and execution of these tasks contained no observable mathematical procedures or principles. In language localizing-nominal and localizing-personal dominated the pedagogy. Local, particularistic meanings were privileged and list-learning activities predominated here. These results have significant implications for the ways in which students were being inducted into the specialized code of schooling. Across the four classrooms, 78% of language tasks and 50% of mathematics tasks with which the learners engaged were personalized, localized and related to everyday categories and experiences (Table 9.3).

Table 9.2 Incidence of specializing and localizing strategies for mathematics and language, aggregated across the four classrooms

Specializing strategies			*Localizing strategies*		
Principling	Proceduralizing	**Total**	Mathematical	Non-mathematical	**Total**
0	10	**10 (50%)**	7	3	**10 (50%)**

Table 9.3 Incidence of specializing and localizing strategies for language, aggregated across the four classrooms

Specializing strategies			*Localizing strategies*				
Complex	Simple	**Total**	Nominal	Personal	Ritual	Mechanical	**Total**
7	3	**10 (22%)**	10	12	7	6	**35 (78%)**

Instructional form – individualizing and communalizing

A consideration of the organization of students for learning, and whether they were individualized or communalized in the pedagogy, describes a particular aspect of the regulative discourse of the classroom. For the analysis all tasks for language and mathematics were coded as to whether students were individualized in the teacher-student interaction or in their grouping, or whether the class was treated as an undifferentiated whole. Each of the tasks was then coded in terms of the differentiation of tasks; whether all learners received the same content (uniform), or whether the content was differentiated. The results are shown in the Tables 9.4 and 9.5.

There was no differentiation of content for different learners in the construction or distribution of tasks. All learners worked on the same tasks at the same time. As in C2005, demarcations within subject areas were blurred (i.e. in literacy there were no clear distinctions between reading, phonics, writing etcetera), and there was no differentiation of tasks with respect to ability in either literacy or

Table 9.4 The classroom organization for the tasks

		Tasks n = 65			
		Teacher E n = 18	*Teacher F n = 18*	*Teacher G n = 15*	*Teacher H n = 14*
Classroom organization	Total homogenous by teacher	18 (100%)	18 (100%)	11 (73%)	14 (100%)
	Total % homogenous	**94%**			
	Total integrated by teacher	0 (0%)	0 (0%)	3 (20%)	0 (0%)
	Total % integrated	**5%**			
	Total specialized by teacher	0 (0%)	0 (0%)	1 (7%)	0 (0%)
	Total % specialized	**1%**			

Table 9.5 Content differentiation in the instructional form of the tasks

		Tasks n = 65			
		Teacher E n = 18	*Teacher F n = 18*	*Teacher G n = 15*	*Teacher H n = 14*
Content – differentiation	Total uniform by teacher	18 (100%)	18 (100%)	15 (100%)	14 (100%)
	Total % uniform	**100%**			
	Total differentiated by teacher	0 (0%)	0 (0%)	0 (0%)	0 (0%)
	Total % differentiated	**0%**			

numeracy. Classroom organization took the predominant form of the teacher working with the whole class (homogenous). Learners seldom worked with each other in groups (integrated), and only on one occasion did learners work individually or in small groups with the teacher (specialized). In this context individual performances were generally not sought, and differentiation between learners (in terms of ability or other criteria) did not occur with respect to instruction.[3] The pedagogy was ***communalized***.

Summary

To summarize, the pedagogy found in these classrooms is characterized by strong framing over sequence, selection and pace, and very weak framing over the evaluative rules. The transmission generally does not draw out the knowledge principles in exposition, and very little (sometimes no) attempt is made to make the requirements for the legitimate production of a text available to learners. In the pedagogy, the hierarchical rules are strongly framed, learners are communalized, and instructional knowledge is undifferentiated. All pupils are treated as the same. The predominant instructional strategy is that of localizing where the tasks incorporate knowledge that is familiar and particularistic, and meanings that are concrete and context-bound. The form of pedagogy has weak potential for inducting students into school knowledge.

Conclusion: a communalizing pedagogy

Consistent with the pedagogy identified under C2005, the analysis found a regulative discourse grounded in a 'communalizing pedagogy' where the teachers worked with the whole class as a homogeneous group, with little or no differentiation of tasks or differentiation of individual performances. In a communalizing pedagogy, close scrutiny of what individual learners produce is not possible, and, consequently, the conditions for the successful production of the relevant pedagogic text are foreclosed.

While learner-centred, progressive pedagogies such as those promoted by both the C2005 and NCS reforms entail a relaxing of the framing over the social relation and a weakening of the boundaries between knowledge, the pedagogy here entailed the near dissolution of specialized knowledge itself and the retention of strong teacher control over the social relation. The autocratic ritualized relations of the traditional pedagogy, identified in classrooms under apartheid and sustained in C2005, endure into the second reform.

The chapter, however, offers a more precise description of this 'traditional' or 'teacher-centred' pedagogy that we know from Chapter 2 to be prevalent across developing countries. The research on which the chapter is based forms part of a broader tradition of classroom research that attempts to produce a sharper delineation of the mechanisms through which classroom processes engender social reproduction (and interruption). This broader work, that draws on concepts drawn from Bernstein, has made a notable contribution by identifying ***specific*** *dimensions of pedagogic practice* favourable to children coming from poorer homes (Morais & Neves, 2001; Morais et al., 2004; Rose, 2004; Arnot & Reay, 2004; Reeves & Muller, 2005). In particular, strong framing over the evaluative criteria, weak framing over hierarchical rules and variable pacing has been emphasized as contributing to working-class success, along with strong classification of school knowledge in order to aid its recognition. This is a hybrid pedagogy, containing both elements of so-called 'teacher-centred' and 'learner-centred' pedagogies. And the dimensions are contrary to the classification and framing modality identified in the classrooms under study in this chapter and Chapter 7. Two reforms later, pedagogic practice was a long way from providing appropriate forms and meaningful learning for socially marginalized children in the newly democratic South Africa.

Notes

1 However, it could be argued that, in this case, the teacher in fact substitutes the textbook for herself; or she recruits a proxy voice – the sequence and selection of the textbook – because her voice isn't able to do the pedagogic work. Neither student nor teacher here appears to be controlling the knowledge but rather the textbook is followed to the word, strongly dictating the sequence and selection. So an initial (iconic) selection in terms of the theme 'trees' is made, but from there the sequencing follows that of the textbook from the top of the page to the bottom.

2 The descriptor for one of the indicators for F^0 for the evaluative criteria reads:
Evaluative criteria: In the introduction/explanation/exposition to a topic/task
F^0 – It appears as if no attempt is made to transmit the concepts and principles in the instructional practice. What counts as a successful production in terms of instructional knowledge is therefore totally unclear. The purpose of the task/activity/discussion is unclear. Learners are unclear as to how to proceed, or they are only given criteria relating to how they should behave.

3 In non-pedagogic tasks, however, there is gender differentiation. For example, girls clean, boys open windows.

References

Arnot, M., & Reay, D. (2004). The framing of pedagogic encounters: Regulating the social order in classroom learning. In J. Muller, B. Davies & A. Morais (Eds.), *Reading Bernstein, researching Bernstein* (pp. 137–150). London: RoutledgeFalmer.

Bernstein, B. (1990). Class, codes and control, volume 4: The structuring of pedagogic discourse. London: Routledge.

Bernstein, B. (1996). Pedagogy symbolic control and identity: Theory, research, critique. London: Taylor & Francis.

Dowling, P. (1998). The sociology of mathematics education: Mathematical myths/pedagogic texts. London: Falmer.

Fitz, J., Davies, B., & Evans, J. (2006). Education policy and social reproduction: Class inscription & symbolic control. New York: Routledge.

Hoadley, U. (2007). The reproduction of social class inequalities through mathematics pedagogies in South African primary schools. *Journal of Curriculum Studies, 39*(6), 679–706.

Hoadley, U. (2008). Pedagogy and social class: A model for the analysis of pedagogic variation. *British Journal of Sociology of Education*, *29*, 63–78.

Hoadley, U. K. (2005). Social class, pedagogy and the specialization of voice in four South African primary schools. Unpublished PhD thesis, University of Cape Town.

Hoadley, U. K. (2006). Analysing pedagogy: The problem of framing. *Journal of Education*, *40*, 14–34.

Hugo, W., & Wedekind, V. (2013). Ordering principles and operating principles of pedagogy: A reply to Zipin. *Southern African Review of Education*, *19*(1), 167–176.

Morais, A., & Neves, I. (2001). Pedagogical social contexts: Studies for a sociology of learning. In A. Morais, I. Neves, B. Davies & H. Daniels. (Eds.), *Towards a sociology of pedagogy: The contribution of Basil Bernstein to research* (pp. 185–222). New York: Peter Lang.

Morais, A., Neves, I., & Pires, D. (2004). The what and the how of teaching and learning. In J. Muller, B. Davies & A. Morais (Eds.), *Reading Bernstein, researching Bernstein* (pp. 75–90). London: RoutledgeFalmer.

Morrow, W. (2001). Scriptures and practices. *Perspectives in Education*, *19*(1), 87–106.

Pedro, E. R. (1981). *Social stratification and classroom discourse: A sociolinguistic analysis of classroom practice*. Stockholm: Stockholm Institute of Education, Department of Educational Research.

Reeves, C., & Muller, J. (2005). Picking up the pace: Variation in the structure and organization of learning school mathematics. *Journal of Education*, *37*, 97–125.

Rose, D. (2004). Sequencing and pacing of the hidden curriculum: How indigenous children are left out of the chain. In J. Muller, B. Davies & A. Morais (Eds.), *Reading Bernstein, researching Bernstein* (pp.91–107). London: RoutledgeFalmer.

10 Reclaiming knowledge[1]

The Curriculum and Assessment Policy Statement

Introduction

> A great deal of political courage will be required to repudiate outcomes-based education (OBE). And this step cannot be achieved by stealth: if the announcement of the new policy does not explicitly mention the dropping of learning outcomes, opposition politicians, media commentators and public intellectuals will certainly ask the question, and if the Minister does not have a clear answer, the latest reform initiative will only serve to deepen the confusion. The temptation on the part of government will be to compromise: to assert . . . that the principles of the 1994 revolution, as embodied in OBE, have not been overturned.
>
> (Taylor, 2009)

Prominent educationalist Nick Taylor made these comments on the possibilities of another curriculum review that was called in 2009. The quote indicates how, by 2009, OBE was not only an educational issue, but had become a highly politicized one. The calls for the review came from two sources: ongoing criticism in the media of OBE by prominent public intellectuals and educationalists, and the persistent poor performance of South African learners on national and international standardized tests such as TIMSS and SACMEQ. In these tests South Africa was out-performed, not only by developed countries, but also by developing countries with a lower GDP and lower spend on education (van der Berg & Louw, 2008). Thus, following the failure of C2005 and problems with the NCS, calls for a third reform were made.

Once again refracting the broader curriculum reform issues through an analysis of the curricula developed for mathematics and reading in the Foundation Phase, the chapter shows how a review of the National Curriculum Statement (NCS) in 2009 finally managed to dispense with OBE and, consequently, open up the possibilities for clearer curriculum content specification. The Curriculum and Assessment Policy (CAPS), as the new curriculum would be called, reasserted the importance of subjects, including closely specifying the teaching of reading, writing and number concept. The third curriculum reform of the democratic era made a decisive shift towards a knowledge-based curriculum.

1998	C2005 Implementation
2000	C2005 Review
2002	NCS Implementation
2009	NCS Review
2012	CAPS implementation

Figure 10.1 Timeline of the reform processes C2005 to CAPS

The curriculum shift was surprising in a number of ways. One is suggested in the quote by Taylor above: OBE had achieved a scriptural status (Morrow, 2001), and to reject OBE was still regarded as tantamount to being anti-transformation. The second reason why the shift was unexpected was that, in many ways, the new curriculum flew in the face of the strong local and broader skills emphasis that had endured since late apartheid. Third, the reform was able to dispense with many of the progressive features of the curriculum that constrained clear statements of expected learning while this progressivism was still very strong especially in the academic field. The chapter begins by considering the broader regulative environment and the discursive features of the recontextualizing field, and goes on to account for the subject knowledge-based curriculum that ensued from the revision. The making of the CAPS asserted the relative autonomy of formal schooling from the political and economic pressures referred to above. CAPS was driven by a particular understanding of social justice in education as being grounded in access to formal knowledge.

The Knower: skilled, emancipated or knowledgeable

By 2009 socially, economically and politically, the South African state and society had begun to unravel in a way that saw widespread xenophobic attacks, service delivery protests and sustained criminality. The fundamental problems underlying this turmoil were those of inequality and the fact that the gains of democracy had been captured by an elite group, while the majority remained dispossessed (Nyamnjoh et al., 2013).

The frustration around education was not just about poor outcomes, but also about the enduring ***inequality*** in educational provision and performance. Nowhere was this seen more starkly than in the poor schooling conditions and outcomes that persisted, especially in former Department of Education and Training (DET) (black) schools. It was in this context that a review of the curriculum was called. The minister declared that she understood there were multiple problems in education. However, "This is our starting point because the curriculum is the main thing in education" (Motshekga, 2009).

The focus on skills in the face of persistent poverty, unemployment and slow growth in the economy had begun in 1997 with a green paper, *A Skills Development Strategy for Economic and Employment Growth*, and was followed by a number of acts of parliament aimed at addressing the issue of skills and skills levies. The policy thrust was evident in the National Development Plan (NDP) (National Planning Commission (NPC), 2012), wherein a 'developmental state', supporting new productive activities in a range of knowledge- and skill-intensive activities, was envisioned (Seekings & Nattrass, 2015). The NDP was a comprehensive policy document setting the trajectory for South Africa in all sectors up to 2030, and once again foregrounded education's task in developing skills. The discourse was familiar:

> Provide skills development for students currently in school with a focus on grooming an entrepreneurial attitude. This should include reviewing the curriculum with a view to encouraging entrepreneurial thinking and creating the skills necessary for start-ups.
>
> (NPC, 2012, p. 143)

However, the document went one step further by suggesting that this review "should consider focusing education into technical and academic streams after grade 8, and establishing vocational and technical training for students in grades 9 and 11" (ibid.). Skills shortages had, for some time, been described as a 'crisis', and the fragmented and uncoordinated post-school education and training sector was blamed for not meeting demands. Schools, it seems, were intended to take up some of this slack.

This emphasis on high skills and 21st century skills was prevalent in more global discourses. These entailed a preoccupation with the changing nature of work and the need to specify and measure different competencies – what they were, how they could be transferred to different contexts and, crucially, how they could be measured. With this intense focus on measurement came a whole industry to support the testing and measuring of every aspect of education. The knower in education became 'the measureable unit' that was an indicator of a country's developmental level and economic viability.[2] A number of African, European and Asian countries had begun to overhaul their education systems along the lines of outcomes-based systems in the context of National Qualifications Frameworks (see Young & Allais, 2016). In other countries standards-based reforms placed similar emphasis on measureable skills and content in relation to their direct usefulness.

At the same time the progressive, learner-centred tradition was alive and well in local discourse, focused on the holistic development of the individual and the release, through education, of the 'natural' potential of learners. This thrust stretched back to C2005, but was given renewed impetus by broader notions such as the philosophically-rooted 'capabilities' approach and the idea of Ubuntu in education with its implications for local knowledge and culturally-informed values and understandings. The emancipatory ideals behind these approaches were also evident in the arguments around the possibilities for digital technologies to enhance learning. Young (2013) explains: "If only, some argue, teachers allowed learners unfettered access to the enormous information resource available on the internet, successful learning would become the norm for all and not restricted to the few" (p. 102–103).

The question of knowledge

Alongside these discourses at the time of the CAPS review the distinct current of curriculum theorizing that privileged the question of knowledge endured. These were the arguments that had informed the review of the NCS, as described in Chapter 8, but were strengthened and refined in a series of publications and the development of ideas subsequent to the reform work there (for example, Muller (2000), Moore (2007), Young (2008), Wheelahan (2010)). The approach to curriculum was framed by a loose, scholarly international group, broadly subscribing to a 'social realist' view of knowledge. This view critiqued both relativist and social constructivist conceptions of knowledge, arguing for a concerted engagement with subject disciplines, how knowledge is structured therein and how this structuring differs across different disciplines.[3] Social realists extended their knowledge arguments into arguments around curriculum, asserting that an undifferentiated view of knowledge (such as that which underpins outcomes-based systems, for example) presents a particular problem for education and for the selection of knowledge for inclusion in the curriculum.

Young's (2007) notion of 'powerful knowledge' attempted to surface the equity implications of a social realist approach to curriculum. He argued that formal education enables students to access (powerful) knowledge that is not necessarily available to them in their everyday lives, especially those in socially marginalized positions. This knowledge enables students to move beyond their particular understandings and experience and gain a more generalized understanding of the world in which they live, or, as Bernstein had it, participate in society's conversation more broadly (in Wheelahan, 2010, p. 13). Reflecting on the fact that the place of traditional knowledge had slipped from view in curriculum considerations, Young (2013) asserted: "The struggle over schooling has always has been a struggle for knowledge; that is what the debate about the curriculum should be about" (2013, p. 115).

The discourses described above – of skills, progressivism and a knowledge-based approach – were circulating across the Official Recontextualizing Field (ORF) (the bureaucracy) and the Pedagogic Recontextualizing Field (PRF) (the arena of academia and educational practice) at the time of the CAPS reform. In Hoadley (2010) I describe the debates and contestation around curriculum at this time in South Africa in terms of different 'modes' operating in the academic curriculum terrain, or PRF, most notably those working in a 'knowledge mode' and those in a 'knower mode'. The knower mode was focused on concerns around voice, indigenous knowledge, issues of integration and pedagogical concerns with constructivism and relevance. The social category of the knower was privileged, authorizing multiple 'voices' and authenticating and valorizing experience. Broadly, this mode was located within a progressivist discourse. The knowledge mode, in contrast, argued largely for a discipline-based approach to curriculum that foregrounded the importance of knowledge boundaries and knowledge differentiation. Here the concern was with access to formal knowledge, particularly for those previously marginalized. This was the knowledge discourse. In relation to the skills discourse, around the time of the NCS, Chisholm (2005) argues that the NCS review had sought a weaker link to the NQF and 'broke the umbilical cord' between the supposedly integrated worlds of education and training. However, the skills focus was prominent in the policy debates that resulted in the NDP, still questioning the role of schooling in directly contributing to economic development.

Arguments of the knowledge mode held sway in the third review that led to the Curriculum and Assessment Policy (CAPS), which remains the current curriculum. The report emerging from the review argued strongly for greater knowledge specification, a rejection of OBE, a focus on the conceptual coherence of subjects, more strongly classified subjects and reduced integration of everyday and academic knowledge in the curriculum. Below I provide a short account of the review process, based on primary documents produced in the process as well as my own experience and interpretation as a participant and a member of the Ministerial Review Committee.

The recontextualizing field and the critique of the NCS

Amidst severe and public criticism of OBE Angie Motshekga, new Minister of the Department of Basic Education (DBE) in 2009, followed up on the leaning towards a revision of the curriculum of the previous minister, Naledi Pandor. She appointed an eight-person Ministerial Review Committee (MRC). The team consisted of two 'overseeing' bureaucrats, two members of the two largest teacher unions (though it was clearly stated that their role was not union representation), three academics and a publisher. Information gathering, as well as legitimation for the review, was gained through a series of large provincial teacher hearings held across the country. The MRC spent days in a 'listening exercise' with hundreds of teachers in packed halls. There was also an extensive process of public submissions where individuals, NGOs, civil society organizations, schools, parents and teachers commented on the revision proposals.

While certainly informed by the voices of teachers and other submissions by education role-players, the review married these concerns with research and with the project to reinstate subject discipline-based principles for the organization of the curriculum that had been initiated in the review of the NCS. In the 2009 process and the development of arguments for the revision, there was a high level of consensus amongst the MRC, without the intrusion of sectoral interests. There was also strong consensus in public submissions and teacher hearings about the problems and possible ways forward – the central one being the call for greater specification of the curriculum content to be taught. A public submission from Linda Chisholm, who chaired the 2000 review, and Cas Lubisi a participant in that review read: "complete the revision that was not completed in 2002 . . . Prescribe standard learning programmes (or syllabi) for each subject at each grade. It is possible to do this in plain language".

Consensus, as well as less interference from other stakeholders, academics, unions or labour made the work of the MRC relatively seamless. Why this was the case is open to interpretation. One argument may simply be that there was policy reform fatigue, and the review process attracted less attention than it may have in another time when more faith was vested in policies to bring about real change. Another argument is that key members of the 2009 MRC had been part of the review and revision processes of C2005. In some ways the 2009 review became a process of addressing the unfinished business of the C2005 review and those members who had been part of both processes amplified the knowledge arguments. In other words, the MRC facilitated the realization of the conceptual arguments made around coherence and progression within clear subject boundaries made in 2000.

The resultant review report was framed in relation to theoretical debates around a knowledge-based curriculum. The notion of 'powerful knowledge' was explicitly invoked in making an argument for the social justice imperative of providing a well-specified curriculum to support teachers and enable students to access formal knowledge in schooling. Citing Young (2007) the report argued:

> What we have learnt is that, despite the good intentions of past efforts, an underspecified curriculum advantages those who are already advantaged – those who already have access to the knowledge needed to improve their life chances.
>
> (DBE, 2009, p. 61)

The report also lodged a direct criticism of constructivist understandings of teaching and learning that had dominated curriculum thinking:

> Though all learners do engage in the construction of knowledge in terms of coming to understand certain concepts, skills and content, it has generally been accepted that these aspects inhere within the subject and not in the minds of learners in the first place.
>
> (DBE, 2009, p. 24)

The political load of OBE became apparent in the deliberations of the MRC, which was reluctant to take a decision on its fate. Members of the Committee were conscious of the anti-transformation associations of abandoning OBE, and they were uncertain whether the Minister would accept this. The recommendation that OBE be abandoned was eventually written into the report at a late stage, and it was with some surprise, after a period of silence, that the Minister declared to the National Assembly, "We've signed OBE's death certificate" (Motshekga, 2009).

The report included a comprehensive critique of OBE. Drawing on the work of a number of critics, (Muller, 2000; Jansen, 1999; Allais & Taylor, 2007; Donnelly, 2005) the report argued that, by focusing on outcomes, the content, or the means for achieving these outcomes, was not sufficiently specified, producing "curriculum and assessment descriptors that are often vague, ambiguous, difficult to measure and low in academic content" (DBE, 2009, p. 38). It argued that the genericism entailed in an outcomes-based curriculum inhibited clear specification of what was to be learnt. The report suggested that outcomes be replaced with 'clear content, concept and skill standards and clear and concise assessment requirements' (DBE, 2009, p. 45). The report also argued that several tenets associated with OBE required scrutiny, including the subordination of textbooks, the ongoing press for integration and the emphasis on groupwork as the privileged classroom organizational strategy. Unusually for a process like this, all the recommendations of the review committee were accepted and the report was endorsed in its entirety and parameters for a curriculum revision clearly established.

Real contestation and conflict arose in the revision process itself, in the writing of the actual curriculum documents. The central conflicts and tension were around who was appointed to revise the curricula, the extraordinarily stringent time frames for revision, weak leadership of the process and very poor and conflicting communication channels. The role of the subject specialists in the writing of the revised curricula was asserted, and there was a complete abandonment of the notion of stakeholder groups for writing that had held sway in the development of C2005 and to some extent the NCS. However, there was significant pushback from bureaucrats responsible for specific curriculum subjects and an attempt, especially in certain subject areas, to gain control over the process. In cases where this occurred (life skills is one example) there was a great deal of continuity between the NCS and the CAPS. In other areas, for example History, subject specialists controlled the redrafting process, with considerable change to the contents and their organization.

The tension between some of the DBE bureaucrats in the curriculum division (ORF), and the members of the Ministerial Project Committee, a continuation from the MRC set up to oversee the revisions, escalated. The new Committee had lost the leadership of the two senior bureaucrats that oversaw the review process and there was no one to effectively establish lines of responsibility and authority for the production and finalizing of documents. There was a lack of clarity around the appropriate involvement of DBE officials in the drafting and finalizing of the curriculum documents. In the end the curriculum documents were completed in a very short time (deadlines partly being set by budget determinants). The outcome of the revision process can probably best be described as uneven, although the principle of clear specification with respect to subject knowledge was upheld. There has as yet been insufficient research, both at the intended and implemented levels, to determine the success of the review.[4] The most common anecdotal criticisms focus on content overload, excessive assessment tasks and unrealistic pacing requirements. More broadly, though, what was strikingly evident in this process was the relative autonomy of the process of curriculum development from both dominant economic discourses (of skills) and the political press to retain OBE.

Recontextualizing rules

The CAPS documents explicitly stated that they replaced the NCS's subject statements, assessment guidelines and learning programme guidelines with a single document. The importance of language was recognized in the CAPS, bringing back the vocabulary of 'subjects' as opposed to 'learning areas' and 'teachers' to replace 'educators'. In this way the CAPS reclaimed *the school* as the reference site of the curriculum, a process begun in the NCS revision. The Minister declared:

> The department will develop a set of simple, coherent curriculum documents per subject per phase from Grades R to 12. This will simply describe the content, the concepts and the skills that are supposed to be taught. Anyone who has taught before will know what we are talking about: the syllabi, which spell out what your aims, your objectives, your learning areas, your methodology and your assessments are in very simple and clear terms.
>
> (Motshekga, 2009)

The use of the term 'syllabi' was controversial given its association with curriculum developed during apartheid and the consequent abandonment of the term in C2005. Its use indicated the new Minister's impatience with ideological debates, which she also addressed directly in relation to abandoning OBE:

> I do not wish to be drawn into simplistic ideological debates on this issue and forced into a disavowal of our goals. The question is how we can disentangle our goals from the outcomes in which they are expressed, and the very concept of outcomes.
>
> (Motshekga, 2009)

There were some significant changes in the subjects at different levels. At Foundation Phase the nomenclature of the subjects was changed (Table 10.1). Significantly, First Additional Language was for the first time separated from the broader area of languages and given priority in weighting. This was an attempt to address the fact that approximately 80% of learners made a transition from mother tongue instruction to English as a language of teaching and learning in Grade 4, and that research had shown that most teachers only started teaching (some) English in Grade 3 (Prinsloo, 2009).

The timetabling of First Additional Language was one of the most decisive changes in relation to the very difficult issue of language, which had a long and troubled history through apartheid[5] and into the democratic era. For the first time since the end of apartheid, the formal timetabling asserted the enduring policy of additive bilingualism and provided a specific time allocation for the teaching thereof from Grade 1 onwards.

Table 10.1 Foundation Phase subjects in the NCS and CAPS

NCS Grade R-3	*CAPS Grade R-3*
Literacy	Home Language
Numeracy	First Additional Language
Life Skills	Mathematics
	Life Skills

Table 10.2 Grade 4 to Grade 9 subjects in the NCS and CAPS

NCS Grade 4–9	*CAPS Grade 4–6*	*CAPS Grade 7–9*
Languages	Home Language	Home Language
Mathematics	First Additional Language	First Additional Language
Natural Sciences	Mathematics	Mathematics
Social Sciences	Natural Sciences and Technology	Natural Sciences
Technology	Social Sciences	Social Sciences
Eco and Management Sciences	Life Skills	Technology
Life Orientation		Eco Management Sciences
Arts and Culture		Life Orientation
		Creative Arts

There were also shifts in subjects in Grades 4 to 6, with a de-emphasis on the subjects Technology and Economic and Management Sciences in the middle (or 'Intermediate Phase') Grade 4–6 band (Table 10.2).

The preamble to the curriculum documents (one per phase per subject) reflects the pragmatic approach taken in the CAPS: four pages provide a background, overview, general aims of the South African curriculum and time allocation. These pertain to all subjects at all levels, Grades R to 12. The critical outcomes from C2005 and the NCS are retained verbatim, but the developmental outcomes that refer to entrepreneurship and career preparation have been dropped. The document also includes a new set of seven principles, two of which refer specifically to knowledge and its specification:

> High knowledge and high skills: the minimum standards of knowledge and skills to be achieved at each grade are specified and set high, achievable standards in all subjects;
>
> Progression: content and context of each grade shows progression from simple to complex.
>
> (DBE, 2011a/b, p. 4)

The only reference to general pedagogical principles is in the statement: "Active and critical learning: encouraging an active and critical approach to learning, rather than rote and uncritical learning of given truths" (DBE, 2011a/b, p. 4). All prior references to learner-centredness, groupwork and constructivist learning techniques have been omitted.

Below I consider the way in which reading and number specifically are constituted in the CAPS curriculum through a close reading of the following documents:

- Department of Basic Education. (2011a). Curriculum and assessment policy statement (CAPS): Foundation phase: Home language grades R-3. Pretoria: Department of Basic Education.

- Department of Basic Education. (2011b). ***Curriculum and assessment policy statement (CAPS): Foundation phase: Mathematics grades R-3.*** Pretoria: Department of Basic Education.
- Department of Basic Education. (2011c). ***National protocol for assessment grades R-12.*** Pretoria: Department of Basic Education.

Balance and proficiency: reading in the CAPS

In the subject Home Language there are four main language curriculum content areas: 'Listening and speaking', 'Phonics', 'Reading and viewing', 'Handwriting and writing' (Table 10.3). The NCS outcomes 'Thinking and reasoning' and 'Language structure and use' have been abandoned as organizing categories. Language structure and use is to be integrated into the other language content areas (and, it is assumed, thinking and reasoning, too).

Reading as a topic within Home Language is strongly classified and integration is dispensed with in the CAPS. A very short paragraph refers to the notion that themes and topics from other subject areas can be selected in order to provide a context for language teaching, after which integration is not mentioned again. Guidance for weighting the time spent on different skills/content is very specific, and clear expectations are set out as to what should be achieved in each term of the year. At the end of the content specification for each topic and each term there are suggestions for informal assessment, as well as specification of content for formal assessment. The latter re-states the content, at times in greater detail. Evaluative criteria are explicit. For example, content/concept/skill specification for Grade 1, Term 2 for phonics is stated as:

> Distinguishes aurally between different beginning and end sounds of words
> Identifies letter-sound relationships of most single letters
> Participates in whole class phonemic awareness activities: blending sounds [h-op into hop]; segmenting words [hop into h-o-p]; consonant and vowel substitution word-play [replace the 'h' in hop with 'm' to make mop]
> Builds words using sounds learnt (-at, -et, -it, -ot, -ut, -ag, -eg, -ig, -og, -ug, -an, -en, -in, -un -am – at least two word families per week) (DBE, 2011a, p. 63).

Table 10.3 Changes in the content areas for Home Language from the NCS to CAPS

NCS	*CAPS*
Listening	Listening and speaking
Speaking	Phonics
Reading and viewing	Reading and viewing
Writing	Writing and handwriting
Thinking and reasoning	
Language structure and use	

Similarly, for the various methodologies stipulated for teaching reading (for example, shared reading), detailed steps and procedures are outlined.

In the CAPS phonics is separated from reading as a specific area of learning, and, consequently, greater specificity than the NCS is provided. A sequence for the teaching of phonemic awareness is set out in detail, including rhyme, syllable units, onset and rime, matching, isolation and substitution activities, with examples provided for each. The curriculum thus suggests a synthetic approach to phonics and the relationship of phonics to spelling is emphasized. The only brief reference to a more contextualized[6] approach to phonics is: "The teaching of phonics is not an isolated activity and should be linked to the Shared Reading programme" (p. 16). But the document provides no further detail on the use of whole texts in teaching of sub-word level features such as phonemes, nor how phonics might be linked to understanding (features of a contextualized phonics approach). Rather, the focus is on developing letter-sound relations, blending and word recognition. Although contextualized phonics and systematic phonics are both recognized as beneficial in the teaching of reading, the evidence around the best way to implement systematic phonics, with which learners, in what order and when and how it should be contextualized is not well-understood (Wyse, 2010) and has as yet not received research attention in South Africa.

Progression (sequence and pace) is strongly framed, with clear increase in complexity across terms and grades. Reading is given the greatest weighting of all the language areas throughout the grades, and progression is seen in the gradual increase in writing and decrease in time spent on phonics as learners progress through the Foundation Phase. Further, progression is usually achieved through increasing complexity in levels of reading skill: automatization at lower levels (i.e. greater fluency), development of reading strategies, greater cognitive challenge in terms of texts interpreted and produced, and the questions posed to texts. There is clear and systematic progression of these aspects across terms and grades in the CAPS.

In the CAPS the language of 'learning outcomes' and 'assessment standards' is abandoned. For each term, content/concepts/skills are listed, followed by suggestions for informal as well as formal assessment tasks. Reading and phonics are allocated a specified amount of time every day, as seen in Figure 10.2 for Grade 1. This daily hour, (much like the literacy hour in the UK National Literacy Strategy), with strict timings for different parts of the hour, is specified differently for each grade. Here we see evidence of the very strong framing over pacing in the document.

Reading & Phonics	Phonics: 15 minutes per day for 5 days (1 hour 15 minutes) Shared Reading: 15 minutes per day for 3 days (45 minutes) Group Reading: 30 minutes per day (2 groups each for 15 minutes) for 5 days (2 hour 30 minutes)	4 hours 30 minutes

Figure 10.2 Reading and phonics time stipulations, Grade 3 (DBE, 2011a, p. 9)

The balanced approach to reading

There is general agreement within the scholarly literature on reading pedagogy that a balanced approach to reading is required. This consists of both teaching of systematic phonics, as well as a whole language 'real books' approach, where exposure to text is fundamental to reading acquisition. Put another way, there is agreement around the need to teach phonics as a separate skill set, and develop reading for meaning, or comprehension (that is located in children's broader language skills). One of the reasons for the radical shift to a whole language approach in C2005 was the previous meaningless recitation of phonics by children in the early grades, without relating this to connected and whole text and with no evidence to suggest that learners were in fact learning to read. The NCS was a hybrid rather than balanced model. CAPS elaborates a more explicit and systematic, balanced approach (although with limitations in relation to phonics, see previous discussion).

The document adopts the well-known view of what constitutes early literacy instruction articulated in the NCS, based on the National Reading Panel's (2000), 'five main components to the teaching of reading': phonemic awareness, word recognition (sight words and phonics), comprehension, vocabulary and fluency. The document provides detailed, practical steps to develop mastery in these skills, with some, but very little, explanation as to their broader purpose or rationale for inclusion in a programme to teach reading.

The balanced approach is also evident in the four curriculum 'requirements' for reading:

- Shared Reading (including Shared Writing)
- Group Guided Reading
- Paired/Independent Reading
- Phonics (including Phonemic Awareness)

Each of these is explained in detail, with specific strategies and steps for approaching them in the classroom. The implicit theory of how students learn to read is through a combination of the development of emergent literacy skills, the systematic teaching of phonics and a range of reading activities that facilitate sustained exposure to text and discussion of text.

Privileged reading pedagogy: proficiency and choice

Given that there is such clear specification of reading in the CAPS, it is possible to interrogate more closely the approach that is implicitly advocated. Moss (2010) distinguishes between reading for proficiency and reading for choice, which extends the distinctions made in the balanced approach. While reading for proficiency focuses on enabling students to make their way through text, fluently and with understanding, reading for choice entails a different kind of literacy activity that aims to develop children's interest in ***reading as an end in itself.*** Moss identifies this in her data in the following way:

> In these events, children would be free to react in a much more open way to the texts in question, without their responses being used to judge their skill. Sometimes teachers would choose texts they hoped their pupils would enjoy, and read them aloud to the class. At other times they would give children opportunities to choose texts for themselves, giving them access to a wider choice of reading materials in a context where they were far freer to choose what they then did with these texts. Neither of these activities would be formally assessed. This is 'reading for choice'.
>
> (p. 222)

Moss argues that both these aspects – enjoyment and choice – need to be part of the official curriculum. However, she points out that it is far easier to itemize and list particular skills in relation to proficiency approaches. With respect to reading for choice it is not so easy to command children to 'like listening to lots of different stories' or 'enjoy reading and listening to different types of books' (p. 227).

The exercise of choice and self-direction is not strongly in evidence in the CAPS. Enjoyment is referenced in the specification of 'read-alouds' through which "teachers can create in children a love of reading and a passion for stories" (DBE, 2011a, p. 18). Although 'Independent reading' is proposed as a means to "encourage reading for enjoyment" the focus is on the activity as enhancing reading for proficiency:

> If children read books on their own they also develop fluency, provided that the books are easy enough for the children to read without help. Short, simple books with predictable text and colourful illustrations are ideal. Some teachers like to give children individual reading to do at home. This home reading should consist of re-reading the group reading book or reading simple, 'fun' books. This extra reading practice, done on a regular basis every day, plays an important role in learning to read.
>
> (p. 14)

Neither independent reading nor 'read-alouds' are given specific time allocations. Nowhere in the curriculum is it specified that children should be allowed to make choices, control what they read, give reasons for their choices or discuss and compare choices with peers. With an explicit focus on direct instruction, proficiency is decidedly the approach taken in the CAPS, even while located within a 'balanced approach'.

The absence of a reading for choice emphasis is understandable. The trajectory of curriculum reform, and the shift from C2005, logically led to a highly specified approach given the poor teaching of reading, when it was taught at all. Reading for proficiency in the context of extremely low literacy levels is more directed and amenable to stipulation, as Moss (2010) argues. The CAPS curriculum is also implemented in a context where mats and reading corners, with a range of books as well as highly literate teachers generally do not exist. This lack restricts the extent to which a culture of choice can be cultivated. In addition, sufficient books are required to relax the framing over selection of texts,

Perhaps of necessity, the curriculum restricts the role of the reader. However, achieving a balance between phonics and reading for meaning, and between more child-directed and teacher-directed activities, is a complex issue. Ellis (2010) argues that the optimum 'literacy learning mix' depends very much on how prepared children are when they come to school. Those children with good letter and word recognition and with extensive vocabulary benefit more from self-directed activities such as those described above. However, children who are not prepared show greater gains with teacher-directed phonics activities which then progress to self-directed, reading-for-meaning activities (along the lines of the 'simple view of reading').

Given that pre-existing literacy and vocabulary skills are known to be very low for the majority of learners, CAPS is probably fit for purpose, emphasizing phonics and teacher-directed reading activities. Child-directed activity, however, is largely eliminated. In the next chapter we explore how the very procedural proficiency approach of the CAPS lines up with classroom practice.

Scripted curriculum: numeracy in the CAPS

The definition of mathematics in the CAPS is almost identical to that of the NCS. The NCS learning outcomes are now termed 'content areas' but remain the same: numbers, operations and relationships, patterns, functions and algebra, space and shape, measurement and data handling. Overview tables are provided that show the specification of concepts and skills for particular topic areas from Grade R to Grade 3, thus making progression explicit. Figure 10.3 below shows how progression across the grades for the representation of whole numbers is stipulated in the document.

The overview tables across grades are followed by overview tables per grade, per term. These tables contain detailed content specification as well as sequencing

TOPICS	GRADE R	GRADE 1	GRADE 2	GRADE 3
NUMBER CONCEPT DEVELOPMENT: Represent whole numbers				
	Say and use number names in familiar context			
1.3 symbols and number names	Recognise, identify and read number symbols • Recognise, identify and read number symbols 1 to 10	Recognise, identify and read number symbols • Recognise, identify and read number symbols 1 to 100 • Write number symbols 1 to 20	Recognise, identify and read number symbols • Recognise, identify and read number symbols 0 to 200 • Write number symbols 0 to 200	Recognise, identify and read number symbols • Recognise, identify and read number symbols 0 to 1000 • Write number symbols 0 to 1000

Figure 10.3 Content overview table for number concept development by grade (DBE, 2011b, p. 19)

and pacing stipulations. Figure10.4 is an example for comparing and ordering numbers for Grade 1 across the four terms.

The document gives a great deal of attention to weighting and time allocation. It provides a table giving proportional weighting of content areas per grade, it provides specification of time allocation per content area per week for each grade and recommends the number of lessons per content area per term per grade. For each content area in each grade 'problem types', which are examples "that the teacher needs to present repeatedly to her class" (p. 66) are provided.

Following the overview tables and pacing specifications, the remaining 390 pages of the 512-page document contain detailed clarification notes/teaching guidelines that state the concept and skill requirements by year-end, the focus for the particular term in question, and notes and examples. The level of detail (similar to scripting) is shown in the extract in Figure 10.5. In these notes evaluative criteria are very explicit – the document clearly signals the conceptual and definitional underpinning of the mathematics to be taught.

Diagrams, photographs and text are all used to provide greater detail and explication of content to be covered. Problem types, common errors and informal assessment suggestions are also provided.

CAPS

TOPICS	TERM 1	TERM 2	TERM 3	TERM 4
NUMBER COCEPT DEVELOPMENT: Describe, compare and order whole numbers				
1.4 Describe, compare and order numbers	Describe, compare and order up to 5 objects • Compare collection of objects according to many, few; most, least; more than, less than; the same as, just as many as, different • Order collection of objects from most to least and least to most	Describe, compare and order up to 10 objects • Compare collection of objects according to many, few; most, least; more than, less than; the same as, just as many as, different • Order collection of objects from most to least and least to most	Describe, compare and order up to 15 objects Compare collection of objects according to many, few; most least; more than, less than; the same as, just as many as, different Order collection of objects from most to least and least to most	Describe, compare and order up to 20 objects • Compare collection of objects according to many, few; most, least; more than, less than; the same as, just as many as, different • Order collection of objects from most to least and least to most

Figure 10.4 Content overview table for number concept development by term, Grade 1 (DBE, 2011b, p. 41)

TOPICS	CONCEPTS AND SKILLS REQUIREMENT BY YEAR END	CONCEPTS AND SKILLS FOCUS FORTERM 1	SOME CLARIFICATION NOTES OR TEACHING GUIDELINES	DURATION (in lessons of 1 hour 24 minutes)
1.1 Count objects	Count out objects reliably to 50. Give a reasonable estimate of a number of objects that can be checked by counting.	Count out objects reliably to 10. Give a reasonable estimate of a number of objects that can be checked by counting.	It is important that learners count the same number of different objects. Example: • Count six counters • Bring me six pencils • Count six buttons Conservation Learners will begin to realise when counting the number of objects, that the number is not affected by their size or position. One could ask: how many stars on each card? The position or arrangement of the stars is different but the number of stars on each card is exactly the same. It is important that when counting concrete objects, learners recognise a small number of objects without counting. Example, recognising • five, as the number of fingers on one hand • three counters, arranged in any way • one to six, from the arrangement of dots on a die This is also known as subitising.	

Figure 10.5 Clarification notes for the topic 'count objects' (DBE, 2011b, p. 95)

Grade 3 Term 2: Exemplar Assessment Task 2

Content area	Topic	Criteria
Numbers, operations and relationships	Number Concept	Counts forwards and backwards in 2s, 4s or 3s to 500
	Calculations	Does addition up to 400 using one of the following • building up and breaking down numbers • number lines • doubling and halving • rounding off to 10

Figure 10.6 Exemplar assessment task Grade 3 (DBE, 2011b, p. 511)

Finally, a section on assessment contains generic information on assessment within CAPS, but also provides exemplar assessment checklists, exemplar rubrics for marking student work and exemplar assessment tasks. Exemplar assessment tasks are provided for all topics for each grade per term. Actual problems are not given but rather the criteria for each topic are specified. An example is given above in Figure 10.6.

These exemplar assessment tasks summarize the specifications, or evaluative criteria, from the document. Multiple representations of the content/skill requirements for learning are thus provided, at varying levels of detail. This would allow for an adept teacher to use the summary tables and a novice teacher to follow more closely the scripted term-by-term specification with clarification notes/teacher guidelines.

In a manner similar to that described above for literacy, the CAPS Mathematics curriculum stipulates content to be learnt in great detail, on a term by term basis across the Foundation Phase. Selection, sequencing and pacing is made explicit and evaluative criteria are strongly framed. Mathematical vocabulary, semantics and syntax are foregrounded and prioritized.

Regarding the presentation of curricular knowledge, C2005 gave only the broadest descriptions of mathematical topics while the National Curriculum Statements provided tightly defined topics, still providing room for teacher variation in sequence and pacing. The CAPS document resembles a script that lays out all topics in the curriculum in a detailed set of teaching guidelines, especially in the extensive set of clarificatory notes.

The strongest criticism of the NCS from teachers, administrators and parents was directed at policy expectations regarding assessment, which the Review summarized as involving an unnecessarily complicated approach, recommending less continuous assessment, fewer projects and a greater emphasis on systemic testing. In the light of this history, CAPS excludes informal assessment from learner records and provides strong framing of evaluation criteria (F^{++}) through the teaching guidelines.

Mathematics in the CAPS document is strongly classified. In the explication of the content there is no reference to everyday knowledge or suggestions for integration with other subjects. The CAPS differs from the NCS in that it distinguishes between 'Solve problems in context' and 'Context-free calculations', thus making a careful distinction between mathematical tasks that are deliberately constructed in reference to the everyday and those that are not. In the NCS a wide range of context-embedded and context-free topics and activities are included under the learning outcome numbers, operations and relationships, in no particular order. In the CAPS 'Solve problems in context' is a distinct topic under the content area numbers, operations and relationships.

The CAPS has very specific guidelines for more individualized classroom groupings in mathematics. It distinguishes between 'whole class activity', 'small group focused lessons', and independent activity. Small group activity is defined thus:

> Small group focused lessons: are most effective when the teacher takes a small group of learners (8 to 12) who have the same ability with her on the floor or at their tables, while the rest of the class is engaged in independent activities. The teacher works orally and practically with the learners.
>
> (DBE, 2011b, p. 11)

The kind of evaluative practice is also suggested:

> The group sessions should be very interactive and learners should be encouraged to **"do, talk, demonstrate and record"** their mathematical thinking.
>
> (p. 12)

An intensive focus on student response in evaluating their performance, as well as the need to differentiate individual learners according to ability, is also specified:

> Close tracking of learners' responses (verbal, oral, practical, written recording) in learning and teaching situations enables the teacher to do continuous assessment, monitor learners' progress and plan support accordingly for learners experiencing barriers to learning.
>
> (DBE, 2011b, p. 12)

> Independent activities should be differentiated to cater for different ability levels.
>
> (ibid.)

The CAPS curriculum for mathematics at the Foundation Phase resembles a script with a very high level of specification of what is to be covered in highly specified periods of time.

Framing of the social relation

Classroom organization suggestions in the CAPS documents are tied to particular content, and where suggestions around pedagogy are given, these are in reference to the teaching of specific skills/content. There are no general references to child-centred teaching, nor any espousal of a particular privileged pedagogic relation. The privileged teacher-student relation can, however, be read in the nature of classroom organization suggested for the teaching of reading and number. For both the use of whole class, small group and individual work is prescribed. Teachers are required to keep a 'close tracking of learner's responses'. The curriculum suggests an individualized relation between teacher and student, where individual learning trajectories are monitored and supported. The pacing of the curriculum, to some extent, pulls in another direction, focused on tight requirements for the acquisition of content within particular time frames. Nonetheless, the emphasis in the curriculum is on the individual student, and the relation between student and teacher is hierarchical, where criteria rest with the teacher.

Model of the learner

Given a proficiency approach taken to the teaching of reading, it is assumed that the learner is one who is yet to learn to read and has had limited exposure to text. The mathematics curriculum also assumes a learner yet to be inducted into formal mathematical learning. The learner is individualized but, unlike the C2005 construction, this is in relation to instruction of content to be acquired rather than the affirmation or privileging of the individual, experiential knowledge that the learner brings to the classroom.

Model of the teacher

There is no explicit statement in the CAPS around the role of the teacher or a particular teacher envisioned by the curriculum, but this can partly be read off the way in which knowledge is presented. The curriculum does not assume that the teacher is able to develop his/her own programme of learning with respect to the selection, sequence and pacing of educational knowledge. It sets out the content to be covered in detail, clearly delineating procedural evaluative criteria for teaching reading. In particular, the mathematics curriculum presents mathematical knowledge to be covered in the form of scripting, with detailed examples of content and how to transmit it.

The foregoing analysis is summarized in Table 10.4.

Conclusion

The CAPS curriculum represents a significant shift in the structuring of the curriculum from the NCS, with priority given to the subject knowledge to be taught. In mathematics the documents provide an elaboration of the NCS content, with specification that approximates scripting. In reading the CAPS takes a proficiency approach to reading, highly specified in outlining the various components of reading and the procedures for teaching these. A balanced approach that

Table 10.4 Summary of the structuring of pedagogic discourse in the curriculum

Instructional	External framing curricular knowledge	F^{e++}	Strong and explicit selection and sequencing with detailed content delineation. Strong per terms and per week pace specifications. Assessment still largely generic, thus not underscoring the evaluative criteria. However, suggestions for assessment of reading and number entailed in content specification.
	Classification between subject and other subjects and everyday knowledge	$C^{+/++}$	Strong demarcation between subjects and between formal school knowledge and everyday knowledge. No emphasis on integration.
	Classification between areas/ topics within subject	C^{++}	Reading and number clearly specified and delineated areas of learning.
Regulative	External framing of social relation (hierarchical rules)	F^{e-}	No stated privileged pedagogic approach or theory, nor specification of learner-centred education. Strong content specification suggests stronger control by the teacher.
	Model of the teacher		Not necessarily competent in the teaching of reading or number. In need of support, but responsible for the transmission of content.
	Model of the learner		Not yet competent in reading or in counting and calculating. Does not assume prior socialization into learning in the home.

incorporates systematic teaching of phonics, as well as specific time allocated for the engagement with whole texts, is outlined.

The CAPS documents have a different image of the average South African teacher in mind compared to the two previous reforms. No assumptions are made regarding teachers' capacity and inclination to devise their own content and sequence and pace it in a way that they see fit. For the first time since the end of apartheid there was recognition of teachers' limitations as primary recontextualizers or 'curriculum-makers', and an implicit acknowledgement of the low levels of cognitive resources in the system. This drew strength from the call from teachers in the review process for clearer specification on what to teach, where teachers emphasized the equity implications of an underspecified curriculum and a strong desire to be doing "the same thing as the school next door" (DBE, 2009, p. 21).

The CAPS curriculum bore a structural similarity to the curriculum forms developed under apartheid – strong classifications and frames. Some of the criticisms straight after its release honed in on this, claiming it represented a return to the past prescriptive nature of curriculum and that it placed excessive limits on teachers' professional autonomy. Despite the very different ideological underpinnings of the two curriculum regimes, there were those who argued that the CAPS attempted to make the curriculum teacher-proof, rooting it in the apartheid construction of African teachers as technicians (Msibi & Mchunu, 2013; Ramatlapana & Makonye, 2012).

A different kind of critique in relation to the scripted nature of the curriculum was beginning to emerge, however, by those who questioned the possibilities of scripting and teacher proofing more generally for shifting teacher practice. Focusing on questions of knowledge as the basis for professional practice, the argument was made that these kinds of highly scripted, content-based interventions were unlikely to work in the absence of the development of teachers' own subject knowledge and how to teach it (de Clerq & Shalem, 2014; Shalem, 2017). The next chapter explores this question in relation to teachers' classroom practices two years after the implementation of CAPS. Would the intended social justice approach of the CAPS emphasizing access to formal school knowledge through clear curriculum specification bear fruit?

Notes

1 Title borrowed from Joe Muller's book, ***Reclaiming knowledge: Social theory, curriculum and education policy*** (2000), a seminal text in debates around curriculum and knowledge.

2 Tomlinson (2013) describes it, perhaps hyperbolically, as an era defined by the power of knowledge economies, skilling and deskilling, credentialism, credential inflation, heightened labour market and accountability cultures and audit forms of assessment which govern policy economies of different scales and impact upon narratives of selfhood in the 21st century.

3 Epistemologically social realists take "a position of fallibilism [which] recognizes that truth is provisional and fallible, but also claims that knowledge can be judged on its truthfulness, not just on who lays claim to the truth or who the truth appears to benefit or exclude." (Hammersley, 2011, p. 484).

4 There was also a concerted effort by some DBE bureaucrats at the end of the process to retain the title of the previous reform, the NCS, and ultimately the CAPS became known as the National Curriculum Statement: Curriculum Policy Statements, with the byline on the cover of each document, "CAPS: structured, clear, practical: Helping teachers unlock the power of NCS". The appellation CAPS has, however, subsequently become the de facto one.

5 Troubled in that, as explained in Chapter 3, black learners were made to learn in their mother tongue as a strategy of racial/cultural allocation, thereafter they were to learn English and Afrikaans. Mother Tongue instruction which was widely recognized later to be beneficial to learners in the early years was thus tied up in these residue understandings making its assertion in policy difficult.

6 Contextualized phonics involves the use of whole texts to locate teaching about the smaller units of language including letters and phonemes in this way providing learners with contexts that makes the activity more meaningful and which provides them with a better understanding of the reading process and the role of phonics therein.

References

Allais, S., & Taylor, N. (2007). *A nation in denial.* Paper presented at the Kenton Education Conference, Phumula, KZN.

Chisholm, L. (2005). The politics of curriculum review and revision in South Africa in regional context. *Compare, 35*(1), 79–100.

De Clercq, F and Shalem, Y. (2014). Teacher knowledge and employer-driven professional development: A critical analysis of the Gauteng Department of Education programmes. *Southern African Review of Education, 20*(1), 129–147.

Department of Basic Education. (2009). Report of the task team for the review of the implementation of the national curriculum statement. Pretoria: South African Department of Basic Education.

Department of Basic Education. (2011a). Curriculum and assessment policy statement (CAPS): Foundation phase: Home language grades R-3. Pretoria: Department of Basic Education.

Department of Basic Education. (2011b). Curriculum and assessment policy statement (CAPS): Foundation phase: Mathematics grades R-3. Pretoria: Department of Basic Education.

Department of Basic Education. (2011c). *National Protocol for Assessment Grades R-12.* Pretoria:. Department of Basic Education

Donnelly, K. (2005). *Benchmarking Australian primary school curricula.* Canberra: Australian Government: Department of Education, Science and Training.

Ellis, S. (2010). The use of evidence in language and literacy teaching. In K. Hall, U. Goswami, C. Harrison, S. Ellis & J. Soler (Eds.), *Interdisciplinary perspectives on learning to read: Culture, cognition and pedagogy* (pp. 193–206). New York: Routledge.

Hammersley, M. (2011). A sociology of truth? *British Journal of Sociology of Education, 32*, 483–490.

Hoadley, U. (2010). Tribes and territory: Contestation around curriculum in South Africa. In W. F. Pinar (Ed.), *Curriculum studies in South Africa: Intellectual histories and present circumstances* (pp. 125–176). Palgrave MacMillan.

Jansen, J. D. (1999). Why outcomes-based education will fail: An elaboration. In J. Jansen & P. Christie (Eds.), *Changing curriculum: Studies on outcomes-based education in South Africa* (pp. 145–156). Cape Town: Juta.

Moore, R. (2007). Going critical: The problem of problematising knowledge in education studies. *Critical Studies in Education, 48*(1), 25–41

Morrow, W. (2001). Scriptures and practices. *Perspectives in Education, 19*(1), 87–106.

Moss, G. (2010). Policy and pedagogy: Proficiency and choice in the literacy classroom. In K. Hall, U. Goswami, C. Harrison, S. Ellis & J. Soler (Eds.), *Interdisciplinary perspectives on learning to read: Culture, cognition and pedagogy* (pp. 219–230). New York: Routledge.

Motshekga, A. (2009). *We've signed OBE's death certificate: statement by Minister of Basic Education, Angie Motshekga, on curriculum review process*, National Assembly, 5 November 2009. Online. Retrieved from www.politicsweb.co.za/politicsweb/view/politicsweb/en/page71656?oid=150055&sn=Detail (accessed 3 May 2010).

Msibi, T., & Mchunu, S. (2013). The knot of curriculum and teacher professionalism in post-apartheid South Africa. *Education as Change, 17*(1), 19–35.

Muller, J. (2000). Reclaiming knowledge: Social theory, curriculum and education policy. London: RoutledgeFalmer.

National Planning Commission. (2012). *National Development Plan 2030: Our future – make it work*. Pretoria: Presidency of South Africa.

National Reading Panel (2000). Report of the National Reading Panel: Teaching children to read: An evidence-based assessment of the scientific research literature on reading and its implications for reading instruction: Reports of the subgroups. Washington, D.C.: National Institute of Child Health and Human Development, National Institutes of Health.

Nyamnjoh, F., Hagg, G., & Jansen, J. (2013). Introduction. In F. Nyamnjoh, U. Pillay, G. Hagg & J. Jansen (Eds.), *State of the nation: South Africa 2012–2013* (pp. 1–34). Cape Town: HSRC Press.

Prinsloo, C. (2009). Building a strong foundation: Learning to read; reading to learn. In S. Pendlebury, L. Lake & C. Smith (Eds.), *South African child gauge 2008/2009* (pp. 60–65). University of Cape Town: Children's Institute.

Ramatlapana, K., & Makonye, J. P. (2012). From too much freedom to too much restriction: The case of teacher autonomy from National Curriculum Statement (NCS) to Curriculum and Assessment Statement (CAPS). *Africa Education Review*, *9*(sup1), S25.

Seekings, J., & Nattrass, N. (2015). *Policy, politics and poverty in South Africa*. London: Palgrave Macmillan.

Shalem, Y. (2017). Scripted lesson plans: What is visible and invisible in visible pedagogy? In B. Barrett, U. Hoadley & J. Morgan (Eds.), *Knowledge, curriculum and equity: Social realist perspectives*. London: Routledge.

Taylor (2009). *OBE, knowledge and politics Curriculum reform in South Africa 1994–2009*. Comment on Draft Report of the Review Panel Strengthening the Implementation of the NCS, Mimeo.

Tomlinson, S. (2013). Ignorant yobs: Low attainers in a global knowledge economy. London & New York: Routledge.

Van der Berg, S., & Louw, M. (2008). Lessons learnt from SACMEQII: South African student performance in regional context. In G. C Bloch, L. Chisholm, B. Fleisch & M. Mabizela (Eds.), *Education and investment choices for vulnerable children in South Africa* (pp. 114–126). Johannesburg: Wits University Press.

Wheelahan, L. (2010). *Why knowledge matters in curriculum*. Abingdon: Routledge.

Wyse, D. (2010). Contextualised phonics teaching. In K. Hall, U. Goswami, C. Harrison, S. Ellis & J. Soler (Eds.), *Interdisciplinary perspectives on learning to read: Culture, cognition and pedagogy* (pp. 130–148). New York: Routledge.

Young, M. (2008). Bringing knowledge back in: From social constructivism to social realism in the sociology of education. London: Routledge.

Young, M. (2013). Overcoming the crisis in curriculum theory: A knowledge-based approach. *Journal of Curriculum Studies*, *45*(2), 101–118.

Young, M., & Allais, S. (2016). Implementing national frameworks across five continents. New York: Routledge.

11 Form and substance

Pedagogy under the CAPS reform

The Curriculum and Assessment Policy Statement (CAPS) was a very different curriculum to both Curriculum 2005 (C2005) and the National Curriculum Statement (NCS). Teachers were now confronted with very strong stipulation of content and closely specified sequencing and pacing requirements of subjects. Precisely what was to be covered was fixed in weekly outlines of subject content. How would this curriculum affect the practices of teachers emerging from 14 years of weakly framed, outcomes-based education? Would there be signs of broader access to the formal knowledge of reading and mathematics or a reproduction of past practices?

While the CAPS aimed specifically to strengthen the classification of the subject, strengthen the framing of evaluative criteria and pace and introduce greater individualization into classrooms, teachers' practice analyzed in the classrooms under study in this chapter shifted minimally. Classification of subjects was stronger in that mathematics and reading were identifiable as bounded and specific activities. However, the chapter explores the nature of the knowledge (not just its boundedness) in order to discern why individualization was surface, pacing extremely slow and the transmission of evaluative criteria still weakly framed.

Sample, method and theory

The Schools Performing Against Demographic Expectations (or SPADE) project was set up around the time of the implementation of CAPS to explore the relationship between particular aspects of schooling and educational attainment in a sample of 14 schools in poor communities. Part of the SPADE project explored the role of pedagogy in contributing to differential outcomes in schools. Drawing on a sub-sample of the SPADE schools, this chapter reports on the pedagogy observed in the classrooms of 14 teachers across four schools.[1] The schools were selected to match the demographic characteristics of the schools reported on in Chapter 7 and Chapter 9.

Two of the sampled schools were in Khayelitsha and the other two in similar, largely African townships located around Cape Town. All schools drew their students from very poor communities in their surrounds. Very similar social problems, unemployment and crime persisted in these communities. Although more formalized housing was evident, very little had changed in the communities since 2003 when the previous study was conducted. The schools themselves were adequately resourced, with sound infrastructure, furniture, books and stationery. Two of the schools were selected by the SPADE study on the basis of their better performance within their particular quintile and former department designation, and two schools performed just below the mean for the same categories of school. This performance was, however, within a low band and the differences in performance were marginal.

The teachers are labeled with a letter for the school and a number for the teacher (Teachers A1, A2, A3, B1, B2, B3, B4, C1, C2, C3, C4, D1, D2, D3). Each teacher was observed and video-recorded in the subjects mathematics and home language (isiXhosa). The framework that was developed for the study is discussed in detail in Appendix B. In the analysis a global classification and framing score was assigned to each of the 14 teachers' lessons. Briefly, to remind the reader, classification refers to the organization of knowledge in the classroom and whether boundaries between subjects is weak (C^-) or strong (C^+) and whether the boundaries between everyday knowledge and school knowledge similarly are weak or strong. Through classification the 'what' of classroom practice is delineated and made potentially recognizable to the students. Framing refers to control over the selection, sequence, pace and evaluation of instructional knowledge, and whether this control lies in the hands of the teacher or the learner. This pertains to the 'how' of the pedagogy and the forms of interaction that enable or disable students in realizing the appropriate production in the pedagogy. Framing of hierarchical rules refers to the nature of the social relation between the teacher and the student, part of the regulative discourse of the classroom or its social norms and rules of conduct, character and manner.

Changing classifications, enduring frames

The pedagogy of the 14 teachers was coded in terms of classification and framing for mathematics and reading. As in previous research, the pedagogy observed across the classrooms was remarkably similar. Consistent with past practices, there was very strong framing over selection, sequence and pace in both mathematics and reading. These aspects of the pedagogy were strongly controlled by the teacher, and student interventions and questions that may have slowed the pace or altered the sequence of content were not evident. Although the pace of the lessons was strongly framed (i.e. controlled by the teacher), the rate of transmission was extremely slow. If 40 to 60 minutes is a standard period, all the lessons vastly exceeded this length with the duration in mathematics ranging from 75 minutes to 200 minutes, and in Language from 68 minutes to 138 minutes. Very little content was covered across long periods of time and there was little or no differentiation in the pedagogy for slower and faster learners. The pacing was an outcome of a pedagogy that treated the class as a homogenous whole and pegged pacing at the slowest learners. This very slow, undifferentiated pacing is characteristic of a large number of South African classrooms (Hoadley, 2012; Taylor, 2014).

Lessons in both Home Language and Mathematics were predominantly oral and there was very little writing. In Language most classes entailed writing five to 10 single words, sentences were written in three classes and a paragraph in one class. Likewise in mathematics very few inscriptions of the lesson were made. Again, this accords with other research that has found a paucity of writing, especially extended writing, in South African classrooms (Dechaisemartin, 2013).

A consideration of framing over evaluation produced some variation, and although still weak was slightly stronger in relation to previous studies. When considering the framing of evaluative criteria, three indicators were used. The interest was in the extent to which teachers made evaluative criteria explicit, which consists of "clearly telling children what is expected of them, of identifying what is missing from their textual production, of clarifying the concepts, of leading them to make synthesis and broaden concepts" (Morais et al., 2004, p. 8). The three indicators were:

1 In the teacher's introduction/instructions for a topic/task
2 In the course of learners conducting an activity or task
3 In the kinds of verbal answers required of learners

What emerged from an analysis of the data in terms of these indicators was that teachers were making the requirements for the production of the appropriate text more explicit (1.), but in restricted ways. They were able to give instructions for procedures, as outlined in the CAPS documents, but did not elaborate on why things were done, on definitions or explanations of content (1.). In the course of conducting tasks, teachers made very little intervention in the responses by learners (2.). In cases where learners read or produced solutions in mathematics, correction was absent or was restricted to simple correction or moving directly to the next learner (2.). Teachers were not seen to seek elaborated verbal responses from learners in the data (3.).

The nature of response was particularly evident in the series of questions that generally followed the reading of a piece of extended text in 12 of the 14 classes. Questions were always orally delivered and answered and generally elicited chorused responses. Teacher evaluation was focused on simple incorrect or correct responses. An example from Teacher B3 shows the restricted patterning of discourse:

Teacher: What is the story about?
Learner: It's a fable about a wolf's tail
Teacher: Is he right?
Learners: [chorused] Yes
Teacher: Which animal called the meeting?
Learner: The lion
Teacher: Is it right?
Learners: [chorused] Yes Miss

In mathematics, likewise, although clear requirements were laid out for activities and tasks, there was no extended engagement with misconceptions or errors. None of the teachers responded to learner productions in any detail, and learners were not required to provide extended verbal responses or reasoning. Inaccuracies were found in the content provided by teachers across the classrooms.

The hierarchical rules, or the mode of interaction between teacher and learners in the classrooms was strongly framed, grounded in authority where control was explicit and non-negotiable rules and assertions defined the moral context of the classroom. Strong hierarchical rules were also evidenced in the fact that not once in the course of all observations did a student ask a question or offer an unelicited comment or response.

Stronger boundaries

What had shifted in both reading and mathematics classes was the strength of boundaries between these subjects and other subject knowledge and everyday knowledge. Reading and mathematics were more strongly classified in the classrooms, the lessons clearly identifiable as relating to these areas of learning. There were minimal references to the everyday knowledge and experience of learners. In Language lessons theme-driven learning was observed in three classrooms (with the familiar themes of animals wild and domestic, and the weather), and the 'free association'-type discourse observed in prior studies was evident in only one class. Otherwise, the Language content across most lessons was clearly identifiable.

Table 11.1 below shows aggregated codes assigned for reading and mathematics across the teachers. It reflects the similarities found across the subjects as well as across classrooms, but of course masks more subtle variations in different classrooms.

Possibly as a result of the strengthening of the classification of the subjects in the CAPS, the roles of the teacher and the learner as engaged in processes of transmission and acquisition were restored. This is linked to the decisive reintroduction of texts into classrooms. Photocopied sheets of extended text, readers, mathematics textbooks and curriculum-based workbooks provided by the Department of Basic Education (DBE) were evident across the classrooms.[2] In the case of literacy, lessons were driven by a written text (either a photocopied sheet (six lessons), the DBE workbooks (five lessons) or readers (five lessons)). Although much of the classroom discourse remained oral, there was more engagement with written text and subject content was made more visible through the introduction of texts. Although still relatively strongly framed, the relationship between teacher and student does not represent the same authoritarianism seen under C2005 and the NCS. This may be linked to the assertion of the roles of teacher and student as transmitter and acquirer, and might also relate to the authority of subjects and texts being re-established in the classrooms. Authority possibly now resided less in the person of the teacher and more in the teacher role and in the knowledge to be learnt.

Table 11.1 Summary of the structuring of pedagogic discourse across classrooms

Instructional	Selection	F^{++}	Teacher has strong control over content introduced in classroom
	Sequence	F^{++}	Teacher has strong control over the order in which content is introduced in the classroom
	Pace	F^{++}	Teacher has strong control over the rate of transmission
	Evaluation	F^{-}	Weak in relation to ongoing observation of and feedback on student work and low demand for elaborated learner response and reasoning.
	Classification between subject and other subjects and everyday knowledge	C^{+}	Strong. Mathematics and reading are clearly bounded subjects and minimal reference is made to students everyday knowledge and experience in most classes
	Classification between areas/topics within subject	C^{+}	Strong. Very few references are made to other subjects, there is very little attempt at integration and minimal evidence of theme work. Reading, numbers are demarcated as specialized content areas within Mathematics and Language.
Regulative	Framing of social relation (hierarchical rules)	F^{+}	Strongly framed hierarchical relation between teacher and students.

From evaluative criteria to knowledge criteria

There was also some shift in the lessons observed in the strength of the evaluative criteria probably related to the strengthening of classification. However, as discussed above, this shift was in relation to the clarity and explicitness of the instructions that teachers gave to students, or the procedures of conducting an activity. Extended feedback by teachers on students' productions was rare, and students were not asked to give elaborated answers or explain their reasoning or thinking. What persisted was a surface treatment of content and tasks. Evaluative criteria remained weak.

In the general use of the notion of 'evaluative criteria' these refer to strong or weak control over the requirements of the pedagogy, rendering these implicit or explicit (or even absent as in the case of 'F^{0}'). This does not tell us about the operation of the instructional discourse, or the meeting of the ***knowledge*** criteria (Muller & Hoadley, 2010, p. 171). Evaluative criteria arguably, are essentially about 'teaching styles'. The focus is in fact on the social relation between teacher and learner, and whether the teacher is ***controlling*** the transmission of criteria.[3] But what of the criteria themselves, and how they are related? What of the 'what'?

Below I consider in turn the knowledge criteria for reading and mathematics in the lessons. I relate this to the grouping of students for instruction. I am interested in whether the more individualized pedagogy suggested by the CAPS is at all evident in the organization of students and the knowledge criteria made available in the classrooms.

All together now: reading instruction across the 14 classrooms

Reading lessons followed a similar structure in each classroom. The lesson started with the joint reading of an extended piece of text. In nine of the 14 lessons the whole class chant-read the reading. This was followed by a whole class discussion, where the teacher discussed vocabulary, phonics or different parts of speech. This was clearly an attempt at the contextualized teaching of these language aspects. The discussion was often followed by a short activity, which generally entailed writing single words (in eight of the 14 lessons the words written down had a common phonemic and spelling feature and were found in the reading text).

A set of simple, oral questions generally followed the joint reading of the text. These questions worked through the narrative of the piece requiring factual recall by the students of the story. There was no interpretation, evaluation or higher level questioning in these exchanges. There was also no appeal to the students' own meaning-making of the story, nor opportunity for them to relate it to personal experience or evaluate it, as in the example given below:

Teacher: What are they going to buy?
Learners: (chorus) Cloth
Teacher: What are they going to do with the cloth?
Learners: (chorused) They are going to sew a dress
Teacher: They are
Learners: (chorused) They are going to sew a dress

In two instances these exchanges commenced with the teacher asking: "Is the story nice?" which was met with a chorused "Yes". The question had a liturgical ring to it. One cannot imagine an occasion where learners might have responded 'no'.

The dominant reading pedagogy in the classrooms therefore was a communal reading of text and a joint production of literal meaning of the text. In two classrooms, however, there was an explicit attempt to introduce more individualized reading instruction, in the group guided reading format. I discuss both in some detail below.

Point to the word: group guided reading

Group guided reading is a particular methodology that is specified in the CAPS to occur daily in classrooms. The intention is that a group of 6–10 learners of similar ability read the same text under the direction of the teacher, engaging in strategies for decoding text on the one hand, and 'text talk' around the meaning and structure of the text on the other. The curriculum document provides detailed steps regarding how groups should be formed and how the reading should be conducted. It offers direction on 'picture talk', 'whisper reading', suggested questions for a first reading as well as instructions regarding discussion: "The discussion could also include a focus on phonics, comprehension or on an aspect of grammar. Discuss the text bearing in mind the range of questions that should be integrated into the discussion to develop comprehension" (DBE, 2011, p. 13).

Teacher C4 took two groups of learners on the mat, for 15 and 20 minutes each. The two groups were given different texts, one more difficult than the other. In the first group (lower ability) each of the six children read the same paragraph over and over. The only comment that the teacher made in the course of the reading referred to book handling ("Hold the book properly"; "This is the way to hold the book") and either stating the word that a learner could not read or mispronounced, or saying 'uh-uh' after which a learner made a new attempt. No alternative decoding strategies were provided, such as pointing out some feature of the word; asking the student to sound out the word (which would seem to be an obvious strategy in a language like isiXhosa that has a transparent orthography); compare the word to another; break the word down into syllables (particularly relevant to Xhosa where syllabification skills are critical for learning to read in a conjunctive orthography (Katz, 2014)); or helping students to find cues in the surrounding text. Phelps and Schilling (2004) point out that these are not just pedagogical choices, but entail a depth of knowledge about word and text structure and reading. Choosing the most effective strategy depends on the teacher's knowledge of the word itself, the type of error and the surrounding text (p. 35).

There was also no discussion of features of text structure, vocabulary or syntax that might have been challenging for the children (DBE, 2011, p. 13). In addition, there was no 'text talk' and no attempt at making connections between the topic of the reading and students' own life experiences. The only reference to the meaning of the text was in a short exchange between the teacher and students when the reading had been completed:

Teacher: What is the book about? [No response from learners]. This book is talking about eyeglasses. Or is it talking about the grandpa's glasses?

Learners: [chorused] The Grandpa's glasses.

The second teacher who used group guided reading in her class, Teacher D1, employed the same mode of correction in her small group reading. With both groups, however, she drew attention to the cover of the books. In the first, she asked students who the author and illustrator of the book was and then commenced reading. In the second group she held up the cover, which showed a simple drawing of a chicken holding a watering can. The following exchange ensued:

Teacher: What do you think the story is about? [pause after no response]. What are you thinking?

Learner: I think the chicken is watering plants.
Teacher: Do you see Usikhukhukazi [name in the title of the book] watering the plants? [no response]. Why is Usikhukhukazi watering?
Learner: He wants to plant.
Teacher: He wants to plant. And?
Learner: [inaudible]
Teacher: And when he has planted. When he wants to plant and when he has planted. Okay, let's read.

It would have been very difficult to predict the story from the cover illustration, especially given that the story was an allegory around saving for lean times in times of plenty. In the story a chicken busies herself in times of plenty, collecting and storing, planting and gathering corn. The chicken in turn asks other animals to assist and they decline. When it comes to leaner times the other animals, however, implore and rely on the chicken who had anticipated lean times to follow those of plenty.

The story had nothing to do with a chicken wanting to plant or watering "that which was already planted". At the end of the reading session the teacher made brief reference to the fact that the animals were lazy, but no further explication or discussion of the meaning of the story was offered. Thus, a device for supporting understanding in reading – prediction based on picture talk – served rather to obscure the meaning of the narrative.

As in the previous group, the learners in this group struggled to read. Here though two learners could not read at all. Teacher D1's initial response was to try and get the learners to read through assertion:

Teacher: That is the wrong word. Read it there.
Learner is unable
Teacher: Point to the words with your finger as you read.
Learner is unable to locate the word.
Teacher: [irritated tone] Read that word
Learner is unable
Teacher: [to the learner sitting alongside] Help him to read.
The two learners read together (the initital reader echoing the leader who has taken over].

In a second instance, Teacher D1 deployed the same strategies: pointing and then paired reading:

Teacher: That is not the word.
Learner tries again and teacher corrects him by saying the word.
Teacher: Point to the word so you can see it properly
Learner attempts
Teacher: You are pointing at parts that you are not reading. That makes it difficult for you.
Learner looks at the book.

Teacher: Read that part you are pointing at. Carry on from 'hayi'.
Learner makes an error

The teacher then instructed the learner to read with the person next to him. Here the inability to read is conveyed as the inability to point at the correct words.

The examples above suggest that the teachers had at their disposal a number of procedures for the teaching of reading – grouping, pictorial predicting, book handling – mostly clearly derived from the CAPS. The teachers, however, failed to integrate these procedures into evident *principles* for the teaching of reading, a set of specialized approaches to assist learners in decoding text and retrieving meaning from the text.

The procedures themselves were very restricted and provided students in these instances with little support in improving decoding. A phonological path of 'sounding out' or breaking down a word was not offered. Further, there were no opportunities for learners to "look at words, explain their meanings, analyse their forms, talk about the characters and events, talk about the pictures, make predictions, and draw inferences" (Pretorius, 2014, p. 70). No reading for meaning, establishing narrative or reading for pleasure was introduced. It was not that there is no benefit to the pedagogy observed. Through this pedagogic strategy learners unlike before were exposed to whole texts rather than words or letters in isolation and some had the opportunity to handle actual books.[4] There is also a chance that these teachers had a better estimation of their students' reading levels given that they have heard the learners read individually. However, the broader affordances of group guided reading were missed, especially the scrutiny and treatment of individual learners' reading competencies and inabilities and engagement around the meaning of the text.

In both lessons the teachers took on a *form* of individualizing suggested by the curriculum: small groups for reading on the mat. However, teacher feedback and intervention was restricted to correcting a misread word or stating the word that a learner was unable to say. As shown above, although differentiation meant different level texts for different groups, the pedagogy was not individualized with respect to transmission.

By not providing a range of skills with which to approach unknown words, the teachers do not transmit knowledge criteria that would develop students' conscious strategies for decoding or retrieving meaning. In both whole class and small group reading the lack of fluency in the actual reading often renders the text a fragmented series of sentences. At others times, reading represents a repetitive and undifferentiated chorusing of words on a page. In this way the texts are hollowed of meaning.

Specialized knowledge of reading

What does the specialized knowledge of reading entail? What are the criteria that students should be given access to? At its most rudimentary it is decoding text, and this includes a wide range of strategies. It is also the development of fluency, both based on and developing vocabulary. All of this underpins retrieving meaning from text, be this literal or inferential. The ability to evaluate texts and the identification of genres and the structuring of text comes later. And alongside this is the development of reading self-regulation in reading for pleasure or choice. So there is a specialized knowledge/skill set for reading, and it is progressive. Identifying these elements of learning to read makes it clearer what students in these classes were being given access to: an extremely basic and impoverished notion of what it means to read and a restrictive set of resources with which to critically and pleasurably engage with text.

Mathematics pedagogy in the 14 classrooms

As in reading, there was a common structure to the mathematics lessons across the classrooms and schools. The lesson generally began with acoustic counting, the recital of sequences of numbers, in different multiples and what the curriculum refers to as "brisk mental starters" such as "the number after/before 8 is; 2 more/less than 8 is; 4+2; 5+2, 6+2 etc" (DBE, 2011, p. 11).

The 'mental maths' and mental starters were followed in most classes by new or previously-introduced content (for example, time, 2D shapes, measurement), and after brief exposition learners would engage in independent seatwork while the teacher worked with a smaller group of students.

Smaller groups were a feature of eight of the 14 observed lessons. While ability grouping was evident in some of these groups, in general the same pedagogic forms and content of the whole class instruction were repeated in the small groups – acoustic counting, 'mental maths' followed by teacher exposition, often around place value. Interaction in these small groups was strongly framed. The teacher did not engage with individual students, and students did not volunteer information, questions or comment. In both whole class and small group students were communalized and as in reading the teacher does not use the intimacy of the small group form of classroom organization to closely engage with individual student productions.

Across these classrooms as in reading the pace was extremely slow, with very little content covered in very long lessons. In addition, teachers covered a range of number concepts, operations and tasks in one lesson with little sustained work on a particular operation or concept. For example in Teacher C2's class the teacher covered: counting and ordering; a number of calculations involving all four operations; a place value exercise; two contextual money problems; an exercise on counting in multiples of 25; an activity focused on sharing; decomposition of number; and a contextual multiplication sum. Although one could argue that this lesson was about consolidation, there was no conceptual or numerical 'anchor' for the many diverse tasks, and clear evidence of learners' inability to grasp some of the content was not addressed. This lack of conceptual connection was evident in the small groupwork as well. An example below is drawn from Teacher A3's class.

> The teacher moves around a group of 7 learners. Each learner counts out beans in multiples of 2s until the teacher stops them. Learners then 'build'

the number from a set of Flard cards. They are then asked to write the number in the workbooks that are next to them on the floor. Finally once each child has had a turn at counting they are instructed to decompose the numbers written in their books into hundreds tens and units. The learners struggle to do this, and the following exchange ensues between the teacher and a learner:

T:	No no one hundred and eighteen. One ***hundred*** and eighteen.
T:	One ***hundred*** and eighteen. Which number do you start with when I say one hundred?
	No response from the learner.
Teacher:	Which number do you start with when I say one hundred? What is this number?
Learner:	one
Teacher:	What number do you start with when you write one hundred and eighteen?
Learner:	One
Teacher:	Write it down
Teacher:	Did you do it right?
Teacher:	You should write it the way you built it in the cards. When you write the number down write it the way you built it in the cards. Nothing is happening here [referring to what the learners are doing].

The students continued to struggle to complete the task. A number of reasons for this could be identified. First, as we see in the exchange above, the concept of place value was not communicated. Thus, 100 in 118 was rendered as '1' by the teacher – a visual rather than conceptual explanation of how to write the number. This was possibly related to the fact that in representing the number of beans with the cards, unit cards were used to make up the numbers even though the students' sets of Flard cards included 100, 10s and unit cards. No clear connection between the piles of beans, the unit cards, the inscription of the number in the book and its decomposition was made. Because the connection was difficult to retrieve, when a student struggled the teacher offered no elaboration.

In the mental mathematics activities the teacher passed over incorrect responses looking to other students to provide the answers. As in reading, evaluation was restricted to silence, 'no' or the provision of the correct response without any engagement with the error or misconception. The beans in the example above remained a concrete pile of beans, and learners' opportunity to grasp the concept of the decimal system, the fundamental basis of number, was limited by classroom practices that deployed visual and concrete representations of number without connecting these to their conceptual reference point in place value.[5]

School knowledge and everyday knowledge

One final example from the mathematics data shows a different relation between school knowledge and everyday knowledge than the one seen in classrooms under the NCS and C2005. In the CAPS classrooms, classification was strengthened, and the lessons were often knowledge-led. However, conceptual understanding was 'trumped' by an experiential or 'spontaneous' understanding of mathematics, as exemplified below.

In a lesson focused on 3D shapes, the teacher sat on the mat with 10 learners. Each learner took a 3D shape from a box. The teacher addressed each learner asking them what shape they were holding. In every case the teacher offered or affirmed the 2-D shape that made up the face of the 3-D object, but did not offer the name of the 3D object. The teacher became snared in everyday perceptual descriptions of the shapes, and while finding 3D shapes in the environment is not inappropriate at this level, the reason for doing this was not clear and the students were given no nomenclature to harness the activity:

Teacher: What shape are you holding?
Learner: [referring to the sphere in her hand] A circle
Teacher: How is it?
Learner: It's green
Teacher: Look at it. How is it?
Learner: [no response]
Teacher: Is it rough or smooth?
Learner: [no response]
Teacher: [moving onto next student] What are you holding?
Learner: [holding a prism] A rectangle
Teacher: How many corners does it have?
Learner: Four corners
Teacher: What is the shape? What does it look like?
Learner: A dog's house
Learner: A cupboard
Teacher: What shape are you holding?
Learner: [holding a cylinder] A bin
Teacher: What is the name?
Learner: [no response]
Teacher: [moving on to the next learner] What shape are you holding?

The teacher in this exchange demonstrated a practice seen across all classrooms, that is, to pass on to the next learner without comment when an error was made. The starting point of the lesson – 3D shapes – was mathematical, potentially introducing students to defining properties of 3D shapes such as faces, edges, and vertices, as a precursor to concepts of volume and surface area. Thus, comparison of the size of shapes, whether they have flat or smooth edges, the shape of their faces and their names (sphere, prism, cone, etc.) is appropriate. However, everyday conceptions dominated the lesson so that no terminology was introduced and 'corners' (reference to angles) was not grade appropriate.

In mathematics the classification had strengthened and the organizational form had shifted. However, there was a surface treatment of the content introduced. In the very mundane, fragmented and often concrete ways in which learners worked with number it was unlikely that they were gaining access to more abstract ways of working with number concept or broader mathematical principles.

Evaluation and individualization

Above I showed how although teachers in both the reading and the mathematics lessons took on the form of an individualizing pedagogy in constituting small groups, the pedagogy of these small groups replicated that of whole class instruction with no apparent close attention and response to individual student productions. In small reading groups the emphasis was on word correction and book handling and in mathematics on correct or incorrect solutions with no elaboration on student responses.

Individualizing requires a shift from 'positional' to 'personal' forms of relation (Bernstein, 1990) – from a relation based on formal positions and roles to one where there is sensitivity to the person and their unique characteristics (especially their learning development and needs). These personal roles are achieved through explicit and complex forms of communication. These complex and explicit forms of communication are not possible where there is a restricted knowledge base, or where the purpose, skill or knowledge to be transmitted and acquired is not firmly established. In these instances, the teacher will probably enact positional forms that attach the student and teacher to formally defined roles and status understandable and recognizable to all in the relation.

It would be a mistake to see individualizing or communalizing only as a cultural attribute although it may have cultural resonances. The data here and throughout the book suggests that communalizing is about a lack of access to specialized knowledge of practice. A lack of access may explain why even when teachers put students in small groups and the students produce individualized performances teachers don't evaluate individually and engage with the students as individuals. Reflexive access to specialized knowledge would be necessary for teachers to appropriately evaluate students in the immediacy of the small group.

The communalizing pedagogy still prevalent in these classrooms is rooted in weak evaluation. Without close tracking of individual learner productions and appropriate judgments and course of action regarding their productions, the teachers were unable to give specific feedback to learners, or demand elaborated responses from them. Likewise, a pace most appropriate to the majority, or a differentiated pace, was not possible without adequate assessment of where individual students were in a trajectory of learning established in the classroom.

The teachers in this sample provided more simple correction (exerting slightly greater control over evaluative criteria) as well as clearer instructions for tasks. However, none of the teachers responded to learner productions in an extended way, and learners were not required to provide extended verbal responses or reasoning for their productions. Thus, transmission of evaluative criteria was weakly framed and knowledge criteria minimally transmitted or not transmitted at all.

The new CAPS curriculum is associated with some shift in the organization of the classroom into more focused groupings of students. However, the fundamental social relation of teacher to whole (communalized) class endured in the pedagogy. What the CAPS curriculum had directly affected was a change in the textual base of the classroom and a pedagogy that was far more subject-specific with strong classifications of number and reading as discrete content areas. In the surface nature of the transmission, however, and uptake of pedagogic *forms*, the substance of the pedagogy in many respects remained unchanged. This substance refers to the discursive aspects of the pedagogy – the underpinning knowledge that constitutes the practice. It was clear in these classrooms that the CAPS alone had not been able to disrupt the enduring forms of interaction that have been identified across time.

Questions of substance: knowledge in pedagogy

There are a number of researchers that in different ways have begun to explore the issue of knowledge in pedagogy. This work pays attention to the ***knowledge principle*** that structures learning and the selection of content, and that provides a logic for its ordering in the classroom (Venkat, 2013; Shalem, 2017). This ordering logic or 'epistemic relation between ideas' (Shalem & Slonimsky, 2010) can be seen in instances of generalization and drawing connections between ideas in pedagogic practice. More specifically, it can be seen when "a teacher marks certain pedagogical moments to state a propositional rule, compares and contrasts between ideas, demands precision of meaning and confers what can and cannot be inferred from a proposition" (de Clerq & Shalem, 2015).

In the lessons analyzed, teachers' references, especially to students' productions, were made to the particular pedagogic instances rather than generalization across time or across instances. The connectivity both in terms of what had gone before and what would come after, ***and*** connections between bits of knowledge was absent. What provides the knowledge principle? For a number of scholars it is the discipline from which the subject is derived (Young, 2013; Winch, 2013). In early years pedagogy identifying the discipline is not straightforward. Reading especially is not a discipline, and therefore identifying its content knowledge is more difficult (Phelps and Schilling (2004). The disciplinary basis for both mathematics and reading is relatively remote at this level, with psychology a significant intervening domain given that the knowledge base at this level is more pedagogical than disciplinary. In any case, defining and describing the knowledge teachers must possess and use to effectively teach reading and writing and mathematics at this level has for a long time posed a significant challenge (Reutzel et al., 2011; Ball et al., 2001). But an additional complication is that knowledge at this level can be described as 'common knowledge'.

The problem of common knowledge

Subject knowledge in the early years of learning mathematics and reading (the basic skills of reading, counting and calculating) is a form of 'common knowledge'.

In other words, many of us have the ability to read and do at least rudimentary mathematical tasks in our everyday lives. The analysis shows how teaching reading and counting and calculating appeared driven by these everyday competencies (that most of us have) rather than a highly specialized, differentiated skill (that teachers should possess). Those of us who are fluent in reading, counting and basic arithmetic cannot differentiate and articulate, or recognize the different skills and concepts involved in early reading and number – text structure, syllabification, morphology, the principles of cardinality and ordinality etcetera.

Thus, in some classrooms we see how counting and calculating is treated as empirical – that is common – knowledge. Venkat and Askew (2012) report on lessons where despite the presence of artefacts that could be used to model scientific aspects of number bonds – for example the abacus with the structure of 10 – teachers repeatedly established number bonds empirically through counting in ones. This is similar to the beans in the example earlier – a pile of ones rather than organized to represent the decimal system. This was also exemplified in the 3D shape lesson, where common knowledge and appellations of 3D shapes ('ball', 'bin', 'cupboard') were not superseded by more specialized terms or conceptual understandings. In this way the fundamental function of early learning to shift learners to abstract understanding is blocked.

In reading, the teacher's fluency and familiarity with reading (common knowledge) appeared to hinder the ability to notice and work with phonemic, spelling and other issues in reading that those unfamiliar with reading (the learners) confront. The knowledge or content for teaching reading is not just about being a competent and fluent reader.

It is very possible that the teachers in this study do not differentiate common knowledge of content from the specialized knowledge required for the teaching of mathematics and reading. These teachers know how to count and order and add and read and write, in a common knowledge sense. They do not deploy a specialized understanding of what underpins these abilities, nor, relatedly, identify and address the ways in which some children are unable to grasp them in the lessons. This may account for the total lack of, or very restricted, responses to learners' errors. A further factor that would aggravate the development of teachers' specialized knowledge and ability to exercise professional judgment is their own reading practices. Both the SPADE project as well as work by Pretorius and Matchet (2004) found that teachers generally did not read (apart from the Bible). This would likely compromise teachers broader access to issues of genre, text structure, as well as how to communicate reading for pleasure and reading for choice.

Specialized knowledge in pedagogy

Because reading and mathematics at this level resembles common knowledge, it is necessary to attend even more closely to the complexity of the knowledge base of specialized teaching of mathematics and reading. What content knowledge in linguistics do primary teachers need to know? Would they benefit from researchers' delineation of different stages of reading or different systemic functions of language (Reutzel et al., 2011, p. 194)? Would they be helped by understanding numbers in terms of oriented length and not just quantity (NRC, 2001)? It is this specialized knowledge that allows for ***upward generalization*** in pedagogy, where pedagogic instances or procedures are not consumed by their context (Bernstein, 1990, p. 179) in the 'stubborn immediacy of the present' (Venkat, 2013). Rather, instances connect with the broader demands of a mathematics or reading learning trajectory that takes its significance from the future (Bernstein, 1990, p. 179). Moss (2010) points out that thinking like this points to

> the relocation of control over knowledge from what is good enough in a particular context, and the judgments which the immediate participants themselves can call on in assessing a particular performance's adequacy, to an externally validated set of criteria which teachers hand on.
>
> (p. 155)

It is these externally validated criteria embedded in the different forms of specialized knowledge teachers require to teach reading and early number that hold the potential to shift pedagogy meaningfully. In the absence of changing the discursive resources of practice, what we see is isomorphic mimicry of forms privileged in the curriculum, teachers taking on the form but not the substance of changed practice. These knowledge criteria also hold the possibilities for shifting the framing over evaluative criteria and relatedly pacing and a social relation that recognizes individual differences. This relation between individualizing, knowledge criteria, evaluation and pacing represents an attempt to describe ***knowledge in pedagogy*** and its operation in the early grades in teaching reading and number, the most fundamental capacities of and for schooling.

Notes

1 The sample for the SPADE project consisted of 46 Grade 3 teachers in 14 schools located in poor communities. For the present study I excluded the (eight) former HOR or 'coloured' schools in order to achieve a closely comparable sample to those of Chapters 7 and 9. HOR schools were also slightly better resourced, generally had different language issues at play in the school and drew students from slightly better off communities than the schools I had previously studied. Two African schools were also excluded on the basis of insufficient video data for teachers in those schools being available.

2 The workbooks, one of the most ambitious and far-reaching curriculum interventions, comprise year-length series of activities in different subjects, reaching millions of children from Grade 1 to Grade 9. See www.education.gov.za/curriculum/workbooks.aspx

3 A range of studies have come up with strong and consistent findings in relation to evaluation – strong (explicit) control over the evaluative criteria are essential to student success in acquiring recognition and realization rules, especially in working-class contexts ((Morais et al, 2004; Hoadley, 2007; Reeves, 2005; Lubienski, 2004).

4 Taylor (2014) reports on large-scale classroom observations for the NEEDU report that "No individual reading by learners was seen in 83% of classes observed by NEEDU, no independent writing in 90%, and in only 5% did learners ask questions.
5 The concept of place value can be defined as: Any number in the decimal system is the sum of the products of each digit and an appropriate power of 10, where the power in question corresponds to the position of the digit (National Research Council (NRC), 2001, p. 98).

References

Ball, D., Lubienski, S., & Mewborn, D. (2001). Research on teaching mathematics: The unsolved problem of teachers' mathematical knowledge. In V. Richardson (Ed.), *Handbook of research on teaching* (pp. 433–456). Fourth edition. New York: MacMillan.

Bernstein, B. (1990). Class, codes and control, volume 4: The structuring of pedagogic discourse. London: Routledge.

Dechaisemartin, T. (2013). Writing matters: The neglect of writing in South African schools'. In N. Taylor, S. van der Berg & T. Mabogoane (Eds.), *Creating effective schools* (pp.157–176). Cape Town: Pearson.

de Clercq, F., & Shalem, Y. (2015). Teacher knowledge and professional development. In F. Maringe & M. Prew (Eds.), *Twenty years of education transformation in Gauteng 1994 to 2014* (pp. 153–174). Somerset West, SA: African Minds.

Department of Basic Education. (2011). Curriculum and assessment policy statement (CAPS): Foundation phase: Home language grades R-3. Pretoria: Department of Basic Education.

Hoadley, U. (2007). The reproduction of social class inequalities through mathematics pedagogies in South African primary schools. *Journal of Curriculum Studies, 39*(6), 679–706.

Hoadley, U. (2012). What do we know about teaching and learning in South African primary schools? *Education as Change, 16*(2), 187–202.

Katz, J. (2014). Graded basal readers in African languages: Using a phonics-based approach to develop early grade reading materials in the transparent orthographies of our indigenous languages, with an additive syllabic approach to those with conjunctive orthographies. Paper presented at the South African Educational Research Association (SAERA) Conference, Durban, July.

Lubienski, S. (2004). 'Decoding mathematics instruction: A critical examination of an invisible pedagogy. In J. Muller, B. Davies & A. Morais (Eds.), *Reading Bernstein, researching Bernstein* (pp. 107–122). London: RoutledgeFalmer.

Morais, A., Neves, I., & Pires, D. (2004). *The what* and the *how* of teaching and learning. In J. Muller, B. Davies & A. Morais (Eds.), *Reading Bernstein, researching Bernstein* (pp. 75–90). London: RoutledgeFalmer.

Moss, G. (2010). Policy and pedagogy: Proficiency and choice in the literacy classroom. Abingdon: Routledge. 220–230.

Muller, J., & Hoadley, U. (2010). Pedagogy and moral order. In P. Singh & A. Sadovnik (Eds.), *Knowledge, knowers and pedagogic modes: Building on the sociology of Basil Bernstein*. New York: Peter Lang.

National Research Council. (2001). Adding it up: Helping children learn mathematics. J. Kilpatrick, J. Swafford & B. Findell (Eds.), *Mathematics Learning Study*

Committee, Center for Education, Division of Behavioral and Social Sciences and Education. Washington, DC: National Academy Press.

Phelps, G., & Schilling, S. (2004). Developing measures of content knowledge for teaching reading. *The Elementary School Journal*, *105*(1), 31–48.

Pretorius, E. (2014). Supporting transition or playing catch-up in Grade 4? Implications for standards in education and training. *Perspectives in Education*, *32*(1), 51–76.

Pretorius, E., & Machet, M. (2004). The socio-educational context of literacy accomplishment in disadvantaged schools: Lessons for reading in the early primary school years. *Journal for Language Teaching*, *38*, 45–62.

Reeves, C. (2005). The effect of 'Opportunity to Learn' and classroom pedagogy on mathematics achievement in schools serving low socio-economic status communities in the Cape Peninsula. PhD thesis, University of Cape Town.

Reutzel, D. R., Dole, J. A., Read, S., Fawson, P., Herman, K., Jones, C. D., et al. (2011). Conceptually and methodologically vexing issues in teacher knowledge assessment. *Reading & Writing Quarterly*, *27*(3), 183–211.

Shalem, Y. (2017). Scripted lesson plans: what is visible and invisible in visible pedagogy? In B. Barrett, U. Hoadley & J. Morgan (Eds.), *Knowledge, Curriculum and equity: Social realist perspectives*. London: Routledge.

Shalem, Y., & Slonimsky, L. (2010). Seeing epistemic order: Construction and transmission of evaluative criteria. *British Journal of Sociology of Education*, *31*(6), 755–778.

Taylor, N. (2014). NEEDU national report 2013: Teaching and learning in rural primary schools. Pretoria: Department of Basic Education.

Venkat, H. (2013). Using temporal range to theorize early number teaching in South Africa. *For the Learning of Mathematics*, *33*(2), 31–36.

Venkat, H., & Askew, M. (2012). Mediating early number learning: Specialising across teacher talk and tools? *Journal of Education*, *57*, 55–77.

Winch, C. (2013). Curriculum design and epistemic ascent. *Journal of Philosophy of Education*, *47*(1), 128–146.

Young, M. (2013). Overcoming the crisis in curriculum theory: A knowledge-based approach. *Journal of Curriculum Studies*, *45*(2), 101–118.

12 Conclusion

Knowledge in pedagogy

Introduction: the changing moral order

The processes of curriculum reform described in this book offer a kind of natural experiment in changes in curriculum policy and the relation to pedagogy in a developing country context. The period under consideration was a time of radical and rapid change, from apartheid to a democratic regime. The different political regimes fostered very different pedagogic regimes, reflected in the understanding of what knowledge was to be distributed to whom.

Under apartheid different groups, based on race and class, were given access to different forms of knowledge: more specialized, academic forms for the white population and more context-dependent, manual forms for the majority of black people. As the moral order changed over the post-apartheid period these distributive rules changed, too. In the transition to democracy there was an attempt to dissolve boundaries between social, economic and knowledge categories, an attempt to create equivalence between head and hand, or knowledge (education) and skills (production). This was manifest in the establishment of the National Qualifications Framework and the first curriculum reform, Curriculum 2005. In the policy reforms that followed producing the National Curriculum Statement and the Curriculum and Assessment Policy Statement, the gradual re-inscription of educational boundaries was evident as the state retrieved the distinctiveness of schooling and a particular educational purpose: the transmission of specialized subject knowledge to all social groups.

How did these shifts at the broad level of official pedagogic discourse translate into curriculum policy and then into actual classrooms? And what was the relationship between curriculum and pedagogy at different times? These are the questions that the book pursued. In this chapter I discuss some of the central findings of the book and draw out some of the implications of the arguments for theory, research and the possibilities of change.

Shifts in the structure of curriculum and pedagogy

Table 12.1 shows in summary form the shifts in the classifications and frames in curriculum and pedagogy across the three successive reforms. Here, at the

Table 12.1 Changes in the classifications and frames in successive reforms, 1990–2011

	Apartheid	*C2005*	*NCS*	*CAPS*
Curriculum policy	C^{+}/F^{+}	C^{-}/F^{-}	$C^{+/-}/F^{+/-}$	C^{+}/F^{+}
Pedagogic practice	C^{+}/F^{-}	$C^{-}/F^{-/0}$	$C^{-}/F^{-/0}$	C^{+}/F^{-}

level of curriculum policy and then at the level of classroom practice, classification refers to the strength of the demarcation of subject knowledge, and framing refers specifically to the evaluative criteria or strength of signaling of the knowledge requirements in policy and the classroom.

The table shows how from apartheid through the reforms of C2005 and the NCS to the CAPS the position of formal school knowledge shifted – explicit under apartheid, backgrounded in C2005, re-emerging in the NCS and again explicit in the CAPS. There was also a shift in the control over and specification of the knowledge to be taught – strongly framed under apartheid, weaker control under C2005 and the NCS where teachers decided on issues of selection, sequence, pace and evaluation of knowledge, to strong control over these aspects again under the CAPS. This was all at the level of intention (curriculum policy). What is clear is that although there is a structural similarity between the curriculum privileged under apartheid and the CAPS (C^{+}/F^{+}), these are underpinned by very different ideologies and the CAPS is the result of the cumulative trajectory of curriculum change sketched in the book.

The C^{+}/F^{+} form has at times been labeled 'traditional', suggesting a 'teacher-centred' approach. A rejection of the curricula under apartheid meant fundamental changes in the classification and framing in the first post-apartheid curriculum, C2005. C2005 took curriculum in the direction of many systems that have massified rapidly – to a learner-centred curriculum, organized in relation to generic learning outcomes. Classification was weak and weak framing gave teachers' control over the ways in which knowledge was selected for teaching. This shift to weak frames can be read as intended to alleviate the pressure on teachers of the C^{+}/F^{+} apartheid curriculum. When it became clear that C2005 could not hold, in the NCS a hybrid curriculum was created, with elements of more strongly classified subject knowledge and enduring weak frames of learner-centredness. The CAPS curriculum returned to the C^{+}/F^{+} form, intent on support for a teaching corps chronically in need of knowledge signaling.

Given these significant curriculum changes, what happens to the pedagogy under each of these curriculum regimes? The table shows pedagogy as a C/F couplet, the C representing the classification of knowledge in the classroom, and the F the transmission of evaluative criteria. The table shows that under apartheid there is a sense of what was being transmitted and acquired as a result of strong subject boundaries (C^{+}). The subject knowledge is recognizable in the classroom. Transmission of evaluative criteria is, however, weak. Under both C2005 and the NCS subject boundaries are blurred and subject knowledge in classrooms subject to radical integration (especially with everyday knowledge) (C^-). Again, transmission of evaluative rules is weak (F^-) and in extreme forms, absent (F^0). Finally, when we come to the CAPS we again have strong classification and weak evaluative criteria. The analyses in the book suggest that the weak framing of evaluative criteria across the reforms is linked to teacher knowledge and access to knowledge criteria for teaching. The teachers in the classrooms in the study don't explicitly transmit the criteria for what knowledge counts or what ideas belong together in the lessons. Thus, despite a shift in the CAPS to strong knowledge signalling, pedagogy in the classrooms under study persistently fails to give learners access to the criteria required for mastery over the skills and content of the curriculum.

The social relation – a communalizing pedagogy

In the shifts sketched above, what happens to the regulative discourse in the classrooms studied, and the nature of the relation between students and teachers? Across all reforms the analyses showed the persistence of a communalizing pedagogy and strong framing of hierarchical rules, an authoritarian relationship. In Chapter 11 I argued that it would be a mistake to see individualizing or communalizing solely as a cultural attribute of pedagogy, although it may have cultural resonances. The analyses in the book suggest that individualizing is not possible without access to specialized knowledge for practice. A communalizing pedagogy is rooted in weak evaluation and restricted access to knowledge criteria for teaching. The rite of rote and the synchrony established between teachers and students in this communalized pedagogy masks the low knowledge content in the transmission processes.

A key distinction used in the book is between the analytically separable instructional and regulative discourse. Progressivism suggests an individualizing at the level of regulative discourse and a weak classification of knowledge and framing of evaluative criteria at the level of instructional discourse such that integration, self-directed learning and the natural potential of the learner can be released. A number of researchers opposed to learner-centred pedagogies argue for more socio-cultural approaches that aim to develop more 'culturally responsive indigenous pedagogies' (Tabulawa, 2013) which may or may not approximate constructivist or learner-centred pedagogies. Guthrie (1990, 2011) asserts that formalism (another term for 'traditional' pedagogy) should be retained, and that this form of pedagogy is particularly effective in schools where resources are very limited. He argues, "In these contexts, the question to ask is not, how can we improve the quality of teaching by promoting alternatives to formalism, but, how can we improve the quality of formalism?" (1990, p. 228).

These are important critiques. But the focus in these arguments is generally on regulative discourse – the social, psychological aspects of the teacher-student relation and the social and cultural norms implicit in various pedagogic forms. In accounting for the enduring practices seen in classrooms the book draws attention to the transmission of knowledge, the instructional discourse or what Bruner

(1963) referred to as the 'logical' (as opposed to cultural and psychological) aspect of pedagogy. In order to effect change in pedagogy, I argue that it is necessary to change the specialized knowledge base of teachers and how knowledge is transmitted in classrooms. Without fundamental change in instructional discourse, the social form or the dominant ways of interacting and communicating in classrooms (regulative discourse) that impede learning are unlikely to be dislodged.

Conceiving of knowledge as integral to the pedagogic relation (not separate to, out there in curriculum, or aside, independent of the social relation) leads to a relational conception of social relation and knowledge transaction. To put it more simply, poor classroom practices are often blamed on regulative features – the teacher is authoritarian, children do not participate, it's all chalk and talk, for example – leaving aside a consideration of how knowledge resources or the lack thereof shape these regulative features.

To draw out the point in relation to Bernsteinian theory specifically, in most formulations Bernstein argues that the instructional discourse is embedded in regulative discourse, and the regulative discourse is dominant. What the pedagogic analyses in the book suggest is that if instructional discourse (classification and evaluative criteria) doesn't shift, then the possibilities for regulative discourse to shift are limited. In this way, in relation to the theory, the priority of regulative discourse over instructional discourse is questioned, and Bernstein's reversal of the order (see Chapter 5) where he argues "Rules of social order, relation, and identity [regulative discourse] are embedded in rules of discursive order [instructional discourse]" applies at the level of pedagogic practice. Instructional discourse *is* dominant at the level of pedagogy.

More than subject knowledge

The conclusions above in relation to the knowledge of teachers refer to more than just subject knowledge, however. Slonimsky (2015) argues "there are *real* structural factors generated by the past, which have significant implications for teachers to change the orders of their practices in a society in the process of transition to a qualitatively different moral order" (p. x). She cites Durkheim in pointing to a crucial structural factor: 'education theory':

> It is not enough to prescribe to [teachers] in precise detail what they will have to do; they must be in a position to assess, and appreciate these prescriptions, to see the point of them and the needs which they meet. In brief they must be familiar with the problems for which these prescriptions provide provisional solutions. This means that it is essential to initiate them into the great problems involved in education for which they will be responsible, no less than the methods whereby it is proposed to solve them so that they may be able to make up their own minds with that knowledge of the issues involved. Such an initiation can only come from a study of educational theory.
>
> (Durkheim, 1977, p. 4, cited in Slonimsky, 2015)

There has been little consideration in developing country research and policy around how teachers 'make up their own minds' about what they do in their classrooms. Nor has there been much effort in making the point of prescriptions (such as those in the CAPS) available to teachers. Further, what is under-researched across developing country contexts are teachers' deeply held implicit theories of schooling and learning, how they account for and explain what they do, what *they* understand as the point of their practice to be. The book opens up the question (though does not directly address it): How does the 'life-world' of the teacher, their socially-grounded values, interests and commitments intersect with the requirements of reform? What pedagogic forms and theories related to their own schooling and socialization into teaching practice, do teachers currently reproduce in classrooms? To what extent has there been opportunity for the interruption of the traditional, restrictive practices they were schooled under in the past?

The structural factors at play obstructing the expansion of our (not just teachers) cognitive horizons are both educational and relate to the broader social structure. The post-apartheid period in South Africa that has been under review in this study has been relatively short. There have been very limited opportunities for teachers to increase their specialized knowledge in the 22 years since the end of apartheid. This stems in part from the first two underspecified curricula (C2005 and NCS) that provided weak direction for teacher initial and in-service training until 2012, but also is a result of the legacy of apartheid teacher training and the low capacity in the system to upgrade teachers' professional competence. There have been very limited significant, sustained or successful programmes to increase teachers' knowledge across the system in the last 22 years (Council for Higher Education, 2010; de Clerq & Shalem, 2014).

The very deep inequality in South African society hinders the redistribution of resources across society, be these social, cultural, intellectual or material. Ongoing physical separation of race and class groupings of people limit the opportunities of teachers, and students, to see, imagine, acquire and generate different practices to those generated under apartheid and reproduced 22 years into democracy.

Who is the teacher in policy?

Given the low levels of teacher knowledge, what kind of teacher is imagined in the curriculum policies? Table 12.2 shows how this has changed across time, from the notion of the teacher as a reproducer of stipulated content under apartheid, to the assumption in the first post-apartheid curriculum, C2005, that the teacher was entirely competent in being a major recontextualizer (curriculum-maker), but requiring socializing into a new radically horizontalized relationship with learners. The NCS which came next was more ambiguous about the assumed competence of the imagined teacher, and focused on the teacher as key to social change. The CAPS, highly prescriptive and at times close to scripted, does not assume teacher competence and privileges no particular student-teacher relation but focuses on specification of content to be covered.

Table 12.2 The shifting model of the teacher in successive reforms, 1990–2011

Apartheid	*C2005*	*NCS*	*CAPS*
Reproducer of stipulated content, not open for critique or analysis. Not necessarily competent in teaching maths or reading	Very competent in teaching maths and in how children learn. Major recontextualizing agent with high levels of literacy. Emphasis on teacher's role in educating emergent citizen and community member. Teachers' role in eliciting existing competences in learners	Competent in teaching maths and in how children learn to read. Not major recontextualizing agent. "envisions teachers who are qualified, competent, dedicated and caring". Key to social transformation	Not yet competent in teaching maths or reading. Reproducer of stipulated content. Not recontextualizing agent

The shifts in the model of the teacher projected in each of the curriculum reforms reflect an increasing acknowledgement of low levels of specialization in the system and the limits to teachers acting as major recontextualizing agents. The series of post-apartheid reforms represent a cumulative process of attempting the appropriate calibration between curriculum policy specification and teacher agency ***in a specific context.***

The teacher in the theory

Bernstein's pedagogic device captures in the sociological big picture the role of education from social structure to individual consciousness (Hoadley & Muller, 2009, p. 74). Or put another way, the processes of the transformation of knowledge into pedagogy. It also offers a delicate theorizing of the dimensions and axes of variation in curriculum and pedagogy in classification and framing. It has a blind spot, however. For Bernstein education is fundamentally about the specialization of consciousness, about the development of an abstracting orientation to making sense of the world. This is in reference to the acquirer or student and it assumes the transmitter or teacher is already specialized with respect to assuring this. This cannot be assumed in a developing country context with a history of poor schooling and teacher training and significant limitations on the cultivation of knowledge resources across the system.

The pedagogic device offers no position for the teacher, and teachers (transmitters) are assumed in the theory to be already specialized. The analyses in the book show how teachers enact pedagogy with evident low levels of specialized knowledge. Thus, teachers may be a key conduit or an obstruction in the process of knowledge becoming pedagogic communication. This potential variation is invisible in the theory. Elsewhere I have raised the issue of teachers' differential social positioning in potentially better understanding existing and possible pedagogic forms (Hoadley & Ensor, 2009). Some initial and important research raises questions about teachers own literacy levels as well (Pretorius & Machet, 2004). The research in this book suggests that in developing country contexts we need to understand better teachers' literacy levels, and the nature of their specialized, professional, pedagogic judgment, their bases and rationales. This would help to inform how we might better enable changes in practice. Extending Bernstein's framework in relation to variation in teacher expertise could provide a fuller account of educational processes in these contexts.

Implications for research

Much of the debate around curriculum and pedagogy in developing country contexts has been "smothered with a blanket of unexamined ideology" (Alexander, 2008, p. 16) that has closed off theoretical considerations of the complexities of teaching. This book embarked on an epistemic investigation of curriculum processes in South Africa as a developing country case. While Bernstein has provided a useful resource in identifying the structuring of pedagogic transmission over time from the macro to micro levels in a developing country context (see also Sprikpash, 2012), Chapters 9 and 11 especially raised the need to develop more fine-grained theoretical conceptions of knowledge and how it functions in pedagogy beyond the high level concepts of classification and framing; a consideration of both the relay (the structure) and the relayed (the content) in curriculum and pedagogy. The work of Shalem and colleagues (Shalem & Slominsky, 2013; Shalem et al., 2014; Shalem, 2017) in this regard, drawing attention to the nature of the systematized knowledge, both propositional and practical, underlying what teachers are required to do in classrooms, advances the field significantly. So too does the work of Bertram et al. (2015) that focuses on the complexity of the professional knowledge base for Foundation Phase teachers, also in a South African context. And as discussed above, the analyses in this book call into question the model which positions the teacher as a neutral relay in processes of education transmission, opening up a space for theoretical development.

In the book I have emphasized the idea that South Africa provides a case of reform in developing countries, and that although with its own peculiar history, its story has broader potential relevance. I agree with Alexander (2014) that much of the research and policy work of the UNESCO Global Monitoring reports, as well as the work of some prominent economists in education, misses the " 'thick description' of close-grained cross-national and cross-cultural comparative studies of school and classroom life and the forces that shape it" (p. 9). Alexander places interaction at the centre of any study or measure of pedagogy, an aspect not easily captured in input-output models. In his view, mainstream indicators frameworks proposed by agencies such as OECD, the EC, DfID and UNESCO are all highly problematic in their approach to pedagogical quality, utilizing indicators in an arbitrary and selective fashion, with high levels of ambiguity. Process, in these accounts remains largely invisible (p. 39). I would argue, however, that process is most usefully considered in concert with these broader accounts that in a way have themselves drawn increasing attention to the importance of gaining credible accounts of process.

In their recent review of research evidence of what works in education in developing countries, Glewwe and Muralidharan (2015) too recognize the limits of input-output models of education, especially in the areas of curriculum and pedagogy, and suggest that "a fruitful area of future research is for researchers trained in rigorous empirical methods (especially in running field experiments) to collaborate with experts in curriculum and pedagogy to improve the empirical evidence base on effective pedagogy in low-income settings (Glewwe & Muralidharan, 2015, pp. 85–86). In other words, we need good educational theory to combine with strong methodology;[1] and theoretically robust qualitative work to become an intrinsic part of quantitative research programmes.

The point about educational theory is also relevant to some of the major proposals that are currently influencing the policy agenda around curriculum and pedagogy – such as 'Teaching at the Right Level',[2] scripting and the 'overambitious'[3] curriculum. These would benefit from ***educational*** scrutiny with an understanding of how the teacher specializes text (content) to time (duration of learning) to development (grade and level of learner) – the fundamental pedagogic action. The current notion of 'structured pedagogy' which is a broad term referring to a range of interventions that include customized curricula, lesson plans and training of teachers in delivering this content tend to construct pedagogy as a malleable, segmented technology. They would usefully pay careful attention to the way in which pedagogic practice can and does change and thus enhance our understanding of how these interventions work and why some appear to be showing emerging favourable outcomes (Snilstveit et al., 2016). Crucially, it would be interesting to know if and how the materials transmit knowledge criteria to *teachers* (see especially Shalem (2017) on scripting), thus providing potentially more enduring changes in the levels of cognitive resource in the system.

Changing practice

Establishing a knowledge-based curriculum clearly has not solved the problem of access to formal school knowledge for the majority of children in South Africa. There are enduring societal and educational dynamics at play that continue to exclude. And there are large numbers of students not able to make meaningful connections between their own everyday worlds and experience and the abstract knowledge of schooling. Teachers too are locked out, having to draw on their own stores of common knowledge in the absence of a stock of professional knowledge for teaching and learning, exemplified in this book in the early grade teaching of reading and number.

Looking at curriculum and pedagogy together over time highlights the fact that changing the curriculum in our enduring context of extreme inequality can only go some way to addressing the poor quality of teaching and learning. It is a crucial signaling system for textbooks, teacher training and for schools for what content needs to be covered. But it cannot compensate for pedagogy. The arguments of the book suggest that a priority is a shift in the cognitive horizons of those teaching in our schools, both in relation to their own specialized knowledge of teaching their subjects as well as acquiring pedagogic forms likely to benefit those learning in resource-scarce settings. This is a complex issue, especially in developing country contexts where particular pedagogic forms have been reproduced between teachers and students over long periods without the opportunities to witness or engage with alternatives. It is also complex in that the understanding and logic underpinning the practice of teachers in these contexts is poorly understood and consequently easily dismissed or incorporated as culturally located. This lack of understanding restricts the possibilities for making meaningful policy and teacher development programmes to change teachers' practice.

Jacklin (2004) points out that "post apartheid education in South Africa provides [a] telling case of the difficulties encountered when trying to undo the historical knot of spatial, social and institutional organisation and the associated distribution of resources including discursive resources" (p. 2). It is these discursive resources, specifically the specialized knowledge of schooling that has been the central concern of the book. In the absence of substantial change in the levels of cognitive resources in the system, especially teacher knowledge, any reform is likely to fail. In the absence of a reduction of broader social inequality and more sharing of material and discursive resources, education can achieve very little. In the space of 22 years, South Africa covered a very wide curriculum spectrum, while in the classrooms studied here pedagogy in certain key respects has not shifted.

Green shoots

Despite the limitations of changes in pedagogy detailed in the analyses, there are some small signs of positive shift in the system. The first, alluded to in Chapter 11, is that although done in procedural and surface ways, teachers have adopted some new pedagogic *forms*, perhaps as a precursor to more substantive change over a longer period of time. The history sketched here is a mere 22 years, very short in education system terms for significant change (Gustaffson, 2012). The second cause for hope is that, albeit very small and from a very low base, there has been some improvement in student outcomes on some of the standardized tests that South Africa participates in, in particular the Third International Mathematics and Science Study (TIMSS) (Reddy et al., 2016).[4]

But perhaps most relevant in relation to the arguments of the book, and the concern with teachers' knowledge, Armstrong (2014) shows in an analysis of SACMEQ III[5] data, that the learners of younger teachers are producing better results. Further, on the teacher tests administered as part of that study, younger teachers performed better than their older colleagues. What is interesting about the analysis is that the same results do not hold true for other countries participating in the test, such as Zimbabwe, Botswana and Kenya. There is something specific to South Africa that makes age (and possibly experience in the schooling system) negatively correlated with performance. It may be that those 20–29 year old (young) teachers who received most of their schooling and their training post-apartheid (and once teacher training had been moved into the university system) are better prepared for teaching. It may be that the levels of cognitive resource in the system are slowly shifting with time.

Envoi: knowledge in pedagogy

In my view, a knowledge-based curriculum is essential for differentiating subjects and delineating the subject-specific skills, concepts and content which need to be taught, especially in contexts of poverty. In this way a curriculum outlines the possibilities for specializing students' consciousness with respect to different subjects and, consequently, gives access to new and different ways of making meaning and organizing experience.

Those who take issue with the arguments for a knowledge-based curriculum often point out its exclusionary effects, with subject discipline knowledge cast as elite and lacking relevance. In response, there are those who invoke the 'powerful' potentials of access to formal knowledge (for example, Young, 2013). In exploring knowledge *in* pedagogy, I argue that whether knowledge is powerful or exclusionary depends on how it is taught and what the learner is then able to do with it. Thus, arguments around knowledge and curriculum are best made ***relationally with pedagogy***. The book has shown a wide range in knowledge specification in the curriculum through the reforms, and a cumulative process towards clearer knowledge signposting for teachers. The cases of pedagogy have shown, however, that real power lies in the transaction of knowledge between teacher and student in the classroom, and the system requires teachers who can recognize and realize these signposts in pedagogy.

Notes

1 In South Africa productive collaborations of this nature have begun to explore system-wide attempts to change 'instructional regimes', for example Fleisch et al (2015).
2 Teaching at the right level requires differentiation of students in order to accomplish appropriate pacing. It depends on the individualizing of students, distributing differentiated tasks to students on the basis of scrutiny of their individual task performance.
3 Here the argument is made that the curriculum in use has often been developed in the first instance for a selective system where only the elite were educated, and the material being taught is too hard for students as the curriculum has moved ahead, leaving students behind. The idea that the problem lies with the curriculum and not with pedagogy is complicated by the studies in this book, locating at least some of the problem in the leaden pace identified in classrooms across time.
4 TIMSS tests Grade 8 learners (Grade 9 in South Africa) on mathematics and science knowledge. South African performance on this test is highly unequal and

South Africa ranks second to lowest of the 48 participating countries. Nonetheless, South Africa showed the biggest positive change, with an improvement of 90 points in science and 87 points in mathematics. South Africa started with very low performance scores in 2003. This upward shift translates to an overall performance improvement by approximately two grade levels between 2003 and 2015 (Reddy, et al, 2016, p. 2).

5 SACMEQ is the Southern and Eastern African Consortium for Monitoring Educational Quality, a cross-national initiative consisting of 14 countries in southern and eastern Africa. SACMEQ tests the numeracy and literacy skills of Grade 6 learners in each of the participating countries. South Africa participated in the second (2000), third (2007) and fourth (2014) rounds of SACMEQ. In the latter two rounds teachers were also tested.

References

Alexander, R. (2008). *Education for all, the quality imperative and the problem of pedagogy*. CREATE Pathways to Access. Research Monograph No. 20.

Alexander, R. (2014). *Teaching and learning: The quality imperative revisited*. Paper presented at the Teaching and Learning for Development: the 2013/14 Education for All Global Monitoring Report Conference. 3 February, Oslo.

Armstrong, P. (2014). Where lies the problem? Teachers or training? In J. Maserow (Ed.), *Taking Equal Education to the classroom* (pp. 112–119). Cape Town: Equal Education.

Bertram, C., Christiansen, I., & Mukeredzi. T. (2015). *Contexts and concepts: analysing learning tasks in a foundation phase teacher education programme in South Africa*. Paper presented at the Third International Social Realism Symposium. Cambridge, June.

Council of Higher Education. (2010). Report on the national review of academic and professional programmes in education. Pretoria: CHE.

De Clercq, F., & Shalem, Y. (2014). Teacher knowledge and employer-driven professional development: A critical analysis of the Gauteng Department of Education programmes. *Southern African Review of Education With Education With Production, 20*(1), 129–147.

Fleisch, B., Taylor, S., Schöer, V., & Mabogoane, T. (2015). Assessing the impact of the RCUP: A report of the findings of the impact evaluation of the Reading Catch-Up Programme. Johannesburg: Zenex Foundation.

Glewwe, P., & Muralidharan, K. (2015). *Improving school education outcomes in developing countries: Evidence, knowledge gaps, and policy implications*. University of Oxford, Research on Improving Systems of Education (RISE).

Gustaffson, M. (2012). More countries, similar results: A nonlinear programming approach to normalising test scores needed for growth regressions. Stellenbosch Economic Working Papers: 12/1.

Guthrie, G. (1990). To the defense of traditional teaching in lesser developed countries. In V. D. Rust & P. Dalin (Eds.), *Teachers and teaching in the developing world* (pp. 219–232). London & New York: Garland Publishing.

Guthrie, G. (2011). The progressive education fallacy in developing countries: In favour of formalism. London: Springer Science & Business Media.

Hoadley, U., & Ensor, P. (2009). Teachers, social class, professional dispositions and pedagogic practice. *Teachers and Teacher Education, 25*, 876–886.

Hoadley, U., & Muller, J. (2009). Codes, pedagogy and knowledge: advances in Bernsteinian sociology of Education. In M. W. Apple, S. J. Ball & L. Armando Gandin (Eds.), *The Routledge international handbook of sociology of education* (pp. 69–78). New York: Routledge.

Jacklin, H. (2004). *Repetition and difference: A rhythm analysis of pedagogic practice.* Unpublished PhD dissertation, University of Witwatersrand.

Pretorius, E., & Machet, M. (2004). The socio-educational context of literacy accomplishment in disadvantaged schools: Lessons for reading in the early primary school years. *Journal for Language Teaching, 38,* 45–62.

Reddy, V., Visser, M., Winnaar, L., Arends, F., Juan, A., & Prinsloo, C. H. (2016). *TIMSS 2015: Highlights of mathematics and science achievement of grade 9 South African learners.* Pretoria: Human Sciences Research Council.

Shalem, Y. (2017). Scripted lesson plans: what is visible and invisible in visible pedagogy? In B. Barrett, U. Hoadley & J. Morgan (Eds.), *Knowledge, curriculum and equity: Social realist perspectives.* London: Routledge.

Shalem, Y., & Slonimsky, L. (2013). Practical knowledge of teaching practice – What counts? *Journal of Education, 58,* 67–86.

Shalem, Y., Steinberg, C., Koornhof. H., & De Clercq, F. (2014). The 'what' and 'how' in scripted lesson plans: The case of the Gauteng Primary Language and Mathematics Strategy in South Africa. Paper presented in SAERA, Durban November 2014. Currently under review.

Slonimsky, L. (2015). Teacher change in a changing moral order: Learning from Durkheim. *Education as Change, 20*(2), 27–43.

Snilstveit, B., Stevenson, J., Menon, R., Phillips, D., Gallagher, E., Geleen, M., Jobse, H., Schmidt, T., & Jimenez, E. (2016). *The impact of education programmes on learning and school participation in low- and middle-income countries: A systematic review summary report, 3ie Systematic Review Summary 7.* London: International Initiative for Impact Evaluation (3ie).

Sriprakash, A. (2012). Pedagogies for development: The politics and practices of child-centered education in India. *Education in the Asia-Pacific Region: Issues Concerns and Prospects, 16,* 179–189.

Tabulawa, R. (2013). Teaching and learning in context: Why pedagogical reforms fail in Sub-Saharan Africa. Dakar: CODESRIA.

Young, M. (2013). Overcoming the crisis in curriculum theory: A knowledge-based approach. *Journal of Curriculum Studies, 45*(2), 101–118.

Appendix A

The 66 specific outcomes of curriculum 2005

Language, literacy and communication

1 Make and negotiate meaning and understanding.
2 Show critical awareness of language use.
3 Respond to the aesthetic, affective, cultural and social values in texts.
4 Access, process and use information from a variety of sources and situations.
5 Understand, know and apply language structures and conventions in context.
6 Use language for learning.
7 Use appropriate communication strategies for specific purposes and situations.

Mathematical literacy and mathematics

8 Demonstrate an understanding about ways of working with numbers.
9 Manipulate number patterns in different ways.
10 Demonstrate an understanding of the historical development of mathematics in various social and cultural contexts.
11 Critically analyze how mathematical relationships are used in social, political and economic relations.
12 Measure with competence and confidence in a variety of contexts.
13 Use data from various contexts to make informed judgments.
14 Describe and represent experiences with shape, space, time and motion using all available senses.
15 Analyze natural forms, cultural products and processes as representations of shape, space and time.
16 Use mathematical language to communicate mathematical ideas, concepts, generalizations and thought processes.
17 Use various logical processes to formulate tests and justify conjectures.

Natural sciences

18 Use process skills to investigate phenomena related to the natural sciences.
19 Demonstrate the acquisition of knowledge and an understanding of concepts and principles in the natural sciences.

20 Apply scientific knowledge and skills to problems in innovative ways.
21 Demonstrate an understanding of how scientific knowledge and skills contribute to the management, development and utilization of natural and other resources.
22 Use scientific knowledge and skills to support responsible decision-making.
23 Demonstrate knowledge and understanding of the relationship between science and culture.
24 Demonstrate an understanding of the changing and contested nature of the natural sciences.
25 Demonstrate an understanding of the interaction between the natural sciences, technology and socio-economic development.

Technology

26 Understand and apply the technological process to solve problems and satisfy needs and wants.
27 Apply a range of technological knowledge and skills ethnically [sic] and responsibly.
28 Access, process and use date for technological purposes.
29 Select and evaluate products and systems.
30 Demonstrate an understanding of how different societies create and adapt technological solutions to particular problems.
31 Demonstrate an understanding of the impact of technology.
32 Demonstrate an understanding of how technology might reflect the different biases and create responsible and ethical strategies to address them.

Arts and culture

33 Apply knowledge, techniques and skills to create and be critically involved in arts and culture processes and products.
34 Use the creative processes of art culture [sic] to develop and apply social and interactive skills.
35 Reflect on and engage critically with arts experience and works.
36 Demonstrate an understanding of the origins, functions and dynamic nature of culture.
37 Experience and analyze the role of the mass media in popular culture and its impact on multiple forms of communication and expression in the arts,
38 Use art skills and cultural expressions to make an economic contribution to self and society.
39 Demonstrate an ability to access creative art and cultural processes to develop self-esteem and promote healing.
40 Acknowledge, understand and promote historically marginalized arts and cultural forms and practices.

Human and social sciences

41 Demonstrate a critical understanding of how South African society has changed and developed.
42 Demonstrate a critical understanding of patterns of social development.
43 Participate actively in promoting a just, democratic and equitable society.
44 Make sound judgments about the development, utilization and management of resources.
45 Critically understand the role of technology in social development.
46 Demonstrate an understanding of inter-relationships between society and the natural environment.
47 Address social and environmental issues in order to promote development and social justice.
48 Analyze forms and processes of organizations.
49 Use a range of skills and techniques in the human and social sciences context.

Life orientation

50 Understand and accept themselves as unique and worthwhile human beings.
51 Use skills and display attitudes and values that improve relationships in family, group and community.
52 Respect the rights of people to hold personal beliefs and values.
53 Demonstrate value and respect for human rights as reflected in *Ubuntu* and other similar philosophies.
54 Practice acquired life and decision-making skills.
55 Access career and other opportunities and set goals that will enable them to make the best use of their potential and talents.
56 Demonstrate the values and attitudes necessary for a healthy and balanced lifestyle.
57 Evaluate and participate in activities that demonstrate effective human movement and development.

Economic and management sciences

58 Engage in entrepreneurial activities.
59 Demonstrate a personal role in the economic environment.
60 Demonstrate the principles of supply and demand and the practices of production.
61 Demonstrate managerial expertise and administrative proficiency.
62 Critically analyze economic and financial data to make decisions.
63 Evaluate different economic systems from various perspectives.
64 Demonstrate actions which advance sustained economic growth, reconstruction and development in South Africa.
65 Evaluate the interrelationships between economic and other environments.

Appendix B

Theory into data

Introduction

This appendix provides a detailed description of how the theory in the chapters on pedagogy (Chapters 7, 9 and 11) was used in relation to the data. What the chapters show is the evolution of the analytic methods in the different researches carried out over time. In each case classification and framing is a central resource, but put to work in different ways. I detail these as follows. The focus is primarily on Chapter 9, the analysis that developed the most elaborated framework for analysis.

Chapter 5 presented the main theoretical concepts deployed across the analyses in the book. This appendix refers to the concepts elaborated there but does not define or discuss them in detail here. The reader should refer back to Chapter 5 if necessary for a discussion of the theory.

Chapter 7 – using the theory heuristically

In Chapter 7 I began with one of Bernstein's more succinct understandings of pedagogy. Pedagogy entails the specialization of space, time and text. In relation to space and time in the chapter I considered the ways in which time and space were bounded and marked out for pedagogic activity, in other words specialized for instruction. In order to consider the specialization of text, I interpreted text to be 'that which attracts evaluation'; the 'privileged legitimate text'; or as I term it in the chapter, 'the knowledge object'. In order to analyze this I used the concepts of classification and evaluative criteria. In analyzing the operation of evaluative criteria in the pedagogy I was focused on whether these were visible. I state there:

> Evaluative criteria can be seen in teachers' mediation of tasks given to learners: in the correction of, or responses to learner productions and in instructions or explanations given to the class, showing what counts or what ideas

> belong together (Shalem, 2017). Evaluative criteria were also discerned in assessment tasks, and the ways in which these were marked. In order for evaluative criteria to be transmitted, the teacher needs to be aware of what the learners are saying, observe what the learners are doing and intervene where appropriate in order to provide markers towards the realization of the criteria of the task.

In my use of classification I was particularly interested in the relation between school knowledge and everyday knowledge given the dominance of the latter in the pedagogy in the classrooms studied. So the theoretical framework developed for Chapter 7 theorized pedagogy in the following way:

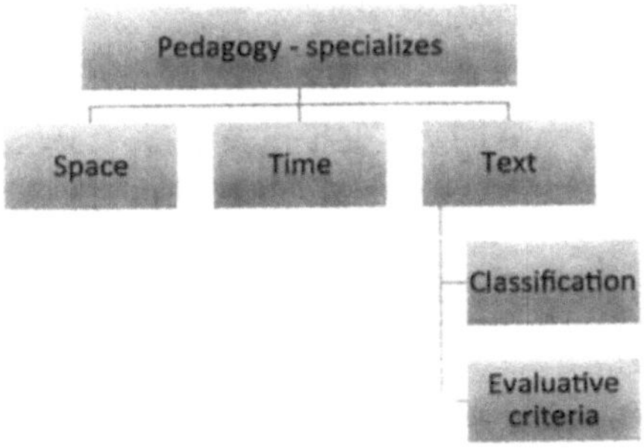

Figure BM2.1 Theorizing pedagogy in Chapter 7

Clearly, the theory in this iteration is used heuristically. The chapter includes my earliest attempts at grappling with Bernstein's theory and dealing with the challenges of using his very abstract concepts to analyze empirical data.

Chapter 9 – developing a 'language of description'

When I came to the research in Chapter 9 I required a far more delicate schema to analyze differences between different social class contexts, the subject of the broader study on which this chapter was based. I was attracted to the work of Morais and Pires (2002) and Morais and Neves (2001), and more generally the work of the Sociological Studies of the Classroom project at the University of Lisbon. They operationalized Bernstein's concepts of classification and framing into fine-grained coding schemes that allowed for the construction and reading of data. As Brown and Dowling (1998) remind us, "the text very definitely does not tell its own story. Rather, its description must be ***biased*** according to an explicit and coherent theoretical framework" (p. 89). This is accomplished through the development of an 'external language of description'.

External language of description

An external language of description is the set of concepts and constructs which allows both for the structuring of data and the reading, or analysis, of that data. Bernstein describes languages of description as follows:

> Briefly, a language of description is a translation device whereby one language is transformed into another. We can distinguish between internal and external languages of description . . . A language of description constructs what is to count as an empirical referent, how such referents relate to each other to produce a specific text and translate these referential relations into theoretical objects or potential theoretical objects. In other words the external language of description (L^2) is the means by which the internal language (L^1) is activated as a reading device or vice versa.
>
> (Bernstein, 2000, pp. 132–133)

The internal language of description is the theory. Moore and Muller (2002, p. 634) describe an external language of description as a 'data-near device', that is, the concepts and constructs that allow the theory to 'read' the data. This external language develops on the basis of deductive and inductive analysis, moving iteratively between the internal language (theory) and engagement with empirical data. The language of description thus developed provides "the basis for establishing what are to count as data and provides for their principled reading" (Ensor & Hoadley, 2004, p. 92).

The question arises, then, as to how and where the theory changes. In this regard, and in order to counter potential circularity in the theory-data relation, Bernstein (2000) introduces the notion of the discursive gap. Moore and Muller (2002) define this gap as lying between the internal and the external language of description:

> The external language must not only be able to describe what is outside the theory in terms relevant to the theory, but also somehow be capable of recognising what is beyond the theory. It must submit to an external ontological imperative that allows that which is outside to 'announce itself'.
>
> (p. 634)

Put more simply: 'Data, via the external language, can thus create a surplus that requires an extension of the theory to make sense of it, or do justice to it' (ibid). At the same time, Moore and Muller (2002) go on to argue, the theory, through its conceptual categories, is able to generate more empirical possibilities than may be evident in a particular instance, raising the "possibility of other ways of doing things" (p. 635). So, the discursive gap provides the space for the development of the theory.

One of the central reasons for engaging with the notions of internal and external languages was that it provided a way of analyzing pedagogy that dealt with common threats to reliability and validity that are entailed in analysing classroom data, where often existing implicit notions of 'good' practice abound (Ensor & Hoadley, 2004). It also provided a more precise 'anatomizing of pedagogy' (Fitz et al., 2006). Finally, as described above, it provided a method for bringing the abstract concepts that I was working with closer to the data, so that the theory could both constitute and read (analyze) the data.

The 'external language of description' I developed for the study reported on in Chapter 9 consisted of a set of concepts and constructs that allowed for both the structuring of data and the reading, or analysis, of that data. This was accomplished through an iterative process, working from data to theory and vice versa. Dowling and Bernstein provided the initial categories, and the data suggested more delicate and specific categories for analysis. For classification and framing a set of 19 indicators was developed in order to analyze the mathematics and language lessons. The conceptual categories are show in the figure below.

Framing	Discursive rules	Extent to which teacher controls **selection** of content
		Extent to which teacher controls **sequencing** of content
		Extent to which teacher controls **pacing** of content
		Extent to which teacher makes explicit the **rules for evaluation** of learners' performances
	Hierarchical rules	Extent to which teacher makes formal or informal the social relations **between teacher and learners**
Classification	Relations between discourses	**Inter-discursive** (strength of boundary between mathematics and other subject areas)
		Inter-discursive (strength of boundary between school mathematics and everyday knowledge)
		Intra-discursive (strength of boundary between different topics within mathematics)

Figure BM2.2 Conceptual categories for theorizing pedagogy in Chapter 9

Table BM2.1 below shows an example of an indicator developed for framing of the evaluative criteria. In the table, framing is expressed in terms of its strength or weakness using standard Bernsteinian notation – F^{++} representing the strongest framing (or teacher control) over the evaluative criteria and F^{--} representing very weak framing. F^0, raised in Chapter 5, 7 and 9 in relation to 'zero pedagogy', is an extension of the theory, and is used to code instances where the transmission of the evaluative criteria is not observable. This is discussed in detail in the book.

Table BM2.1 Examples of coding scheme: framing over evaluative criteria

5. *In the course of learners conducting an activity or task*	F^{++}	F^{+}	F^{-}	F^{-}	F^{0}
	Evaluative criteria very clear and explicit	***Evaluative criteria quite clear and explicit***	***Evaluative criteria quite unclear and implicit***	***Evaluative criteria very unclear and implicit***	***Transmission of evaluative criteria not observable***
	The teacher constantly moves around and monitors what learners are doing and makes comments. To the whole class and to individuals she repeatedly goes over what constitutes an appropriate performance.	The teacher makes some points either to the whole class or to individual learners so as to clarify what is expected of them in the task.	The teacher makes a few comments during the course of the task and looks at some of the learners work, or attends to learner productions; however, this is not sustained and the criteria for a successful production are not made explicit to all.	The teacher looks at a few learners' work when it is brought to her attention. She rarely or never attends to their productions. Rarely she makes a comment to the learner. These are not extended to the whole class.	The teacher engages in other work in her space and is not seen to look at what the learners are doing. She makes no comment on the work as it proceeds. No action is taken to ascertain what the learners are doing.

A further example of an indicator developed for framing of pacing is shown below. Note framing of pacing concerns who ***controls*** the pace, not whether it is fast or slow:

Table BM2.2 Examples of coding scheme: framing of pacing

	F^{++}	F^{+}	F^{-}	F^{-}
3. In the learners doing activities/ tasks	*Always or almost always controlled by the teacher*	*Mostly controlled by the teacher*	*Learners have some control over the pace*	*Learners have substantial control over the pace*
	The pace at which learners work through tasks is always or almost always strictly controlled by the teacher. Injunctions to 'hurry up' or 'work slowly' and mention of time are frequent, and the teacher doesn't vary the pace according to learners' productions. The teacher always or mostly defers or ignores learners' questions and interjections, or learners make no interjections.	The pace at which learners work through tasks is mostly determined by the teacher. Time is mentioned quite often and on occasion the length of an activity is stipulated beforehand. The teacher accepts few learner interventions and questions. She answers questions briefly and moves on. Occasionally she varies the pace in response to learners' productions.	Learners work at their own pace. The teacher exercises some control over pace, but remains open to its variation. The teacher accepts some learner interventions and questions. She pauses the lesson briefly to make sure that all learners are ready to move on before doing so. Setting of parallel activities for learners who have finished may occur.	Learners work at their own pace. The teacher places no pressure on them to finish in a stipulated period. She may give them opportunities to 'catch up'. The teacher accepts most or all learner interventions and questions and discussion may be extended or deviate as a result. Learners decide when they are ready to move on to other work. Setting of parallel activities for learners who have finished may occur.

Nineteen indicators like the ones shown above were used to code the data for the various dimensions of classification and framing. The full set of indicators can be found in Hoadley (2005).

Dowling's strategies

In chapter 7 I augment the Bernsteinian framework with concepts drawn from Paul Dowling, who, in relation to pedagogy, is concerned with how knowledge types are distributed. These types are contained in domains and distributed through strategies, and sociologically he is concerned with the operation of these strategies and the differential distribution of knowledge types to different groups. Recruiting Dowling selectively, I consider specializing and localizing strategies. "Specializing is the construction of abstract message with respect to a specific topic or setting" (Dowling, 1998, p. 147). I attribute a slightly different meaning to localizing than Dowling, defining these strategies as those that distribute context-dependent messages.

Dowling's (1998) strategies were adapted to consider how the tasks set by the teachers in the classroom related to the specialized discourse of mathematics or literacy. For the concepts of localizing and specializing strategies, a network was used in the analysis of the mathematical and language tasks contained within the lessons. The networks are shown in Figures BM2.3 and BM2.4. Localizing tasks are those that the learners are able to do without deploying the specialized knowledge of mathematics or language. The 'mathematics element', 'language purpose' or concept is absent. These tasks incorporate knowledge that is familiar and local, and meanings that are generally particularistic, concrete, and context-dependent. Specializing tasks, on the other hand, refer to a particular mathematics or language element or concept. Tasks incorporating specializing strategies are rule-based or rule-governed; tasks that are characterized as localizing are spontaneous or mundane.

In the data, at the Grade 3 level, tasks that incorporated localizing strategies often resembled 'play' or games. They generally required learners to do things that they enjoyed, and which they knew how to do (recite a well-known verse, colour in a picture). They did not incorporate knowledge that the learners were not familiar with, and were not designed to produce a cognitive shift (although they may indeed have produced this unintentionally). Specializing strategies required learners to apply knowledge in a novel way, practice a concept or skill in relation to particular contexts, or rehearse a new concept.

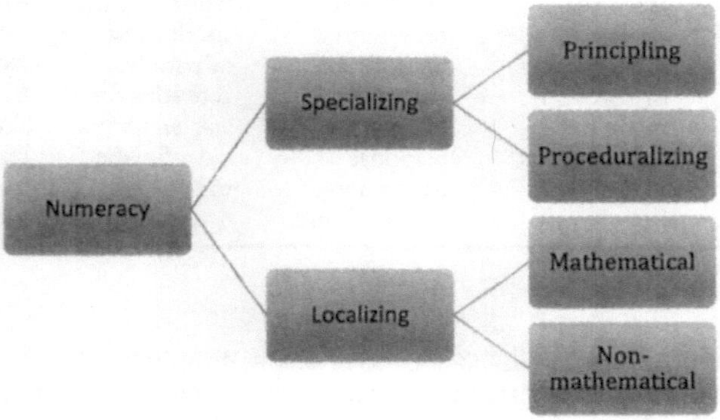

Figure BM2.3 Network for the analysis of mathematics tasks in Chapter 9

For mathematics, at the second level for specializing strategies, the distinction between proceduralizing and principling strategies is made. Specializing-principling strategies entail a rule-based or rule-governed performance on the part of the learner, where novel applications of knowledge, operations, or skills are required, or in oral work, reasoning, justifications, or explanations. Here learners need to show the understandings, competences or reasoning behind the mathematical tasks in producing the legitimate text for evaluation.

With specializing-proceduralizing strategies, the focus is on the procedure required for the production of legitimate texts for evaluation. These strategies require learners to practice a concept or perform an operation without necessarily engaging in the principles for the generation of texts, "exchanging instructions for definitions" (Dowling, 1998, p. 146), and reducing the level of abstraction of knowledge. Localizing strategies distinguish between mathematical and non-mathematical localizing strategies. Localizing-mathematical displays mathematical content, but the principles and procedures for completing the task are absent or the mathematics concepts for use in approaching the calculation remain implicit. In other words the task 'looks like mathematics' but transmits no mathematical procedures or concepts. Localizing-non-mathematical are tasks such as colouring-in or chanting, where there is no mathematical content visible.

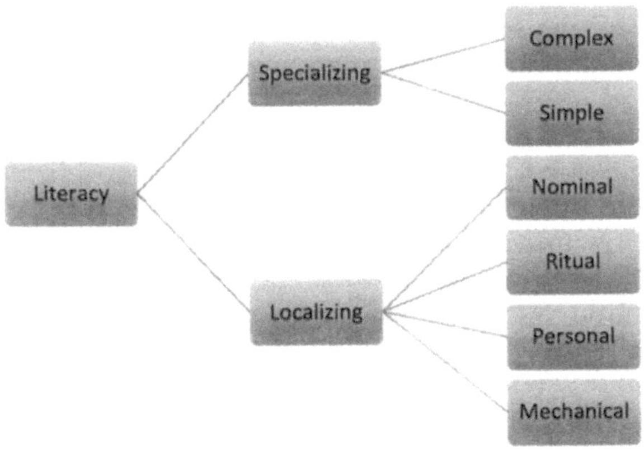

Figure BM2.4 Network for the analysis of literacy tasks in Chapter 9

In literacy, localizing is disaggregated in relation to four possibilities. Localizing-ritual refers to tasks that do not require the exercise of any particular rule relating to literacy. In the data many of these tasks entailed mimicry, a common strategy deployed by the teachers, where learners repeated words and phrases after the teacher, and were not required to produce texts of their own (see the tree example below). This is the 'rite of rote' referred to earlier. Localizing-nominal consists of the teacher and learners naming things. A clear pedagogic trajectory from these kinds of exchanges is not retrievable; rather, the pedagogic process consists of building up a series of words and images, often in relation to a theme.

The third category, localizing-mechanical strategies require learners to reproduce, imitate or copy the exact text of the teacher or other resource, for example, copy off the board, colour in, draw or copy from the textbook without doing any kind of operation beyond this. Finally, localizing-personal refers to tasks that require spontaneous responses consisting of particularistic, local meanings, and not regulated by any obvious rule generating their description, nor the mode of description. Here, any response is acceptable and in the data the teacher often proffered no evaluative comment.

Localizing strategies can represent what was identified in Chapter 7 as a form of initial, segmental pedagogy, aspects of which one may find in the home and in early socialization activities. They are not empty of pedagogic content or potential but, in relation to early grades learning, they do not appeal to the specialized knowledge and they do not require specialized performances on the part of the learner.

Instructional form – individualizing and collectivizing

Finally, an important component of the analysis drew on the work of Pedro (1981) in characterizing the instructional form of the pedagogy. For the coding of the instructional form three options regarding the teachers' interaction with the class were identified: homogenous, where the teacher worked with the class as a whole; integrated, where students worked with each other in groups; and specialized, where the teacher worked with groups of students or individual students.

In relation to the treatment of content, each task was also coded as to whether it differentiated between different members of the class or groups (where it did it was always on the basis of ability, although they could also refer to sex, language, religion etcetera) or treated the class as uniform, with an undifferentiated task structure. These categories are shown in the coding network in Figure BM2.4. The interest in the analysis was the extent to which the teacher individualized learners through engaging with different groupings and allocating different content, or treated the class as a homogenous whole.

This analysis of instructional form was especially useful in allowing me to analyze the individualizing/communalizing practices of the teacher.

Chapter 11 – into subject content

In the third and final chapter analyzing pedagogy I once again use classification and framing to provide a global characterization of the pedagogy that makes the classrooms analyzed there comparable to those of Chapters 7 and 9. But here I confront a problem not uncommon in the use of Bernstein's theory, in that it is developed to describe the structuring of the relay of educational knowledge, but not the relayed (knowledge) itself (the distinction is explained fully in Chapter 5). While Dowling addressed this issue to some extent in the way I deployed his theory in Chapter 9, his strategies and domains remain at a more abstract

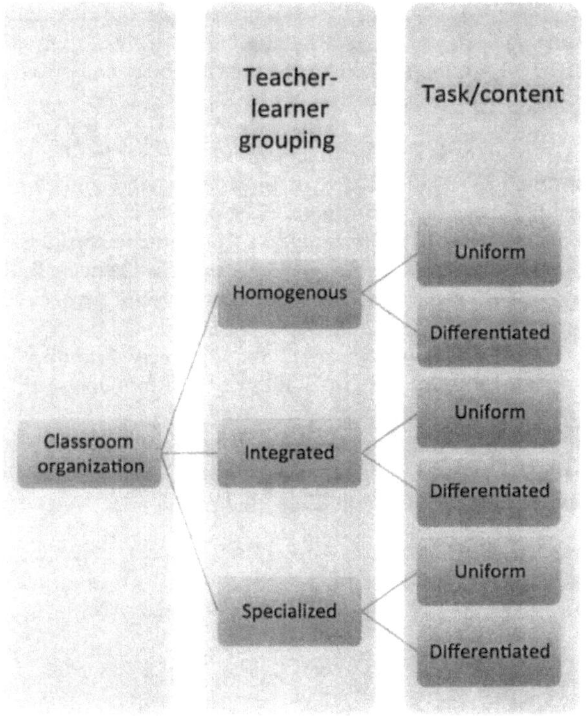

Figure BM2.5 Scheme for the analysis of instructional form in Chapter 9

level describing the forms that the distribution takes. In this chapter therefore I move on to a range of reading and mathematics literature in order to describe the 'knowledge criteria', not just framing over evaluative criteria. I also explored in this chapter the ways in which different dimensions of Bernstein's theory interact – being particularly interested in the relationship between instructional discourse, regulative discourse (communalizing/individualizing) and knowledge criteria. The use of the theory here is more exploratory, opening up possibilities for further development in work going forward.

References

Bernstein, B. (2000). Pedagogy, symbolic control and identity: Theory, research and critique. Revised edition. Oxford: Rowman & Littlefield.

Brown, A., & Dowling, P. (1998). Doing research/reading research: A mode of interrogation for education. London: Falmer Press.

Dowling, P. (1998). The sociology of mathematics education: Mathematical myths/pedagogic texts. London: Falmer.

Ensor, P., & Hoadley, U. K. (2004). Developing languages of description to research pedagogy. *Journal of Education*, *32*, 81–104.

Fitz, J., Davies, B., & Evans, J. (2006). Education policy and social reproduction: Class inscription & symbolic control. Oxford: Routledge.

Hoadley, U. K. (2005). Social class, pedagogy and the specialization of voice in four South African primary schools. Unpublished PhD thesis, University of Cape Town.

Moore, R., & Muller, J. (2002). The growth of knowledge and the discursive gap. *British Journal of Sociology of Education*, *23*(4), 627–637.

Morais, A. and Neves, I. (2001). Pedagogical social contexts: Studies for a sociology of learning. In A. Morais, I. Neves, B. Davies & H. Daniels (Ends), *Towards a sociology of pedagogy: the contribution of Basil Bernstein to research* (pp. 185–222). New York: Peter Lang.

Pedro, E. R. (1981). *Social stratification and classroom discourse: A sociolinguistic analysis of classroom practice*. Stockholm: Stockholm Institute of Education, Department of Educational Research.

Shalem, Y. (2017). Scripted lesson plans: What is visible and invisible in visible pedagogy? In B. Barrett, U. Hoadley & J. Morgan (Eds.), *Knowledge, Curriculum and equity: Social realist perspectives*. London: Routledge.

Index